MIND OVER
EXPLICIT
MATTER

MIND OVER EXPLICIT MATTER

QUIT PORN AND IMPROVE INTIMACY THROUGH NEUROSCIENCE

DR. TRISH LEIGH

W Publishing Group

Mind Over Explicit Matter

© 2025 Patricia Leigh

Published in Nashville, Tennessee, by W Publishing, an imprint of Thomas Nelson.

Published in association with Christopher Ferebee Agency.

Thomas Nelson titles may be purchased in bulk for educational, business, fundraising, or sales promotional use. For information, please email SpecialMarkets@ThomasNelson.com. Any internet addresses, phone numbers, or company or product information printed in this book are offered as a resource and are not intended in any way to be or to imply an endorsement by Thomas Nelson, nor does Thomas Nelson vouch for the existence, content, or services of these sites, phone numbers, companies, or products beyond the life of this book.

The information presented in this book is the result of years of practice experience and clinical research by the author. The information in this book, by necessity, is general in nature and is not a substitute for an evaluation or treatment by a competent health care specialist. If you believe you need medical intervention, please see a professional as soon as possible. While the stories in the book are true, names and identifying characteristics of some individuals have been changed to preserve their privacy.

Illustrations by Murphy Credle

ISBN 978-1-4003-4706-3 (audiobook)
ISBN 978-1-4003-4705-6 (ePub)
ISBN 978-1-4003-4699-8 (softcover)

Library of Congress Control Number: 2024944741

Printed in the United States of America

24 25 26 27 28 LBC 5 4 3 2 1

To Sam
Your struggle and success have taught us both so much.
We are both better because of it.

CONTENTS

CONTENTS

PART 4: HARDWIRE: MAKING YOUR BRAIN REWIRE STICK

INTRODUCTION

As you read this, you may be at a crossroads, trying to determine whether it's worth the effort to give up porn. You might wonder whether you even *can* succeed at leaving porn behind. Unwanted, secret sexual behaviors may have you stuck feeling anxious, unfocused, and with your mind constantly pulling you back to sexual thoughts. Maybe you find some comfort knowing that you are not the only one who struggles with this issue. Or perhaps you feel the shame of discovery, the discomfort of realizing your habit's impact on those you care about most, or the pain that you may even be hurting yourself. Maybe you feel relief in having taken the first step toward freedom by picking up this book. If you are ready to leave the pull of porn behind and step into a purposeful, fulfilling life, then this book is for you. No matter where you are on your journey, I am glad you're here.

In this book, I want to take you on an adventure to find the Real You—the person you innately know you are, deep down inside. That person is strong, independent, vital, and healthy. That person is who you have always wanted to be; that person no longer has their life hijacked by addiction, trauma, or fear. The path to self-discovery does not have to involve running away from pain, but rather running *toward* purpose. It can propel you into authentic living, joy, and happiness. I know this type of transformation can happen. I have experienced it myself and have seen it happen to my clients.

As a cognitive neuroscientist, brain-health coach, neurofeedback provider, communication pathologist, and certified sex addiction recovery coach, I have dedicated my life to helping people heal their brains and overcome porn addiction. I help individuals just like you every single day. I will not sugarcoat it: this journey can be a winding and rocky road packed with potential stumbles and setbacks. But if you set your mind to it, you will join countless others at the apex of a most worthwhile expedition of radical personal transformation.

Our voyage will be grounded in science, research, and professional expertise in addition to stories and anecdotes of others who have escaped porn's clutches. This will help you process and integrate the information along the way. Knowledge is power; once you know *how* something works and *why* it works, you will be inspired and empowered toward positive change.

This book has something for everyone. If you are married or in a committed, long-term relationship, the experiential vignettes will include some of the relationship dynamics that can be upset by porn addiction. There is also a dedicated section for those not in a relationship (whether by design or not), and the personal takeaways will be applicable for you too.

If you're a religious person and want to leave porn for moral reasons, the principles in this book align with the spiritual beliefs of the world's predominant religions. Recovery, in and of itself, is a spiritual journey. However, I will incorporate personally meaningful transformational concepts with neuroscience at every step of the process. If you are not religious, this book is still for you.

Although compulsive porn use impacts more men than women, evidence suggests that since the internet came on the scene, problematic porn use has been closing the gender gap.[1] So, if you are a woman struggling with porn and masturbation, there is a dedicated section for you, but rest assured that the lessons and exercises throughout are effective for women too.

I took my first step toward learning about personal transformation when I returned to university for my doctoral studies. I signed up for a self-development training program, like the one I offer in this book, and I worked with a coach to discover and foster my talents, reprogramming my mind and ultimately reducing my undesirable habits while embracing life in the present. Along the way, I learned that fear is the driving force of survival, and in times of stress, it can lead us into thoughts and behaviors that do not represent our highest selves. I knew then that I wanted to leverage my education and experience to help others free themselves from destructive behaviors and embrace their authentic selves.

After meeting with clients struggling with porn addiction, I began learning about the neurological components behind it, and it terrified me. At first, I struggled with sharing the information, much less making it part of my life's work, because of how it might be received. I knew that I could be chastised for talking about porn or lumped in with others who speak about the topic self-righteously. But the more I learned about the dangers of porn, the more I realized I could not remain silent and sit on the sidelines. So, I stepped out and began developing tools that have been proven to help people conquer porn addiction for themselves.

The irony is that the road to becoming a sex addiction coach helped *me* immeasurably. It has grounded me in the most personalized, authentic version of myself, rather than the inflated, false version I made long ago. Book-smart but closed off was how I survived in the world for too many years. Starting at a young age, as one of six children, I recognized my emotional needs weren't going to be taken care of by others, so I learned to have very few of them. I wore a persona of strength and intelligence to make myself feel safe, secure, and valued among my family members. In my sex addiction training, I dared to look at the parts of me that needed healing and embarked on an astounding transformative process. In doing so, the journey has done for me what I hope it can do for you, and it has solidified this as part of my purpose in life.

Not only that, but I also recognized that, because of the taboo nature of porn, I would receive more ridicule than praise for sharing what I learned about porn use. I felt like I had a burning secret that I couldn't keep inside anymore, even if it made some people uncomfortable. There is a tsunami of porn addiction upon us, impacting millions of people worldwide and by extension their health, work, vitality, and relationships. Hiding behind the mask of "I'm fine" lie the harmful effects of porn addiction. Effects that have the potential to destroy a person unless they do something about it.

I call my approach Mind Over Explicit Matter. It is a strategy I have developed through my work with thousands of people from all over the world who have participated in my program. It is a holistic, step-by-step course to help people heal their brains and end their porn addiction. The approach consists of a combination of four therapeutic disciplines synergized for high levels of recovery success: neuromodulation, cognitive behavioral therapy (CBT), mindfulness, and positive psychology. Each piece is scientifically proven to be effective, and I have seen true transformational power through their coalescence.[2] It is a neuro-bio-psycho-social approach that addresses your brain, body, mind, and relationships.

In part 1 of this book, I will share the "brain basics" you need to understand for part 2, where we will discuss how to unwire your brain from porn and quit it successfully. This includes information about how your brain works and how healing takes place through the wonders of neuroplasticity, which refers to the brain's ability to change itself. This will allow you to feel better and perform at higher levels. Then, in part 3, I will give you the steps to build off that knowledge base so you can rewire your brain to move forward with all the neuroscience techniques, strategies, and tools you need to build the life you have always desired. "Brain hacks" are scattered throughout the text to help you apply the ideas directly to your particular situation. I recommend that you have a journal handy so that you can process and apply the strategies to your life with greater ease. Part 4 of the book helps you to hardwire the new, healthier brain performance pattern permanently to allow you to sustain a life of integrity and healthy sexuality. To overcome porn addiction, you must unwire your brain and its self-sabotaging habits before you can rewire it with new, self-flourishing ones and ultimately hardwire those changes into your brain for long-lasting success.

This book is filled with some of the best ideas I have come across in my years of study—some you won't find anywhere else. It addresses all four areas of the neuro-bio-psycho-social approach while integrating theory with practice to help you heal your brain and find the authentic version of yourself.

The key to this change is, in fact, your own mind. It is the greatest tool you use to create your life. It guides your thoughts, feelings, actions, and reactions. A product of your brain's electrical performance pattern, it is the voice you hear inside your head leading you toward, or away from, healthy behaviors.

I will teach you how to use your mind in a healthier way to forge a more fulfilling life. If you follow each step, you will start observing and weighing your actions, thoughts, and inner monologue like never before. You will learn to process and understand your feelings and emotions while discerning how to be intentional in your thoughts and actions, creating meaningful goals, and, more importantly, knowing how to act upon them. Through enhanced brain performance you *can*—and *will*—establish the desire, commitment, and motivation to succeed. If you show up and do the work, I know you will leave this self-sabotaging habit behind and break the chains holding you back from your full potential.

———

Overcoming addiction is a serious issue. It necessitates a complex and integrated approach at three levels of your consciousness—unconscious, subconscious, and conscious—challenging you to do the following:

1. **Unconscious:** Heal your brain. You will need to adjust your brain's performance pattern, electrical energy, and flow of neurotransmitters to break a negative habit (a downward spiral) and create a positive one (an upward spiral) in its place.
2. **Subconscious:** Resolve underlying issues of which you may not be fully aware but that are holding you back.
3. **Conscious:** Change your thought system despite having to use your distorted thought system to start that process.

The Mind Over Explicit Matter approach is designed to help you accomplish these three challenges by giving you the knowledge and action steps to heal your brain performance pattern, integrate your mind, develop healthy sexuality and communication styles, and improve your relationships. The tools in this book will help you find the most authentic realization of yourself, the identity eager to emerge from behind the false persona your ego uses to protect itself. This self is your *true Self* and is more enlightened than the self you are living as right now. You might think of this as being superconscious: living the authentic, innate aspect of yourself expressed above and beyond your current levels, stepping into the version of yourself who no longer needs to rely on the escapism of porn. This Self won't have to keep secrets anymore or feel any more shame. This Self will feel your mind and your brain working with you, not against you.

The best part about this journey is that you will not have to do it alone. You will have me to help guide you as you make this uphill trek toward the mountain's pinnacle. So congratulations on being here. I know what a commitment it is to start this journey, and I am immensely proud of you for taking this giant first step. Take time to celebrate this progress as your first small win. As you will learn in this book, celebrating small successes is critical to fruition on the journey ahead.

Change is hard. We all know that. A research study found that 55 percent of people were able to maintain personal change one year later, but only 47 percent of those trying to avoid a behavior, such as porn, were successful compared to 58 percent of those who were adding a positive behavior, such as exercise.[3] Quitting an undesirable behavior is harder. Notably, when people had some support, their success rates increased significantly. The primary reasons for relapse were lack of control, stress, and negative emotions.[4] But I always say, "Where there is a will, there is a way," and scientific studies support this.[5] I will show you how to summon the will while I point to the way. It takes a healthy brain, commitment to change, discipline, and consistent execution to engage and evolve into a healthier version of yourself. But transformation is more straightforward when you have the right tools and learn how to use them. So let's get started—together.

PART 1

BRAIN BASICS:
THE POWER OF
KNOWLEDGE

CHAPTER 1

COMPULSIVE PORN USE AND HYPERSEXUALITY

*What lies behind us and what lies before us
are tiny matters compared to what lies within us.*
RALPH WALDO EMERSON

"I WATCH PORN!"

Meet Sam. He has just turned forty-five. And he is at the top of his game. After years of barely getting by, he has recently been promoted at work after outranking every one of his colleagues in sales and customer service. There is even a plaque on the wall with his name on it. I watch as Sam pulls up in his Mercedes-Maybach convertible—black on black on black. Standing tall, lean, and confident, decked out in his designer clothes, he opens the door for Krissy, his gorgeous wife. They laugh together as they enter the building and make their way to my office. Sam gently brushes a piece of his wife's long blonde hair from her face, and they share a smile. I invite them in, and they take a seat in my office. Sam is confident and at peace. His life seems idyllic, but we both know it wasn't always this way.

Five years earlier, Sam had arrived at my office under very different circumstances. On that day, there was no laughter. He had sat down in that same chair but with his back bent over and his head in his hands. He was riddled with shame.

Sam is a client and friend, but I had never seen him as I did on that fateful day.

I greeted him in my usual upbeat, enthusiastic way. "Hi, Sam!" Though he raised his head slightly, he did not answer. Unusually paralyzed in the office chair, he was pale, a look of panic in his eyes. After a few more moments of silence, the words spilled out with a mix of anguish and simultaneous relief: "I watch porn!"

"Porn?" I replied with both curiosity and confusion. At that point in my career as a neurofeedback therapist, I primarily helped people overcome anxiety and attention issues using brain-training technology. I had never had a client divulge information about porn use. In fact, I hadn't given it much thought. But then Sam shared a recent experience I have since found to be all too common in millions of homes and offices across the country, if not also the world.

A few weeks earlier, at his home, Sam was alone. Or he thought he was anyway. It was nearly dinnertime, and Krissy was working the grill outside while the rest of the family was upstairs. Sam was down in his man cave, sitting in front of his eighty-five-inch big-screen television and holding the remote control. He wasn't watching a game or a movie or even idly flicking through the channels. Instead, he was surfing online porn, trying to choose a scene out of the seemingly infinite number available. He just couldn't help himself.

Meanwhile, busy with dinner preparations, Krissy passed by

the window to the downstairs room. She saw Sam and what he was watching. He had thought it was his secret sexual habit. But she knew about it. She had even asked him to stop twice before. He had assured her that he had. But he hadn't. Now she was at a loss, feeling betrayed and overwhelmed. The next day, Krissy confronted him. "Is this the cause of the problems in our relationship?" she wondered aloud. "Is this why we've grown so distant?" She told Sam that he needed to get help, or she was leaving.

She came to suspect that porn had deeply impacted their marriage, and they'd had no idea. Sam wouldn't come to recognize this for quite some time. Sure, Krissy had noticed Sam's behavior had been a little weird. Some days he seemed to become angry and irritable without provocation, even lashing out at her and the kids for relatively insignificant things. Other days, he would come home almost manic, buzzing around in an energetic mood, delighted with life. These mood swings were understandably confusing to Krissy, but she hadn't made the connection to Sam's porn habit. And he hadn't either.

Sam was unsure of what to do, or who to see, for help—that is, if he really needed help. Was porn a genuine problem or was Krissy overreacting? Was their marriage truly in jeopardy, and if so, could it be repaired? And even if he wanted to stop watching, could he? After weeks of arguing back and forth, Krissy demanded Sam call me. She hoped that I could figure out the underlying neurological issues behind porn use and how they were impacting Sam. She also knew that I would be nonjudgmental and hold their story in confidence. When he came to me that day, I wasn't yet specializing in helping people recover from porn addiction, so I listened and referred Sam to a colleague. To his credit, he called. But of course, my interest in understanding porn addiction and my desire to help Sam and Krissy were sparked. And this brings us back to that first meeting in my office, his head in his hands.

Sam may have felt defeated that day, but his disclosure was a major accomplishment. Although he didn't know it then, he had reached the first critical stage on a path of self-exploration and understanding: he admitted he had a problem. But the question was, how big of a problem was it? Sure, he admitted that the amount and type of porn he had been watching was probably not good for him or his relationships, but he still didn't believe he had a "real problem" that warranted help from a professional. And so, like many others, he left my office determined to beat his pornography "habit" on his own. And, just like many before and after him, he failed.

At first, Sam half-heartedly went through the motions of quitting by himself, in which he'd stop every so often only to start up again shortly afterward. Then he tried a little harder, vowing to stop watching "cold turkey," but that proved futile. He followed that with a more moderate approach, reducing his porn use—both the amount and the intensity of the scenes—only that didn't work either. Two years went by, and Sam was still watching porn. Just as before, it was his little secret, hidden from those he loved. He even lied to Krissy, something he thought he would never do, telling her he hadn't watched in years when in fact he had watched the day before. He manipulated her whenever she got too close to discovering the truth. He developed tactics of watching porn when Krissy went out. On occasion she returned home unexpectedly. He'd nervously jump up, deny his reality, and gaslight her into thinking she was wrong to question him because she was unreasonably controlling. She began to believe she was overbearing and paranoid, but in fact she was correct about his behavior the whole time. He feigned working on recovery to the detriment of his brain, relationship, work, and life.

Finally, when Sam's marriage became increasingly strained due to his continued erratic behavior, lies, and manipulation, Krissy prepared to leave. Realizing he was about to lose his family, Sam decided to commit fully to quitting. He returned to my office and began his journey to overcome porn use and repair his relationship.

———

What Sam didn't know was that while he was trying and failing alone, I was on my own journey of discovery. His initial visit piqued my interest so much that I began to study under the most influential sex addiction professionals in the country, achieving my certification as a sex addiction recovery coach. Incorporating my knowledge base of brain dysregulation and the use of technology to enhance brain healing, I was easily able to integrate the behavioral aspects of porn addiction into what I already knew about brain dysfunction. I felt as if all my professional training had culminated into my true purpose: helping people heal from porn addiction.

I have found that my neuroscientific approach is an incredibly powerful solution. Thus, upon Sam's return, I was fully prepared to help him quit porn, heal his brain, and improve almost every aspect of his life. In time, Sam kicked his habit, saved his marriage, and created the life he'd always dreamed of. We will continue to follow Sam's story so you can see what he experienced following this process and how he ultimately accomplished his goals of joyful, authentic living.

If you have struggled on and off with porn over the years, and have unsuccessfully tried to quit by yourself, there is another, easier way. If you have found yourself lying to your wife, boyfriend, parents, or employer to cover your behavior, feeling shame and anxiety because of it, I want you to know there is hope and achievable success to be gained. Overcoming porn addiction can be challenging, but with a strong scientific approach, you can break free and flourish.

A PORN ADDICTION EPIDEMIC

I am not a huge fan of the word *addiction* because it can feel too unrelatable to some people and overly identifiable to others, who might believe they can never fully recover. However, it gives us a common language to communicate the devastation that a consistent porn habit can have on your brain and life. So I've found the term helpful when discussing porn use. But what does "porn addiction" mean?

The International Classification of Diseases (ICD), the global standard for diagnosis of health issues, has identified compulsive sexual behavior (CSB) as a disorder that includes pornography use, compulsive masturbation, and sex with anonymous partners.[1] The negative impact and harmful effects from compulsive sexuality, including porn use, can include mental and physical health issues such as anxiety, depression, erectile dysfunction, and delayed ejaculation.[2]

Porn users have a dysregulated brain mechanism that manifests as a sexual compulsion, an irresistible craving that urges a person to watch porn, usually beyond their conscious wishes.[3] It is in the family of obsessive-compulsive-related challenges, which scientific research has demonstrated to be neurological in origin. Here's how it works: An obsessive thought about sex comes into your mind from the need to regulate mood—namely, to offset stress, perceived boredom, or other emotions.[4] The obsessive thought persists until you act out a compulsive behavior to reduce the thought and make it go away. Because the underlying brain performance pattern has changed from optimal to dysfunctional, these urges increase in quantity and intensity as you continue to use porn.

I simply refer to compulsive sexual behavior disorder as *hypersexuality*: the feeling of needing sex all the time. In the Internet Age, hypersexuality manifests itself primarily through porn use, most times coupled with masturbation. The high level of mental stimulation from porn combined with increased physical stimulation from masturbation drives a continual need. You have an idea to watch porn and masturbate, which consumes you until you do. The more you engage the thought, the more you have it, and the loop continues on and on.

Many people confuse this compulsion for a high libido or sex drive but—let me be clear—they are not the same thing. Unlike a high libido, hypersexuality derives from a dysregulated brain performance pattern. Most people find porn and masturbation during their childhood or adolescent years, with an average first exposure reported at age twelve and a range all the way below ten years of age.[5] A recent study reports that 69 percent of teens have been exposed to porn, with up to 37 percent of that group doing so intentionally and 66 percent unintentionally.[6]

After first exposure, the brain begins to change how it functions. With continual use, those hypersexual brain pathways become reinforced. Not only does watching porn change how those children view sex over their lifetime, but it also alters their brain chemistry within the initial exposures. This early neurochemical alteration impacts brain performance and keeps the kids returning for more porn throughout their adult lives. Porn changes their brains and lives forever if they keep watching. The seeds of neurobiological addiction are thus planted the *first few times* you consume pornography and then are watered over time as your habit continues.[7]

Porn use is widespread. In one recent study, over 85 percent of participants between the ages of twelve and eighty-five said they view porn.[8] Porn use can be harmful even at low consumption levels (such as once per week).[9] This is because porn hits the sweet spot in being pleasurable and unassumingly dangerous even as it leads toward addiction. Not only is it extremely addictive to the brain, but it also includes the triple As—accessibility, affordability, and anonymity—for anyone with a phone or computer. Videos on porn websites are viewed over two hundred times more than YouTube videos, and porn sites themselves receive more traffic in the US than Instagram, X/Twitter, Netflix, Pinterest, and LinkedIn combined.[10] Yes, I said *combined*.

YOU ARE NOT ALONE: 85 PERCENT OF PEOPLE OF ALL AGES SAY THEY WATCH PORN.

With 96 percent of young adults encouraging, accepting, or neutral toward porn when talking with friends, and very few young people speaking up against it, porn use will continue to increase dramatically into the foreseeable future.[11] Shockingly, teens and young adults aged thirteen to twenty-four believe not recycling is worse than viewing pornography.[12] The first generation of children raised on the internet, smartphones, and social media—known as "digital natives"—are just now reaching adulthood. Thus, we are only beginning to witness how pornography will affect their lives and the generations to come.

WHY SHOULD YOU QUIT PORN?

Simply put, porn damages the brain, which inherently impacts the chronic user's ability to think, feel, perform, and relate at optimal levels.

Porn use is directly linked to:

- an increase in sexual dysfunction in men and women alike;[13]
- a significant rise in erectile dysfunction among young men;[14]
- higher impulsivity, emotional dysregulation, cognitive rigidity, and poorer judgment;[15]

- difficulty controlling sexual cravings regardless of situation;[16]
- excessive preoccupation with sex;[17]
- objectification of others,[18] leading to increased sexual coercion and abuse;[19]
- committing acts of sexual promiscuity, deviance, and violence;[20]
- low self-esteem, loneliness, anxiety, and depression;[21]
- less interest in sex with one's partner;[22]
- an increase in anal sex, which has negative effects on relationship well-being;[23]
- decreased body self-image,[24] and being more critical of a partner's body;[25]
- challenges building intimacy, causing relationship harm;[26]
- a greater risk of cheating on a partner;[27] and
- more than twice the occurrence of heated breakups or divorce than people who do not use porn.[28]

Porn use has been demonstrated to have a wide variety of negative effects in many areas of brain function, relationships, and physical and mental health. Porn use *is* impacting your life.

For Sam, porn use led him not only constantly back to the screen but also to "check out" young women when he was at work or other places around town, even when his wife was standing right next to him. Due to porn, Sam would low-key criticize his beautiful wife's appearance, feeling unsatisfied with her and their sexual relationship. Krissy was distraught and shared with me that she felt placed in a no-win situation. How could she live up to the image of a porn actress? How could their sex life compete with dozens of professional porn actors?

What Sam, and so many other people addicted to porn, did not realize is that the pull toward sexual media isn't really about sex; it is about heightened pleasure in the brain due to the neurochemical response that is linked to the content on the screen. It is based on fantasy, not reality. Subsequently, the porn user begins to substitute, or even prefer, the higher-level stimulation from sexualized media instead of lower, healthier, more balanced pleasure from a real-life sexual experience with a partner.

PORN ADDICTION AND WOMEN

Inherently, porn addiction differs slightly for most women, with a preference for the building of arousal from more suggestive, mood-based erotica that contains emotionally charged sexual content.[29] Brain-imaging studies support this difference and suggest it's what has made it so easy for erotic fiction, such as the Fifty Shades trilogy, to become so popularized.[30] In fact, there was an immediate 80 percent increase in the sale of sex toys—mostly whips, spanking paddles, handcuffs, and blindfolds—with the release of the Fifty Shades series.[31]

Some sex therapists promote a women's sex-empowerment movement based on this phenomenon, not taking into consideration that it promotes painful victimization of women for the pleasure of their male counterparts.[32] A significant increase in sex-toy injuries was noted during the first two years of Fifty Shades' release, with 83 percent of the injuries being related to foreign body removal.[33] This has led scientists to comment on the dangerous nature of constructing extreme, marginalized, and harmful sexual fantasy practices as fun, fashionable, and exciting.[34]

Consistent exposure to explicit matter can lead women to be more open to sexual acts that demoralize themselves or induce pain and suffering. Women who view porn are more likely to endorse rape myths—the notion that women cause and enjoy rape—through their thinking and actions of partaking in rape scripts with a higher number of sexual partners.[35]

With an increased acceptance of these sexual attitudes, pornographic scenes are now being reinforced in television shows more than ever. *Game of Thrones* rose in popularity within the fantasy genre but has been criticized for capitalizing on the fantasy "in which every woman, no matter her power or fortune, is likely to be sexually violated in front of the viewer's eyes."[36] The normalizing of sexualized violence against women became a cornerstone of the show's storylines, with the producers receiving harsh critiques because they chose to add brutality to the scenes even though it was not in the original writing of the story.[37] I distinctly remember the first, and last, time that I watched the show. I walked into the room as my husband was watching. As I sat down next to him, a scene of a young woman about to be raped by five or six men was on the screen. I walked out. Although it isn't directly porn, viewing sexual-violence-fantasy media impacts women and their perspectives toward themselves, their partners, and sexuality.[38]

Women porn users have been shown to have greater dissatisfaction with their genital appearance and monitor their own bodies more during sexual experiences, with lower body satisfaction leading to decreased sexual esteem.[39] With increased porn use there was also decreased affection within their relationships and more depression and loneliness.[40] Women felt more pressure to perform porn-influenced sexual acts while at the same time feeling worse about their body because their partner was more critical of it.[41]

Increased sexual fantasy about someone other than a partner was found to occur in 80 percent of women, and it was related to having a higher number of sexual partners and a higher incidence of cheating on one's partner.[42] So what does all this mean? It means increased sexual fantasy and its popularization in the media increases hypersexuality.

FAKE NEWS ABOUT PORN

Have you ever wondered why there isn't an overabundance of articles on the harmful effects of pornography if it is scientifically proven to be detrimental to people's lives? Well, the multibillion-dollar pornography industry has established a vast and in-depth disinformation campaign to create confusion and cause doubt in the mind of the public and decision-makers. *Dis*information is bigger and more harmful than its subtler counterpart, *mis*information, which is simply twisting facts. Disinformation includes the elements of disrespect, insult, and contempt, in this case with the intent of discrediting the factual basis of porn's harm on mental, physical, and relational health.

The disinformation playbook has four known components: (1) challenge the problem, (2) challenge causation, (3) challenge the messenger, and (4) challenge the policy.[43] Often the porn industry will pay scientists to attack messengers who try to communicate the problem of porn consumption, its cause, and how to recover from it. Recovery from porn addiction is bad for the porn industry's business. Understanding these tactics can increase preparedness and promote resilience when faced with disinformation. The playbook is designed to confuse people, and it works.[44]

Disinformation by seemingly qualified professionals can make it difficult to know what is true. I want you to understand three ways you might be exposed to disinformation so that you can recognize it and learn how to discern the fake news of accusations, twisted misinformation, and deliberate disinformation. This way you can stay empowered on your porn recovery journey.

First, generative artificial intelligence (AI) is being used to produce summaries of "facts" to make it easy for users to access information on the internet. Due to the amount of disinformation that has been reported in a variety of ways from falsified research by scientists who are paid by the industry, it can be very difficult to determine what is true from false.[45] Don't believe everything generated by AI. Dig deeper and be sure that the source is a benevolent messenger with a reputable guardian organization behind them.

Second, astroturfing is a deceptive marketing technique that is used by offending professionals as they generate unsolicited comments to confuse public opinion, meaning you might read comments on social media, news articles, or interviews of professionals claiming that porn is healthy.[46] You might read negative reviews of professionals you believe to be positive messengers. This is deliberate to make you question the intent of well-meaning porn recovery organizations. Offenders, for the most part, attack the messengers with ill intent. One helpful strategy is to filter comments for helpful information versus attack messages.

Lastly, identifying offenders can help you begin to see who the players are in the disinformation campaigns. When you encounter a few loud and disruptive voices that speak to the merits of porn use, this can be a red flag that you are dealing with a motivated offender.

By recognizing false attacks and the misrepresentation of well-meaning porn addiction recovery professionals who are associated with capable guardians, you will begin to discern helpful information from disinformation.

As a messenger, I have personally been a target of malicious disinformation campaigns. My credentials have been denounced and distorted. I have been falsely reported by offenders to a variety of organizations and government agencies for violating FDA regulations, all of which are not true. I have been lied about and slandered online by players in the campaign. So I want you to know these are known tactics to confuse you and convince you porn is good for you when, simply put, it is not.

NORMAL, BUT NOT HEALTHY

"But isn't porn use normal?" you might ask. Maybe, but it's certainly not healthy. We live in a world where all kinds of things that are not good for our health and well-being have been normalized, including, but certainly not limited to, porn and hypersexuality. Processed foods, alcohol, and drugs, both pharmaceutical and illicit, are all consumed at alarming rates. But what differentiates porn from most other unhealthy vices in our society is that, if you want it, you can find it almost immediately at all intensity levels. This is why people, young and old, are now constantly and passively consuming explicit content to entertain themselves through fantasy to improve their moods. In such a world, you could say watching porn is both normal and unhealthy.

So, maybe asking whether porn is "normal" is not actually the right question. Instead, we must ask whether it is beneficial. Based on my studies and those of others, the answer to that question is undoubtedly no. I have observed the ways in which getting stuck in a pleasure-seeking consumption loop can steal a person's ability to live to their full potential. And I want to help people live lives filled not only with pleasure but also with happiness and joy.

In the pages that follow, we'll dive into the science of how porn alters the brain, how those alterations have devastating effects on people's lives, and how you can free yourself by rewiring these neural pathways.

But for now, let's start with just the basics.

THE NEUROBIOLOGY OF PORN ADDICTION

The human sex drive is one of our most vital biological imperatives, hardwired into our bodies and brains. At the heart of this imperative is a neurotransmitter called *dopamine*: the "feel good" brain chemical. It's the pleasure-giving and pleasure-seeking driver in our brains. It is also one of the primary factors most responsible for pushing us to satisfy our natural desire for sex. Whenever a person has sex, or even thinks about having sex, dopamine is released in the brain.

IT IS THE DOPAMINE "HIT" THE BRAIN NEEDS, NOT SEX.

But porn fulfills our biological desire for sex in a fabricated and disruptive way. Neuroscientists classify pornography as a supernormal stimulus because it floods your system with rushing rivers of dopamine, giving your brain an unnatural high that it would not encounter otherwise.[47] There are four distinct Ds in the dopamine cycle of porn addiction: dopamine drip, dopamine deluge, dopamine drowning, and dopamine drought.

Thus, for Sam and others addicted to porn, it is the dopamine "hit" that the brain needs, not sex. When Sam feels the dopamine drip of an urge to watch porn, he is sensing the internal neurobiological change associated with the shift toward higher dopamine levels in his brain. This shift happens in response to his need for mood enhancement. As he moves toward consuming porn and masturbating, his brain releases a higher flow of dopamine in the dopamine deluge, the second D in the cycle. As he stays in a porn session, his brain is bathed in high levels of dopamine for a longer timeframe, which I refer to as dopamine drowning. Afterward, he is left in a dopamine drought state when he reengages with the world. With continual porn use the dopamine cycle is perpetuated, reinforced, and heightened.

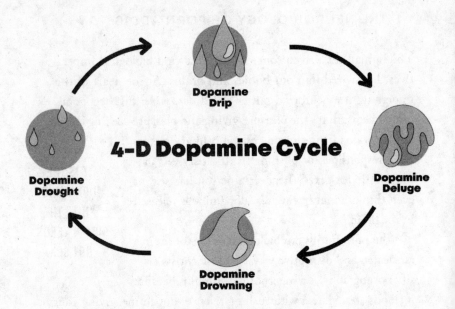

HOW PORN USE BECOMES PORN ADDICTION

Porn use typically begins as a pleasure-seeking activity but increasingly becomes more about avoiding stress, pain, or anxiety. In fact, it actually creates more tension within a person's life due to a real-world dopamine-deficit state of affairs. With lower levels of dopamine being derived from healthy, real-world sources, as would have occurred without porn use, the user becomes disenchanted with their work, relationships, and hobbies. With increased consumption over time, porn use transitions to abuse and ultimately to addiction. For many, strife becomes a way of life.

Thus, there is a growing desire to continue to create an unreality—a fantasy—to offset the ever-increasing pain and discomfort of the stressful reality. Masturbation starts to serve as a mood manager. Your brain becomes hardwired to need it and to need larger and larger doses of it as time goes by. The scientific word for this process is *desensitization*, and it leads the porn viewer to seek out novel and more graphic situations to get the same level of arousal as before. Before you know it, real-life sex with a real-life partner starts to pale by comparison.

Psychologically, the constant pleasure-seeking, which uses and takes from others, induces more shame and discomfort. Enhanced shame derives from the uncontrollable need to return to sexual behaviors that are kept secret and often cross moral boundaries. Before long, the pain and fear of being discovered that is held within gets projected toward the world and those within it.

How Porn Use Becomes Porn Addiction

Like Sam, you might find yourself living a kind of paradoxical existence, with dual identities. I often refer to this as the Dr. Jekyll/ Mr. Hyde effect, based on Robert Louis Stevenson's classic novella in which the seemingly smooth-talking, high-statured Dr. Jekyll spends a lifetime repressing his ravenous, evil inner urges personified in his alter ego, Mr. Hyde. On the one hand, there is the Dr. Jekyll persona: the good father, husband, and businessman who is respected by his family and community. He presents a face of serene happiness and confidence on social media and in public. And on the other, Mr. Hyde hides just around the corner. He is down in the dark man cave by himself, being served by a webcam girl, masturbating to porn, and typing online searches for fetishes that he would be mortified for others to discover.

Or maybe you're Mrs. Hyde, in your apartment, locked in your bedroom with porn while your roommates hang out in the living room. You tell yourself that it is not a big deal because you're not having sex or at risk of getting pregnant. It is just a way for you to relax, and it helps you sleep. This double life can be extremely exhausting and stressful, oscillating between pleasure and pain, arousal and shame.

All of this sounds like bad news, doesn't it? Well, it is. But there is good news too. Porn addiction stems from your brain, and neuroscience has demonstrated that brains have neuroplasticity, which means they can be rewired. So if you're feeling overwhelmed or exhausted by your porn use, misuse, abuse, or addiction, you can learn to heal your brain and free yourself to live the liberated life you dream of.

CHAPTER 2

YOUR PORN BRAIN

The journey of a thousand miles
begins with a single step.
LAO TZU

A FAMILIAR PATTERN

It was Sunday afternoon, about a year before Krissy finally confronted Sam about his porn use. He was cranky. He had been at home with Krissy and the kids since Friday afternoon. His family had been having a great weekend. They spent Saturday morning playing games, joking, and laughing. Then they went to the pool, returning to make and eat dinner together before watching a movie. On Sunday, they had an enjoyable brunch, eating together and talking before taking their dog hiking in the woods. But Sam was not present emotionally. He was primarily in his man cave—just wanting to be alone.

Sam recalled that Friday evening had been fairly relaxing, but the rest of his weekend had been just OK. Saturday, he did some odd jobs around the house while watching TV, and his wife was annoying him about everything on Sunday. His kids were particularly obnoxious too. They kept making messes and wouldn't stop talking. He wondered why they were all so abrasive. He had difficulty dealing with them and decided to watch football all day instead of engaging with them. At this point, he never would have considered that it was him, not them, who was the problem.

Monday morning came. Sam was still not happy. Krissy asked him why he had been so upset. He snapped at her and told her he didn't have a problem; she did. This was one of many times over the past few years that their week began with this pattern. Krissy knew it would shift again the next day. She didn't know why, but she knew it would. Sam didn't see this pattern at all or realize it was happening. At least not yet.

Behind the scenes, there was an explanation for Sam's behavior. Sam had watched porn and masturbated on Thursday morning like he usually did. His routine for a while had been to watch porn on Tuesday and Thursday mornings after his family left for the day. So, on Friday, he was still feeling good. But by Saturday and Sunday, he was hitting a low point.

Sam's kids would joke they never knew which version of their dad they'd get on a Friday night. Sometimes he was the life of the party; other times he was an irritable drill sergeant, barking orders at anything that moved. Everyone was aware that his behavior was erratic and upsetting; it was just that no one knew the underlying cause. As it turned out, if he had watched porn that Thursday, he was happy. If he hadn't, it was the opposite. Even when we acknowledge problematic external behaviors, it is hard to change them until we discover what lies at their roots.

THE POWER OF KNOWLEDGE
TO TRANSFORM

I firmly believe that knowledge is power. Knowledge can transform the seemingly inexplicable into the readily observable and improvable. It can help you make sense of who you are and figure out what you can do to create the life you want. The initial motivation for change is fueled by understanding. So to break the chains of porn addiction, let's take a moment to learn how your brain functions with porn so you can understand what's happening when you unwire, rewire, and hardwire your brain.

When your brain pattern is dysregulated, using a less-than-optimal operating mode, it swings like a pendulum between high-speed and very slow-energy patterns. Pendulation, as such, leaves your life swinging, too, with your behaviors and emotions fluctuating in response. It's just like we saw with Sam on Friday night. He was driven to a lowered energy state, in which he needed frequent self-soothing, including the familiar sensations of masturbation and porn, to feel better.

The human brain is staggeringly complex. It is the product of millions of years of evolution. Contained within your skull is an organ composed of around one hundred billion neurons—an organ some scientists consider the most complicated thing we have ever encountered in the known universe.[1] Not surprisingly, there is still so much to learn about how the brain functions. Thanks to decades of research, however, we have already learned a great deal about how various electrical and chemical pathways in the brain shape our emotions and behaviors.

The many neurons in the brain communicate with each other through neural pathways that involve chemical messengers known as neurotransmitters. These neurotransmitters affect your mood, arousal levels, and behaviors.

In concert, three primary neurotransmitters (dopamine, serotonin, and oxytocin), known as the "happiness trifecta," make up an ideal neurochemical cocktail when they are produced—at healthy levels—within authentic experiences that lead to a sensed feeling of happiness.[2] Dopamine contributes to pleasure, serotonin to joy, and oxytocin to connection.

Dopamine, the molecule of more, motivation, and pleasure, can prompt you to seek out and repeat pleasurable activities.[3] At healthy levels, it can put you in a good mood while helping you maintain focus and motivation toward meaningful work, satisfying relationships, and hobbies you enjoy. At unhealthy levels, however, it can derail you from your life's purpose and set you on a constant pleasure-seeking roller coaster. If you give your power to dopamine, it will take it and run insatiably in the direction of short-term pleasure over long-term joy and happiness.

The dopamine pathway, or reward system, in your brain makes you feel satisfied after eating and having sex with your partner. Life-sustaining activities are essential for the survival of the human species; dopamine rewards you for performing them.

Abuse of this reward system can lead to different types of behavioral addictions, including gambling, shopping, and internet addictions, especially pornography.[4] Remember, porn use is not the same as sex with a partner. The unnaturally high levels of dopamine linked to porn and masturbation not only negatively impact your pleasure by taking you away from shared, partnered sexual experiences, but they also harm you. High dopamine levels are the reason for the long list of negative effects caused by porn you saw in chapter 1, including low mood, depression, decreased self-esteem, irritability, social awkwardness, difficulty concentrating, decreased family interaction, and an increase in unhealthy sexuality.

YOUR BRAIN'S GEARS

A healthy brain follows a natural biological clock based on the rising and setting of the sun; we call it the circadian rhythm, and it contributes to a healthy baseline arousal state. The brain shifts in and out of its three natural arousal states, achieving (1) low arousal (sleep), (2) medium arousal (calm alertness), and (3) high arousal (a stress response designed to protect you when necessary). In this way, your brain acts like a car shifting in and out of braking, neutral, and accelerating throughout the day. When cycling along with circadian rhythms, your brain is in an optimized state of neurological regulation, which leads to strong self-regulation skills that allow you to be aware of your own emotions and behaviors while gauging the impact of them on other people within social contexts.[5] This allows you to feel relaxed, maintain focus, and interact with other people in an emotionally healthy way. The optimal brain performance pattern can be measured, analyzed, and visualized using an innovative, advanced technology called quantitative electroencephalogram (qEEG), also known as a "brain map."[6] Neurological dysregulation happens due to the disruption of circadian rhythms and contributes to mental and physical health issues, such as addiction, anxiety, depression, trauma, and attention and arousal dysfunction.[7] Each of these dysregulated brain performance patterns can be viewed on a qEEG brain map.

Compulsive porn use has been shown to disrupt circadian rhythms, causing a dysregulated brain pattern that can lead to stress, emotional volatility, and sleep issues, all of which can increase the desire to watch porn and masturbate.[8] Essentially, your brain can use too much braking, which causes exhaustion; too much neutral, which can make you feel depressed; and excessive acceleration, which can lead to anxiety. In turn, your brain acts like a manual transmission stuck in gear.

THE PENDULUM EFFECT

Due to the dopamine deficit outside of your porn use, your brain oscillates back and forth between the high arousal state of stress activation and the low arousal state of exhaustion, *except* when watching porn. This "wired and tired" brain pattern makes you feel anxious, exhausted, and in need of more dopamine. Once porn is used again, with high levels of dopamine coursing through your system, you can become stuck in artificially induced neutral, with its numbed-out, euphoric state. However, you will feel stressed, overwhelmed, and fatigued when the flood dries up again. I call this the pendulum effect. Fast then slow. Stressed then exhausted. Up then down, just like Sam and his unstable moods and manic behavior. Your brain becomes taxed and exhausted. As the iconic physicist Galileo

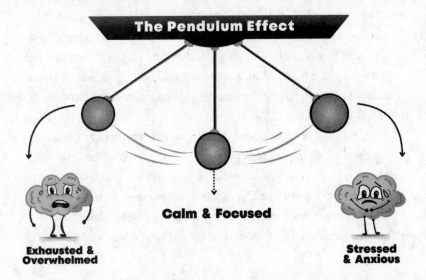

The Pendulum Effect

Calm & Focused

Exhausted &
Overwhelmed

Stressed
& Anxious

observed, the distinguishing characteristic of a pendulum is that its momentum *must* propel its force to the opposite, but equal, extreme. This means that however high the pendulum swings toward anxiety, it will swing equally high in the direction of exhaustion.

Overload results in what I refer to as "strained brain," in which your brain becomes stuck in wired-and-tired states semi-permanently. With every slip back into porn, you reinforce the strained-brain pattern. Every step away from porn leads to healing it. This brain pattern must be soothed and stimulated simultaneously. It craves more dopamine to offset stress and boredom by artificially shifting into neutral once again—which is something I call "drained brain." In the drained-brain pattern, the pendulum is stuck in the middle, not able to move at all. Porn is very good at doing that for you, which is why your brain wants to go back to it, to stop the pendulum from swinging for a little while. However, with increased porn use and its related high levels of dopamine, your brain can become semi-permanently stuck in neutral due to the desensitization of the dopamine receptors in the reward center of the brain.[9] This is a leading cause of sexual arousal dysfunction (SAD), including erectile dysfunction (ED).[10] In this state you may feel depressed and unmotivated and suffer from a lack of overall arousal. Once you optimize your brain pattern, you won't feel the incessant need to watch porn anymore, nor will you feel stuck, low, and frustrated.

HOW CAN THE BRAIN BE
UNWIRED AND REWIRED?

Neuroscientists have identified a well-known phenomenon referred to as Hebb's law, which states that "neurons that fire together, wire together."[11] Every experience a person has gets written into their brain cells, or wired into the brain's topography, if you will. Each time the

NEURONS THAT FIRE TOGETHER, WIRE TOGETHER.

same experience is repeated, the connection in the brain is strengthened. In this case, the neurons that fire with each instance of porn use help to build and reinforce the neural pathways back to porn with continued use.

Unwiring is the opposite of Hebb's law and is scientifically called anti-Hebbian learning theory, and it helps the brain to discriminate between rewarding versus nonrewarding behaviors.[12] Stop watching porn, and the neural pathways back to porn die off. At the same time, if you establish new healthy thoughts and actions, you will capitalize on neuroplasticity to make significant positive changes in your life, which will help you reach your full potential.

Ivan Pavlov and his drooling dogs popularized learning concepts known as classical and operant conditioning, which can be used to stop a self-sabotaging habit and induce a new, healthier one. Pavlov taught his dogs to salivate on cue by rewarding their behavior. A stable, but unwanted, behavior pattern, such as watching pornography, can be destabilized and eradicated through lack of reinforcement, and a new, healthier behavior, such as reading a book, can be established in its place through positive reinforcement. The brain will chase down the reward you give it, so it is important to give it a healthy one. Up until now you have been reinforcing the behavior of a porn habit with a high dopamine reward. We will shift the reward you currently receive from compulsive sexuality to healthier dopamine rewards associated with your work, relationships, and hobbies.

EPIGENETICS AND NEUROMODULATION TECHNIQUES

Advances in neuroscience and technology now make it possible to improve brain performance patterns strictly at an unconscious level, without you thinking about it or using your body in any particular way. As we've already discussed, your brain can heal itself using its own changeability, called neuroplasticity.[13] Remember, neurons that fire together, wire together. For those struggling with addictive behaviors, it has been shown that the reward system in the brain changes the way that it functions, needing more dopamine due to the addiction. Emerging fields of integrative health care, such as psychoeducation, mind-body practices, and biofield electromagnetic therapies, can improve brain performance and the way a person feels and performs.[14] This is known as *epigenetics*, with the prefix "epi" meaning "over."[15] We can elevate our brains and minds *over* explicit matter.

Did you know that you can rewire your brain without trying? Advanced technologies, called *neuromodulation*, target the dysfunctional brain areas and are projected to be the preferred method of healing neurological disorders, including addiction, since they are drug-free and flexible.[16] Neurofeedback, also called qEEG-guided biofeedback, monitors the electrical energy pattern in your brain and allows you to gain more control over it through feedback that is presented to you through sights and sounds. It reinforces the use of a new desired brain pattern while not reinforcing the undesirable one. In this way it can teach a person's brain, unconsciously (without using the mind and body), to reduce or enhance the use of any given gear in the brain. As you wear sensors on your head, they read how your brain is performing as you simply watch video and listen to audio. As the feedback changes, or modulates, your brain adjusts its own performance based on what it is seeing and hearing. It is a passive treatment that uses neuroplasticity that we will explore deeper. You don't have to try; it does the work for you.

Applying neurofeedback to compulsive porn use helps your strained brain, with its fast and slow speed domination, to be destabilized while the use of medium brain speeds, to feel calm and focused, are reinforced. For people with drained brain, the stuck brain pattern can be guided by technology out of unhealthy arousal back to a healthier brain performance pattern. Neurofeedback has long been shown effective to reduce anxiety and depression and can facilitate addiction recovery.[17]

DID YOU KNOW THAT YOU CAN REWIRE YOUR BRAIN WITHOUT TRYING?

Two decades ago, when I was a university professor, I researched and implemented a wide range of neuromodulation techniques. Neurofeedback proved to be the most enjoyable and powerfully effective of them all. I want you to know about it because porn addiction can create a neuro-rigid, stuck brain pattern that can be difficult to move toward the healthier, optimal pattern. This is why so many people try to quit porn and fail. The lack of success is because they are using a biopsychosocial approach while ignoring the neurological aspect. With the power of neuromodulation techniques on the unconscious brain, a person recovering from porn has a much greater chance of succeeding quicker and with less resistance. I have seen it firsthand for Sam and the rest of my clients. It is a crucial aspect of healing your brain from porn.

PORN'S INSIDIOUS NATURE

Over the years, Sam's porn use escalated and made him anxious, depressed, less motivated, angry, irritable, and overly sexual. It even gave him erectile dysfunction, though he did not know it was due to porn. All of this came on so gradually that Krissy, who had been with and adored Sam for fifteen years, didn't trace his changed behaviors back to anything in particular. This is what makes porn use so dangerous. It is insidious. It sneaks in unassumingly, damages your brain, changes your thoughts, morphs your actions, and begins to ruin your life.

Sam's weekly porn use helped him focus during his workdays and deal with family weekends. But his feeling good depended on his porn use. If he missed a day, his mood was off. Over time he needed additional days of watching porn just to feel all right. Thus, his habit escalated from Tuesdays and Thursdays to every day. From there, it quickly became a morning habit, once his wife left, and an evening habit, to relax before bed. Before Sam realized it, he watched porn on and off, multiple times a day, almost daily. His brain needed the constant flood of dopamine from frequent, consistent, and intense porn sessions. Scientifically, this is a known component of addiction and is referred to as *escalation*. It is driven by an increased need for more dopamine due to tolerance building in the brain.

In the dopamine-induced, numbed-out state he was in, Sam left porn open on his computer and his phone browser, and out of need, he went back into the man cave for a Sunday evening porn session even though his whole family was home. He did all of this without thinking twice about it. This is how his wife ultimately discovered the extent of his porn use. His guard was down because his brain began to deteriorate from the consistent deluge and drowning of dopamine. Porn made him feel good, but it was damaging his brain. His motivation decreased, so he stopped working as much, and he became trapped in the loop of constantly going back to porn and masturbating in a futile attempt to feel better. The silent tsunami had overwhelmed Sam's life, and it was time to turn it around.

THE SILENT TSUNAMI OF PORN ADDICTION

I remember when the deadliest tsunami ever recorded in history happened in late 2004. A magnitude 9.1 earthquake happened eighteen miles under the ocean floor. The force caused an eight-hundred-mile-long rupture, and the tsunami spread in every direction.[18] The damage was catastrophic. As I completed my sex addiction recovery training, the devastation of that tsunami stuck in my head. The devastation of porn was something I felt nobody was talking about, but everybody should be.

Porn is likely affecting the vast majority of people, whether because they themselves use porn or because porn is affecting someone important in their life. The negative impact is spreading in every direction, and no one understands the proverbial earthquake that has happened below the surface.

The tsunami engulfs your life, first under the surface within your nervous system as continued dysregulation in your brain. Then the inner disruption begins to show itself on the outside in the form of mental and physical health issues. Eventually, it inundates every aspect of your life. You may have difficulty engaging in your work, your relationships become strained—where there once was happiness, now there is damage and loss. Like large waves on the ocean of life that have been created by disruption under the surface, the impact of your pornography habit crashes down on you, upheaving your existence. Not only that, but your porn addiction doesn't only affect you; it impacts everyone in your life. With a 91-percent global increase in porn consumption since 2020, the tsunami of porn addiction is at risk of creating a massive negative wave effect of physical and mental health issues for men and women worldwide.[19]

There are six stages to the porn tsunami's progression in a person's life:

1. Neurological dysregulation is caused by the first porn exposure and subsequent reinforcement through continued viewing.

2. Emotional dysregulation emerges due to neurological dysregulation.

3. Porn use continues for mood regulation via self-soothing and stimulation.

4. Addiction then occurs through tolerance building, escalation, and reinforcement of dysregulation in the brain.

5. Next is the development and persistence of mental and physical health issues.

6. And there is also decreased relationship satisfaction and stability.

Six Stages of the Silent Tsunami of Porn Addiction

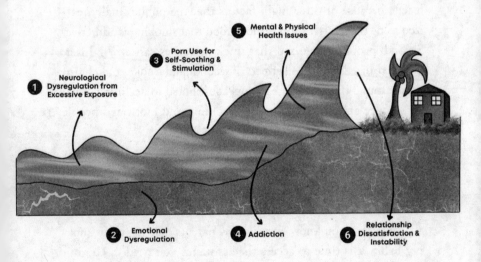

IMPETUS FOR CHANGE

Change is difficult—especially when you have been dependent on an addictive behavior for a long time. Take smoking for example. I remember when my parents quit smoking in the 1980s. Initially, each would sneak behind the garage to smoke as they were trying to quit, but they eventually had success by getting assistance and support from others. What made them commit to stopping? Knowledge.

Today, we know that for the first half of the twentieth century, nobody, even physicians, thought smoking was harmful. Disinformation campaigns, as we have already looked at, made it even more difficult for people to understand the harmful effects, making it much more challenging to commit to cessation and then succeed. But in 1964, smoking reached its peak and then began to recede because of three main factors that the public finally realized to be true. First, people understood that smoking is addictive. Second, people recognized that smoking causes cancer. And last, people realized that the ill effects of secondhand smoke could harm those around them.[20] These factors contributed to declining social acceptance and attitudes toward smoking, and motivated people toward change.

This is precisely why I want to remind you that (1) porn use has been shown to be addictive; (2) it contributes to sexual arousal dysfunction, especially in young men; and (3) it is a risk factor for relationship satisfaction and stability at any level of use.

Now that you know, just like my parents quitting their smoking habit, it is time to access the assistance you need to commit and succeed. That starts with the recognition that compulsive porn use stems from a dysregulated brain performance pattern: strained brain. It is imperative to interrupt the brain pattern that perpetuates your habit and establish new habits to rewire the brain and sustain healthy dopamine levels for a lifetime. In doing so, you will improve your brain health, mental and physical well-being, and, quite possibly, your relationships. This will effectively recede the silent tsunami of porn in your life, and if enough people collectively engage in the healing process, it could recede the global tsunami altogether.

Using neuroplasticity, we can reverse the tsunami of porn in your life and the lives of others in six intentional steps:

1. Regulate underlying dysregulated brain patterns using neuromodulation techniques.
2. Increase emotional intelligence and self-regulation through new action steps.
3. Quit porn for good because there is no more need for self-soothing and stimulation.
4. Establish a healthy lifestyle, including healthy sexuality, through improved thoughts and behaviors.
5. Live authentically and purposefully with integrity for optimal well-being.
6. Enjoy improved relationship quality and stability.

To progress through these stages, we will move through the first two levels that are under the surface: the unconscious brain performance patterns and the subconscious thought processes that you might employ. Then we will move toward consciously quitting porn and creating a healthy lifestyle with proven neuroscientific strategies. Above the surface we will use your improved mental and physical health to superconsciously create the most authentic version of your true Self so you can realize its fullest potential for lasting happiness.

Brain Hack Number 1
Recede the Silent Tsunami and Establish Calm Waters

Reflect on the idea of the silent tsunami of porn addiction, and in a journal draw a wave and label the six steps to receding the tsunami in your life. Then draw the calm beach and ocean, highlighting what your life will look like when you have quit porn for good.

CHAPTER 3

WHAT IS HEALTHY
SEX ANYWAY?

Find out who you are and do it on purpose.
DOLLY PARTON

WHEN SEX IS EVERYWHERE

Sam thought about sex *all the time*. Hardly an idle moment went by when he didn't think about it. He started to watch more porn—morning, noon, and night. He would masturbate most mornings before work. He started edging, which means watching porn without orgasm to achieve elevated levels of dopamine for an extended period. Sometimes he would edge several days in a row, slowly building the dopamine levels in his brain. This would extend the exhilarated feeling until he finally ejaculated days later. It would also result in more significant crashes when he was away from the screen, which meant increased anxiety, irritability, and anger. And so, he flooded his brain with dopamine day after day without knowing that was what he was doing.

Sam's unguarded state is called the *narcissistic bubble*. Influenced by dopamine dominance, all your sexual desires appear as if they should be yours for the taking. This keeps your brain laser-focused on pleasure-seeking, searching for the next dopamine fix. This "bubble" can creep over you in an imperceptible manner with increased porn use. But self-awareness and accountability for your behavior go increasingly down as you keep trying to feel good. Joe, a client of mine, put it like this: "My wife walked in on me masturbating to porn, and I just looked up at her and kept going." It wasn't quite that bad for Sam, but almost.

HAVE YOU EVER BEEN IN THE BUBBLE?

Explicit matter isn't restricted to full-blown pornography accessed on specific porn sites. Comfortably in the bubble, Sam could keep the dopamine flowing throughout the day using lower-level sexual media as well. He would scroll TikTok, looking at women for an hour here and there. After that, YouTube would provide more porn-adjacent content that remained socially acceptable at work or in public, but he could still feel a micro-surge of dopamine within his brain. The feeling is what he wanted, no matter what was on the screen. On X/Twitter, he would follow his favorite porn performers, and on Instagram, he could enjoy still images on and off all day. What Sam didn't know is that although social media might seem harmless, sexual media was surreptitiously firing up the porn neural pathways in his brain, keeping him in the bubble and leading him back to porn. He would discover this connection later as he tried to quit porn consumption for good. Have you ever been in the bubble?

———

Sam's porn consumption habits began to shift. Not only did his need escalate to greater intensity, but his craving for erotica increased unwittingly and far beyond his moral values. It was as if he were having an out-of-body experience as he watched his fingers type into the search bar terms for acts he would never ordinarily want to see—morally unacceptable sex acts, including those involving sexual violence and featuring very young women.

Anytime his wife would come into his office or man cave, before Sam inadvertently let his guard down, he would immediately click out of whatever window was open on his screen. The trust between them started to break down, and so did their sex life. Sam unconsciously tried to get his wife to participate in some of the ramped-up, aggressive, dopamine-producing sex acts he had seen on the screen. After watching these acts thousands of times, they were normalized to Sam's distorted mind, and he thought his wife would want to do them. She did not.

He would also wake her up early in the morning to have sex. Then he would be mad at her when she didn't want to do it or if she just lay there, unmoving. One time he woke her up at 4:30 a.m. for sex without even realizing it was that early. Many porn users wake up their partners for sex in this way. The purpose is rarely to connect with their partner but rather to get that hit of dopamine that will reduce their stress or regulate their mood for the upcoming day. Sam was objectifying his wife by using her like this. He was inadvertently turning her into a sex object to be used purely for his pleasure.

But Sam was objectifying more than his wife. Lust increased as he constantly stared at other women sexually. He began making sexual comments publicly and frequently initiated sexual conversations. This is another aspect of hypersexuality—almost *everything* becomes sexual. On one family vacation, Sam couldn't stop checking out the women around him, even while at the dinner table with his family—and even after Krissy asked him why he couldn't take his eyes off the female servers' bodies. Sam did not apologize.

Instead, he snapped at her, telling her she was insecure and asking, "What do you expect me to do? Wear blinders out in public?"

Sam often said he was "appreciating the beauty of gorgeous women." This is a ubiquitous thing for hypersexual men to say. But it is a justification—a rationalization for the objectification of women and the need for a "high." In reality, Sam was not appreciating female beauty. He was obsessively looking at buttocks and breasts for extra dopamine hits while on vacation with his family (a stressor) and away from porn (which he used for stress relief). It was only in retrospect that Sam realized this was a big pattern for him: the less he had access to porn, the more he lusted after women.

Porn addiction was different for Layla. She was exposed to explicit matter at a young age and continued in secret from then on. Like many other females addicted to porn, she had difficulty reconciling the exciting and stimulating response she felt inside with the appallingly graphic scene she viewed on the screen. The societal sexual double standard (SDS) set out for women enhances the internal conflict they feel due to the continual need to watch porn.[1] Many women who view pornography report increased negative body image, face pressure to accept rape myths, and experience sexual assault and domestic violence.[2]

Layla started watching videos of how to French-kiss and within a matter of weeks was watching a variety of sexual acts. Before long, watching pornography had become an uncontrollable habit for her. She used porn every night to relax. If she was more stressed, she would watch porn a few times throughout the day. "I was disgusted with myself. I hated my own mind," she told me. But she couldn't stop. After years of "shame tearing her apart on the inside," she finally told her secret to her three best friends. With their encouragement, she told her mom and began the road to healing.

SEEKING HEALTHY SEXUALITY

Knowing the difference between compulsive, addictive sex and healthy sexuality is crucial for success in rewiring your brain. You must leave the first behind and develop the second. This will help you experience authentic pleasure, intimate connection, and overall happiness. But learning to stay out of an addictive sex pattern and embrace a healthy view of sexuality takes time. In comparing addictive and healthy sex, it is helpful to learn fifteen key distinctions between the two.[3]

Addictive Sex

1. Originates from shame-based sexuality
2. Takes advantage of others and compromises your integrity
3. Confuses intensity for intimacy
4. Reenacts trauma and cements arousal patterns in the brain (neurorigidity)
5. Requires a level of dissociation
6. Is organized around the past and future (i.e., euphoric recall and fantasy)
7. Relies on self-loathing and self-destruction
8. Seeks power and control
9. Is covert and manipulative
10. Serves to avoid feelings at all costs
11. Is fraudulent
12. Creates a tolerance that requires more stimulation
13. Requires compartmentalization

14. Is rigid and routine
15. Is without meaning and devoid of eroticism or a spiritual connection

Healthy Sex

1. Is mutually respectful and honoring
2. Reinforces a congruent sense of self
3. Recognizes vulnerability as the road to intimacy, intensity, and eroticism
4. Allows for exploration, flexibly making meaning of the sexual act (neuroplasticity)
5. Requires you to experience the feelings in your body
6. Demands the experience of the present moment and staying relational
7. Relies on self-love and nurturance
8. Seeks surrender and vulnerability
9. Is direct and requires risk-taking
10. Requires the willingness to feel deeply
11. Demands honesty and creates congruence
12. Requires self-confrontation for growth
13. Demands truth and authenticity
14. Is a joyous celebration of life, partnership, and your spirituality
15. Creates meaning and embraces your erotic self as a pathway to spirituality

Moving from addictive sex habits into healthy sexuality usually cannot be achieved overnight or at the flick of a switch. Healthy sexuality is close to impossible to achieve when your mind is hypersexualized and operating from a dysregulated brain pattern. Just understanding what healthy sexuality looks like is not enough. But it is a start, and the more you distance yourself from addictive sex habits, the more attainable healthy sexuality will become.

Brain Hack Number 2
How Does Addictive Sex Show Up in Your Life?

In a journal, reflect on the difference between addictive sex and healthy sexuality. List instances of one, the other, or both in your life, and evaluate how addictive sex impacts your ability to thrive.

FINDING THE REAL YOU FOR BETTER SEX

We all create identities to help us feel safe and secure in an uncertain world. Your identity is a construct of yourself that you generated when you were younger to establish stability and a sense of self. A great deal of identity development occurs for us during adolescence and young adulthood and revolves around our values and goals for the future.[4] Identity formation can be influenced by positive feedback from your family and community as well as stressors, including trauma, family dysfunction, or difficult childhood experiences.[5] For some, identity serves mostly as a protective mechanism for feeling safe in an unpredictable life situation. Hypersexuality might have been infused

MOVING FROM ADDICTIVE SEX TO HEALTHY SEX USUALLY CANNOT BE ACHIEVED OVERNIGHT.

into your identity at an early age due to your porn use. Men with hypersexuality have very different sexual behavior patterns than men with healthy sexuality.[6] Their desire for sex is driven more by negative emotions and exposure to sexual imagery, namely porn. This is due to the patterned use of porn and masturbation to deal with such emotions. Hypersexual men are much more likely to use porn or masturbate when they are stressed or in a bad mood. The lack of emotional regulation skills also can lead to the use of more sexually aggressive or coercive behaviors, whereas men with high emotional regulation skills do not show this proclivity.[7]

Men with healthy sexual behaviors demonstrate more desire to be with their partner as a result of their positive mood. Healthy sex with your partner is mostly enjoyed when you are in a good mood, not bad. Porn and masturbation are a coping strategy related to a low ability to deal with emotions. Learning to increase your emotional maturity can improve your sex life and relationship satisfaction. When you learn to deal with life's challenges in different, healthier ways instead of porn, then you can also learn how to truly enjoy sexual experiences with your partner from a standpoint of well-being. But first let's better understand how you came to lose touch with the ability to regulate emotional issues.

YOUR THOUGHTS, BELIEFS, AND ATTITUDES CONGEAL INTO YOUR IDENTITY.

The Real You was preprogrammed, before porn use, for the purposes you were uniquely designed for. That is why the true Self is thought of by many people as a spiritual entity—because it is not programmed by the features and functions of the world, but rather it is the innate and divinely inspired programming you were born with. This Self feels first and then responds intentionally based on purpose. This version of you can enjoy vulnerable, erotic sex with your partner, feeling free to connect in a loving, intimate way. Often this Self gets buried under the conditioned thoughts and learned responses that your Dr. Jekyll and Mr. Hyde personas use to feel safe and not have to feel difficult or intimate emotions. Hypersexuality is one of these distorted mechanisms. I think of our conditioned habitual, repetitive behaviors as manifestations of our past programming recurring over time. For some people it is going to porn to help them regulate emotions, for others it is bottling emotions up and not talking about them. It can come from three primary sources, or the *three Ns* of development: nature, nurture, and what some researchers call 'ndividuality (but I prefer the term navigation).[8]

Nature corresponds to your familial predispositions. Brains don't fall far from the family tree. You were born with a brain that operates like others in your family, and you engage with the world in a similar way to your parents and ancestors.

Nurture relates to your environment. In this case your programming can be learned from your parents, culture, community, or religion. Shame, although strongly associated with porn use, can also arise from your upbringing, specifically surrounding sexuality.[9] If your parents never talked with you about healthy sexuality and it was considered a taboo subject even into adulthood, you may feel an inherent sexual shame. Sexual shame can also arise from your self-programming in response to the environment you lived in as a child.

Navigation refers to the way in which individuals negotiate their way through the world differently. You program your identity as you react to the world that you encounter. For example, I was self-programmed to stay busy, in a subconscious attempt to prove my worth. To this day, if I'm taking a break and someone walks into the room, I have the impulse to jump up and be productive. But one of the amazing things about this phenomenon is it also means that if you take a new action while navigating, then you

YOUR TRUE SELF IS BASED UPON YOUR FEELINGS, NOT YOUR THINKING.

can learn to think about the world differently and walk within it with new hope, behaviors, and confidence. Your new navigation pattern can help you create the life you want.

Brain Hack Number 3
Your Past Programming

In your journal, explore past programming. Write down the following:

- **The Aspects of the False Identity You Will Leave Behind:** Identify the "you" you have become and all that currently comes with it: porn use, anger, optimism, moodiness, lack of motivation, financial success, relationship problems, alcohol or drug use, fitness levels, working hard or lack thereof—everything. Don't leave anything out. Which pieces represent the false persona you have made? Now, write a letter to this version of yourself, releasing any aspects that are holding you back, so you can make room for the new, improved version: the Real You who we will rediscover and unleash within these pages.

- **Your Past Programming:** Keep track of what you say to and how you interact with others. Be aware of any hypersexual behaviors. Ask yourself, *Is that what I want to do? What are my knee-jerk reactions? Why do I act in this way?* Identify the self-programmed, conditioned responses you have developed as a way of navigation—especially those related to porn use and masturbation—in order to release them.

Your current identity is the persona being played out and reinforced by your routinized actions. Whatever the various sources of your mind's programming, it is likely outdated. Let's create new habits, new thoughts, and new routines for a new life. Actor Jim Carrey has often spoken publicly about how he realized, through acting, that the person he considered himself to be was very much like the characters he portrayed—a set of characteristics acted out on a daily basis.[10] Thus, identity is *pliable*: you can change it to be the truest version of yourself. You can rewire your brain using advanced technology to enhance neuroplasticity. The increased malleability will strengthen your resolve to take new, healthier, purposeful action steps. We will break that old identity into pieces, and then I will challenge you to create a new and improved one.

YOUR INNER CHILD

Your new identity will be your authentic, true Self—the Real You— and it will not include hypersexuality. This originated when you were very young but was stunted due to disruptions in your programming, such as trauma, emotional dysregulation, and porn use. This true version of yourself, known as the *inner child*, can be healthy or wounded by childhood experiences. A healthy inner child, who can use strong emotional regulation skills, has been associated with optimal well-being across the lifespan.[11] If your inner child is wounded, the healthy version can be reclaimed through brain regulation and cognitive behavioral techniques that we will explore together later in these pages. Once discovered, this true, healthy inner child can be reprogrammed to function to your greatest benefit on a day-to-day basis as the healthy adult, the full-potential version of you. This will include feeling your emotions, including painful ones, and using them to continually grow. The added benefit is that you will no longer use sex as a soothing mechanism—you will be free to enjoy it on its own merits.

Tapping into your authenticity as the healed inner child is crucial for long-term success in maintaining sexual integrity. Get back to the Real You. When you do, you will not need to go to something outside yourself, like porn, to regulate your mood and state. Finding your true Self and having the courage to live your life with purpose and filled with happiness is essential to living without the escapism of porn. How you identify yourself will dictate who you become. Think of the Real You as more than you are right now. More grounded in your power. Together we will find that inspired Self and revive him or her. It's going to be a beautiful thing.

Brain Hack Number 4
Who Is the Real You?

Discover who you were meant to be. In your journal, write down the following:

- **Your Healthy Inner Child:** Think back to when you were young, to that child within you. Give him or her a name (e.g., "Little You"). Give him an identity with characteristics. Think about Little You and write down as much as you can remember about her. Who is he? What are her dreams? What charges him up?
- **What You Love:** Write down the things you love to do now as the adult you are. Free-flow write, nonstop, and try to list at least fifty things you like to do. *You.* Not your mother, boyfriend, wife, or friends, but You! What fires you up? What gets you up in the morning? What activities help you feel calm and focused?

HAPPY SEX

Emotional intelligence, which is the ability to manage your emotions to handle your relationships with improved judgment and understanding, has four distinct pillars: self-awareness, self-regulation, social awareness, and social management.[12] Challenges can be overcome, conflict defused, intimacy built, and the flames of love fueled through this important skill involving healthy interpersonal communication. A healthy interactional style includes being honest, trusting, and responsible, and consistently using strong emotional regulation to stay calm and engaged relationally. At times it involves knowing what you want or need and expressing it with empathetic assertiveness while remaining open to discussion and compromise. Importantly, porn use can be more easily avoided through improved emotional intelligence. Difficulty identifying your own emotions and then dealing with them in a healthy way has been related to the development and maintenance of sexual performance and enjoyment difficulties in men and women.[13] Improving emotional intelligence has been shown to decrease SAD (sexual arousal dysfunction), improve sexual satisfaction, and increase positive relationship feelings overall. When you increase your emotional intelligence, you can enjoy *happy sex*.

The first pillar of emotional intelligence is self-awareness, which I have already indicated can be very low if you are addicted to porn. You've subconsciously designed your porn habit for just that reason, to keep you numb and unaware of your feelings. Well, the solution lies where the problem is. As self-awareness increases, you can begin the journey of self-discovery and self-reliance.

The second pillar is self-regulation, which is your internal ability to respond intentionally, or not to react erratically, to your emotions in an unhealthy way. Mastery of self-regulation allows you to move through the world with greater confidence and ease. It also means not using porn or masturbation to deal with stress and boredom. Healthier mood regulation techniques are essential for improved self-regulation. Once assured in your skin, you can better understand what is happening with others around you through developed empathy and compassion.

Empathy and compassion lead to improved social awareness—the third pillar—which is a powerful tool for establishing intimacy and increased levels of security and connection. Once aware of your own needs and the needs of your loved ones, you can make new choices in how you convey your thoughts and listen to others, and therefore interact more intentionally.

Improved social management (the fourth pillar) guides you toward better communication, collaboration, and conflict resolution skills. With new insight and abilities, you can navigate the world of relationships more healthily and enjoyably. You can also enjoy a more satisfying sex life with your partner, in addition to enjoying your relationship more overall too.[14] Men who can identify their own emotions and express them, not suppress them, were shown to have lower depression and anxiety, higher relationship satisfaction, fewer relationship conflicts, and higher levels of sexual desire for their partner.[15] The female partners of these men reported less conflict and greater relationship satisfaction too. Improving emotional intelligence can directly impact your relationship and sex life.

Here is an example from my life that I learned on my own journey of improved emotional intelligence. One day I had the epiphany that my husband and I are completely different human beings. Shocking, I know. But, up until that point, I thought of us as in "a relationship." On this fortunate day, I realized that he was in a relationship with me, and I was in a relationship with him. We have two different relationships. Let that sink in.

I assume I had the realization on this given day because,

Four Pillars of Emotional Intelligence

Self-Awareness	Self-Regulation	Social Awareness	Social Management
Conscious understanding of your thoughts and feelings.	Ability to manage behavior in response to your feelings.	Ability to empathize with others.	Manage your emotions to connect and build intimacy with others.

through this work, I had increased my self-awareness to the point that I had built strong self-regulation skills. My brain was ready for increased social awareness, which led to improved social management. So I stopped seeing us as in a relationship and started seeing my own and his individual viewpoint much more strongly. I considered his needs in every situation we were in, not just my needs or the "needs of our relationship," which is not a real thing anyway. Our relationship doesn't have needs in and of itself. We each have needs within it, and I now see that those needs are rarely the same. This was incredibly powerful for me to transform our life together into a healthier version of mutual consideration and love. Now, I reflect on what he needs in consideration of what I need, and he has developed the same capacity. We are far from perfect in doing this, but we always practice it.

Here's another excellent example of emotional intelligence as it pertains to sexuality. Roger, a fifty-year-old client of mine, found himself lusting after women whenever he went out. He didn't mean to, but he couldn't help it. He would even plan trips to the mall where he could enjoy a bevy of people to check out for dopamine hits, and then he would return home to masturbate after inducing a heightened state. As he focused on increasing self-awareness of his behaviors and the driving forces underneath them, he realized that this behavior was something he had been doing since his teen years. He considered it harmless until he finally looked at it for what is was: a mood regulation habit related to the porn he had been watching for so long. He stopped going to the mall and instead took his wife out to dinner, enjoying intimacy and camaraderie that led to better sex.

Past patterns can show up in the present and color the future in ways you do not want. When you shed light on them, especially when you work intentionally on your self-regulation and relationship management, they will dissipate and enable you to leave porn behind and create an authentic life of happiness and joy.

Brain Hack Number 5
Think of a Time You Lost It

The times when you lose your cool can be the most informative regarding your emotional intelligence and your repetitive, conditioned, reactionary behaviors. They can be opportunities for growth. When you get mad, upset, or don't get your way, your wounded inner child typically shows up and acts out in his or her usual way. What does that look like for you? The last time you got mad, what did you say and do? This will help you see what you can do differently next time.

HOW TO UNWIRE, REWIRE, AND HARDWIRE YOUR BRAIN

Now that we have covered how porn use has pulled you into hyper-sexuality, let's consider what is necessary to guide you out. To heal your brain and end your porn addiction, you must marry the theories about how your brain works to the practices that will rewire it. Practitioners and teachers sometimes refer to this crossing-over of theory and practice as *integration theory*.[16] This scientifically developed approach shows that you can be successful when you know what to do, how to do it, and why. Understanding how your brain works and how it can be healed enables you, in turn, to use its incredible capabilities to unwire unhealthy habits and replace them with healthy ones. Knowledge educates, empowers, motivates, and inspires you. There is no guesswork.

This self-actualization process is also about integrating your mind, body, and new identity that is informed by your healed inner child, the Real You. You will let the adopted self-sabotaging identity fade and get back to your true Self.

We know that, ultimately, porn use is about coping with life, not sex. When you live a purposeful, authentic life that is all your own, you won't need to self-soothe with porn. You will build new, better habits and possibly enjoy healthier sex. This process will entail a personal transformation that spans your past, present, and future.

The first phase of our approach is to unwire your brain. That starts with neurologically picking the proverbial lock on your brain, the neurorigidity caused by the wounds of the past. This frees the brain and creates neuroplasticity, making future change more manageable. That's a tall order, but I will show you exactly how.

It's easier to leave a harmful habit behind when building positive habits in your present life. Once you've identified where you want to go in the future, you can forge your new path in the direction of your dreams. Once your brain is functioning with enhanced neuroplasticity, we will explore the present and how you use your brain in your daily activities and habits.

The second phase is to rewire your brain using new pathways and programming through actions that improve your brain and mind and increase its use of optimal energy patterns. It's about changing your routines and your thought processes, as well as your behaviors and actions.

The third phase involves projecting into the future to create the best version of yourself and hardwire your brain to fortify those new pathways that keep the optimal energy balance in place. In the future, you will establish healthy sexuality, set goals, and keep your personality fully integrated. This hardwiring process will be cemented through regular activities and action steps. When you set the intention to change and then take the relevant action, you will come to expect that your efforts will bear fruit. The changes will gradually become more accessible and easier to enact. The ultimate goal will be to help you better regulate your brain from within. The better your brain performs, the easier it will become for you to keep yourself in check. And the fantastic thing? You won't even have to *try* to keep yourself in check.

SEX IS EVERYWHERE, BUT IT DOESN'T HAVE TO BE

It takes some work to leave behind the version of yourself that you have become and finally find your true Self. When you revisit some of your past's most challenging, traumatic, and uncomfortable parts to resolve them, you will be one step closer to the healthier, authentic you. When you do this, you begin the unwiring process.

As your brain unwires, hypersexuality decreases. Although our society is filled with sexual images, your brain will not need them as it did before. Your mind won't want them anymore either. It will be transformed over the need for explicit matter. The compulsion to constantly search for sex will be diminished. Engaged in real-world, enjoyable activities, you will have more mental space for other interests, like those you identified earlier. Sex with your partner can be arousing and enjoyable, and you won't need self-soothing through masturbation and porn. Now that you know the basics of how porn impacts the brain, you are empowered to control your brain, so it doesn't control you. Together, let's embark on our journey of unwiring, rewiring, and hardwiring.

PART 2

UNWIRE:

CONFRONTING YOUR BRAIN'S PAST

CHAPTER 4

THE HIJACKER: THE IMPACT OF TRAUMA, ABUSE, AND NEGLECT ON THE BRAIN

Although the world is full of suffering, it
is full also of the overcoming of it.
HELEN KELLER

GROWING UP TOO SOON

Sam's life growing up was like that of a lot of boys. Family life was a bit chaotic, and he struggled to find his place. He was often left home alone and learned early on to care for his own needs, since it didn't feel like anyone around him could or would help. No one talked about their emotions or processed their feelings.

Sam's dad was away at work most of the time, leaving his mom overwhelmed with the kids. They had just enough money to get by.

Sam's mom would take out her stress and frustration by yelling at him, chastising him, and sometimes even hitting him.

Sam grew up quickly. Like his parents, he just had to cope and make do. During his teen years, he worked three jobs while attending school to pay for his own things. Although his parents were never terrible to him, he knew he couldn't count on them for much, especially the emotional challenges that he struggled with, like bullying, peer relationships, and paving his own way with little support.

Through his recovery journey, Sam came to understand many important aspects of his childhood. He realized, in hindsight, that he felt angry most of the time but learned to hide it with a smiling face. His world felt out of control, and he would grasp at straws to maintain feelings of power. Regretfully, this meant he could be brutally mean to his younger siblings; he found he could exert more force over them than on anyone else.

Growing up, Sam would be angry and frustrated by how his parents and siblings treated him, but then he would apologize for his anger and "grin and bear it," feigning happiness and elation. At the same time, he found porn, which gave him the high he had otherwise been faking. And so, even as a teenager, he formed two personalities to help him survive—his Dr. Jekyll persona to maintain safety in his home and neighborhood, and his Mr. Hyde persona to soothe the anger of his wounded inner child. Sam had been hiding his true Self from himself and others his whole life. That covert aspect of Sam's personality saved him in childhood, but as an adult, it was harming him, not saving him.

LEARNING FROM THE PAST

We are all the products of our childhoods in some way, and who we are is often shaped by how we learn to navigate the world as young people. Our minds become fragmented as we try to please the important people in our lives, losing touch with who we are. As a grown-up, Sam didn't even realize that his put-together exterior (Dr. Jekyll) and his need to run down to his man cave to relieve the stress of it (Mr. Hyde) were two sides of the same coin—two masks protecting him from the inner pain of his childhood that he had been dragging around inside for decades.

WHEN YOU LET GO OF THE PAST, YOUR BRAIN WILL BE FREE TO RISE ABOVE PORN.

As we begin to unwire our brains, we will dig into our pasts and unearth any unresolved or lingering issues that might still affect us. It could be abuse, being a middle child, or some general family dysfunction. You are only going to stay in the past as long as you need to so that you can release and resolve any trauma that is locked in your brain, mind, and body. When you release the trauma, your brain will let go of the neurorigidity it is used to and will be entirely free to use neuroplasticity to rise above porn and achieve your full potential. Because of the nature of this process, it can be helpful, even imperative, to work with a professional coach, counselor, or therapist to guide you through your healing journey. Professionals have the skills to move you through an important healing process. Emotionally intelligent friends or family members can be a good start. Remember how Layla broke the secret of her porn addiction by telling friends, who encouraged her to tell her mom, thus enabling her to get the professional help she needed to succeed?

You can work through those traumas to integrate them, releasing the hurt caused by them but retaining the eventual adulthood wisdom the experience may have offered you. Famous researcher Brené Brown found that people who live joyful, authentic lives maintain the perspective that people are "doing their best" with the emotional intelligence skills they have developed.[1] Remember, one person's personal best is not always enough for another person. But inherently, it is still their best.

Consider Olympic athletes who cannot beat their best times or scores in an event until they get a coach who teaches them new, more advanced skills. That is our goal here—improved emotional intelligence skills that lead to increased empathy, understanding, and self-compassion. You will learn to forgive your parents and others who may have wronged you. This can even hold true in the context of neglect and abuse in that it is transmitted within families from generation to generation.[2] People who witness violence between their parents or experience abuse when they are young are much more likely to mistreat their own children.[3] Men who were sexually abused in childhood have a significantly higher likelihood of becoming a perpetrator in adulthood.[4] Programming is passed on. Therefore, it is important for you to better understand not only the programming of others but also yourself and your internal motivating forces, so you can forgive others for how they have treated you and forgive yourself for how you have treated people, including yourself. You will be able to look at yourself in the mirror and say:

> There are people who treated me poorly in the past. Unfortunately, there are also times that the less emotionally intelligent version of myself has treated others in ways I am not proud of, but that was due to my emotional capacity at the time.
>
> They were doing their best. It is all they knew how to do. I was doing my best at the time with the tools that I had. Now I can and will do better because I am learning to raise my emotional intelligence and use new and better tools. My mind is elevated. My capacity has grown.

You can look at the past, release it, and learn from it to grow. Your past does not have to dictate your future. It can be a place to learn from in order to help you create a new future. You can improve the regulation levels in your brain to use the highest levels of consciousness, intentional thought and action, and the divinely inspired purpose of superconsciousness. Through your newfound emotional intelligence skills, you can become the best version of yourself and stay connected to the healed inner child within you for authentic living. It might hurt to do this in the short run, but you will learn that the pain will make you stronger in the long run if you use it correctly. The pain won't kill you; it will make you the resilient person you have always wanted to be. Pain can be a great teacher if you are willing to learn.

HOW YOUR PAST CREATES THE HIJACKER

You may not have had a driver's license until you were sixteen, but you were behind the wheel of your life well before that. Eight psychosocial stages of development across our lifespan are widely accepted by the scientific community as stages that arise as an individual grows, facing new challenges and decisions across multiple turning points in their life.[5]

Each stage is defined by a positive or negative psychological tendency depending upon the experiences within it and how a person handles and internalizes them. During this time, identity is impacted in either a helpful, adaptive way that encourages growth and development or an unhealthy, maladaptive fashion. Maladaptive behaviors stop you from adjusting to new, especially difficult, circumstances in a healthy way. They can include coping mechanisms like nail-biting, daydreaming, oversexualization, and self-injurious behaviors. Porn use itself can be considered a maladaptive strategy to soothe emotional dysregulation.

The healthy development of the earlier psychosocial stages

61

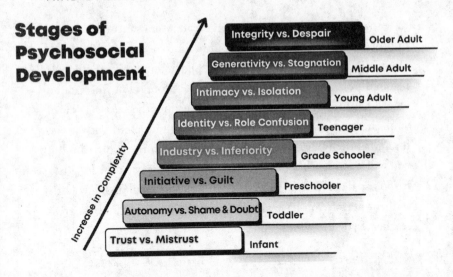

Stages of Psychosocial Development

Increase in Complexity

Integrity vs. Despair — Older Adult

Generativity vs. Stagnation — Middle Adult

Intimacy vs. Isolation — Young Adult

Identity vs. Role Confusion — Teenager

Industry vs. Inferiority — Grade Schooler

Initiative vs. Guilt — Preschooler

Autonomy vs. Shame & Doubt — Toddler

Trust vs. Mistrust — Infant

creates trust, autonomy, initiative, industry, and intimacy because of positive nature, nurture, and navigation of the experiences. However, if adverse childhood experiences (ACEs), such as neglect, trauma, or abuse, take place at one or more of the critical earlier stages, not only is that stage negatively impacted, but subsequent stages can be disrupted too.[6] This may lead to mistrust, shame, doubt, guilt, inferiority, confusion, and isolation.

So, when you were young, you might have felt free to explore and be the confident driver of the proverbial car of your life. You had the whole world in front of you. Just imagine you are in your vehicle and have your hands firmly on the steering wheel. You are the person you were born to be. Envision yourself when you were four, seven, or nine years old. You were free to be yourself.

Then something happened and your brain and nervous system couldn't process it with an emotionally healthy strategy. It changed the way you progressed through the developmental stages, taking you off track from the positive course and onto the maladaptive one. You might have experienced bullying, abuse, neglect, or family dysfunction of some kind. It might even have been porn exposure itself. Even the constant feeling of having nobody to depend on, like Sam had, can overwhelm the child-sized version of yourself. Dealing with these types of experiences was beyond the capacity of your young mind, and nobody was there to help you work through it.

These experiences can effectively result in an inner wound to your mind. Such wounds change you; they dysregulate your nervous system, setting the pendulum brain effect into motion. They create the need in your brain to eradicate the discomfort that ensues.[7] Porn use becomes an unhealthy regulating mechanism.[8] Getting rid of that discomfort, even for a moment, becomes a goal of your young emotional self.

When you found porn and masturbation, it scratched that itch in the perfect way. The discomfort of your adolescence, whatever it may have been, could be forgotten for a time, and you could feel good. Really good. That authentic version of yourself who felt uncomfortable was pushed down and squelched so you wouldn't feel bad anymore.

So as you are cruising down the highway of your life in the driver's seat, the pain of your childhood experiences and the pleasure of porn derailed you from your original intended journey. You were pushed into the passenger seat of your car by your wounded inner self. Ignoring the discomfort of your mind (Dr. Jekyll) and secretly scratching the itch to soothe it (Mr. Hyde) became a way of life that has stuck with you for years, possibly decades. It may be a driving force for you up until this very day.

The Hijacker—the wounded, maladaptive version of yourself—has taken over the vehicle of your mind and is now in control. He did it to help you survive, but now he has had you stuck in survival mode for far too long. The Hijacker still feels the intense need to protect himself from the wounds inside and the world outside. But now it is time for you to thrive.

IT'S JUST PORN. IT'S HARMLESS. I HAVE A HIGH LIBIDO.

Until now, you may not have understood the complex inner workings of your porn habit. You may have thought, *It's just porn. It's harmless.* Or, *I have a high libido.* But no. That is not it at all. The Real You wants to come out and shine. He is stuck in there, buried by pain and discomfort. She is screaming for your attention. Every urge to watch porn is a call for help. Every time you desire to masturbate or check out a woman, the child inside is speaking to you. He says, *Do the work for me; free me from this cycle. It's time to end the madness of survival. We can thrive in the life we have always wanted. Let me out so we can!*

Sam was operating on the softly spoken commands of his own wounded inner child for a long time. From the outside, Sam appeared confident and energetic. But on the inside, he was terrified of failure. The fear that he could never measure up led him to try only moderately toward achieving his goals.

And then, layered on top of the fear was the brain devastation caused by porn use. With both issues at play, Sam lacked motivation because he had been in survival mode his whole life. First as a compensatory pattern and then as a default mode. He had been faking contentedness, hiding pain while constantly seeking pleasure, and allowing himself to simply get by. He had given the wheel of life over to the Hijacker.

It is likely that your brain has also been hijacked by this inner child, who has not yet processed the unresolved traumas of the past. That precious child inside you—Little You—wants nothing more than to escape the pain-pleasure cycle for good. Now is his chance.

BIG T, LITTLE T

Traumatic stress is a complicated subject that can often be misunderstood. What is stressful to one person and traumatic to another depends on how the experience is reconciled within their nervous system.[9] "Big T trauma" refers to disastrous-level experiences, such as threatened death, sexual abuse, and violence, whereas "little t trauma," although considered to be equally traumatic, might involve bullying, housing insecurity, and parental neglect.[10] Some people hold on to fear, anxiety, and depression following a difficult experience, whether large or small, because their nervous system does not truly process it. Others become acclimated to a higher level of traumatically stressful experiences throughout childhood, leading them to misgrade those experiences as easy for them to deal with. Some people don't realize that what they experienced in childhood was, in fact, traumatic stress. The brain will try to protect you from such experiences, allowing you to undermine the effects those experiences have had on the way you interact with others and move through the world. The trauma can remain stuck in your brain and is manifested in your mind and body.[11]

STRESS RESPONSES

The stress response to traumatic experiences shows up in four main ways in your behavior: fight, flight, freeze, and fawn.[12] You have probably heard of fight-or-flight but might not have encountered the terms *freeze* and *fawn*. As outlined below, most people default to one or two stress responses when experiencing trauma. Let's investigate them as they relate to your porn use so you can learn to recognize and diminish your stress by responding to difficult situations with increased emotional intelligence.

Four Main Stress Responses

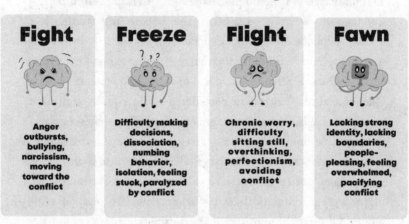

Fight	Freeze	Flight	Fawn
Anger outbursts, bullying, narcissism, moving toward the conflict	Difficulty making decisions, dissociation, numbing behavior, isolation, feeling stuck, paralyzed by conflict	Chronic worry, difficulty sitting still, overthinking, perfectionism, avoiding conflict	Lacking strong identity, lacking boundaries, people-pleasing, feeling overwhelmed, pacifying conflict

Fight mode is when you approach challenges as they come toward you. You are ready to fight. Vigilance dominates so you can feel safe from threats. Unfortunately, you might perceive threats everywhere even as you try to stay safe. You might have an angry outburst, show a sense of entitlement, be unable to consider others' perspectives, or try to control or demand perfection from others—all to create feelings of safety. But hypervigilance is exhausting to the brain and necessitates escapism through eventual freeze. Mental health labels for people stuck in fight mode include personality disorders, narcissism, and conduct disorders.

Flight mode, when used chronically, can be equally exhausting—overthinking, overdoing, and overworking to avoid feelings of fear. People in flight tend to be constantly on the go and micromanage details to create safety. Rushing around to offset anxiety is a flight response that can look like overachieving. Heightened anxiety due to addiction can perpetuate the flight response. Constant fleeing can also result in sporadic freeze episodes to provide a reprieve. Labels in the mental health realm that encompass flight stress responses include obsessive-compulsive disorder (OCD), bipolar disorder, attention deficit hyperactivity disorder (ADHD), and mood disorders.

Freeze is the equivalent of an animal playing dead upon threat for survival. It helps a person avoid conflict and fear by putting off the inevitable for a while, or indefinitely if you stay stuck. The lifeless feeling of freeze involves escapism, numbing, spacing out, brain fog, lack of motivation, feeling "unreal," and laziness while trying to hide from the world. Escaping into porn to avoid the perpetual stress and anxiety of being in a fight-or-flight mode can be a type of freeze response.[13] Labels for the freeze trauma response include dissociative disorders, depression, and attention deficit disorder (ADD).

Fawning is a compensatory stress response where the individual, often subconsciously, acts in ways to please, appease, and pacify the threat in their life to try to keep themself safe from further harm. Actor Will Smith wrote about this phenomenon as the impetus for his early prowess for acting.[14] He, his mother, and his brother suffered repeated physical abuse at the hands of his father, "Daddio." Will Smith said that he could perceive Daddio's moods and would "act funny" to avoid the anguish of watching his mother suffer abuse or the pain of being struck himself. He fawned to reduce the chaos of his childhood home, and it worked. In doing so, he began to hone the skill of acting from a very young age and eventually became one of the leading actors in Hollywood.

Fawning, like any stress response when used too much, can be dangerous if it becomes your maladaptive coping strategy for a lifetime. You may not recognize it is keeping you stuck in a self-defeating survival mode. Unless, of course, you dare to see it for what it is—a stress response—and grow from it, which is what Will Smith has done on his journey of self-discovery. In the infamous "slap that could be heard around the world," Will Smith came to the defense of his wife by hitting Chris Rock on a live, televised broadcast. Perhaps an overstep of no longer fawning by approaching, Smith engaged in the conflict of his wife being disparaged within the moment it occurred. Fawning is often labeled as codependency or a victim mentality.

No matter how it manifests in the mind or body, the stress response in the brain has evolved to protect you and help you cope with events in real time. When you experience trauma and avoid or relive the event over and over, the stress response gets stuck. After experiencing an event, the emotions associated with it should last sixty to ninety seconds, what is now known as the 90-second rule.[15] Research shows that the ability to process daily stressors as they occur decreases the risk of chronic health issues.[16] If your brain processes that event, the emotions move through you. If you don't, the emotions get stuck and create a chronic stress response. Allowing your emotions to be felt, processed, and integrated for learning can be essential to living a life of joy.

Brain Hack Number 6
What Are Your Default Trauma Stress Responses?

In your journal, reflect on your childhood and discern which of the four trauma responses you used most often. There might be two equally used stress responses. Do those responses show up in your life today? Can you create safety in adulthood and learn to respond differently by staying with your complicated feelings and working through them in a healthy way?

FEEL, THINK, ACT

Personally, I default to flight. In the past, if I was dealing with difficult emotions, I was out the door. I still feel the pull to run when things get challenging. I have recently realized how prevalent fawning responses have been in my life too. I never considered myself a people pleaser and was shocked to discover my survival pattern of conflict avoidance where I would ignore difficult issues and make everything all right for everyone else, many times ignoring my own needs in the process.

Survival Mode

> Avoid Feeling Out of Fear → Negative Thinking Keeps
> Fear Going → Act in Habitual Maladaptive Ways

Instead of those default survival modes, I have learned to pause, check in with myself, take a breath, approach, and engage. I remain engaged in resolution until the road forward is identified and traveled. After years of this work, I can sit with my feelings and figure out what they tell me. Then I can use them to formulate my thoughts on proceeding toward the best positive outcome for all. The solution comes from the use of the optimal brain pattern, that of problem-solving, creativity, and thriving. I refer to this as *thrival mode*.

Thrival Mode

> Feel Your Feelings → Think Solution-Oriented
> Thoughts → Act in New, Healthy Ways

We will use this information to help you move through the world confidently, without defaulting to a chronic stress response, especially regarding the freeze response of watching porn. We will do this in two ways. First, we will investigate and then reduce the amount of stress in your life. When you determine where your stress is coming from and then act to alleviate it, there will be less need for survival mode. Financial, professional, relational, and parenting stress dominate the stressors that can make you want to escape into porn. Also, remember that continual porn use and the residual shame it induces can contribute to the anxiety you feel within. If you do not know how to explore and resolve stress in your life, it might be best to work with a brain-health coach or counselor to help you address the issues that are keeping you in a chronic stress response.

Second, we will build a toolbox of healthy stress-reduction exercises and activities so that you can offset stress daily to keep your brain in thrival mode. The upward spiral will keep ascending from there. You will learn to identify and articulate your emotions so you can think healthy, solution-oriented thoughts to take new actions to break the cycle. In doing so, you will stop simply surviving and begin thriving.

DEFENSE MECHANISMS

On top of the unresolved trauma, your childhood wounds may be reinforced by defense mechanisms that you developed when you were young but carried into adulthood to protect yourself from getting emotionally hurt. These defense mechanisms were first identified by Sigmund Freud in the nineteenth century and are characterized as "unconscious resources" used to decrease internal conflict and stress within oneself.[17] It is thought that if a person becomes aware of these mechanisms, they can learn not to default to using them, which can provide an improved quality of life. Primitive defense mechanisms develop earlier in life and are almost always used in an unconscious manner. They are considered a less mature type of defense mechanism and often are used by younger children and adolescents, but they may become maladaptive for adults. Primitive defense mechanisms include:

- Acting out in detrimental behavior
- Avoidance of thoughts, feelings, people, places, and situations
- Conversion of emotional distress to physical illness
- Denial by dismissing reality
- Copycat behavior by acting like others instead of authentically yourself
- Projection of blame onto others
- Regression to childish behaviors
- Repression of memories
- Paranoid behavior, often confusing reality for fantasy or imagination
- All-or-none/black-or-white thinking

High-level defense mechanisms are more evolved and mature. They tend to reflect a healthier relationship with reality. Following are some examples of high-level defense mechanisms:

- Anticipation of problems before they arise
- Achievement- and recognition-seeking to offset negative feelings
- Displacement of emotions by calling others to offload one's own burdens onto them
- Humor to combat negative emotions
- Intellectualization by excessive thinking or overanalyzing to distance emotions
- Blocking off feelings so as not to experience them
- Rationalization by justifying one's own or others' behaviors

- Sexualization by overly sexualizing nonsexual experiences
- Suppression by blocking out experiences entirely

Both types of defense mechanisms help a person deal with anxiety.

Brain Hack Number 7
Identifying Your Defense Mechanisms

In your journal, determine which of the previously given lists of defense mechanisms you still use as an adult. Why do you need to respond that way? How are these defense mechanisms no longer serving you? Together we will develop healthier ways to respond soon.

When you leave porn behind, you can become an emotionally mature version of yourself. This new, emotionally healthier version can heal the wounds of your inner child using thrival mode.

When you change your current behaviors, you effectively rewire your brain into the positive feedback loop of consistent improvement. It's called reparenting your inner child. It is your chance to parent Little You as you wish someone would have done when you were a child, and can lead to improved health and well-being across the rest of your lifetime.[18] You can give yourself the love, support, guidance, and understanding you needed when you were young. You are now older, wiser, more emotionally mature, and can handle difficult emotions.

YOU CAN GIVE YOURSELF THE LOVE, SUPPORT, GUIDANCE, AND UNDERSTANDING YOU NEED.

CHAPTER 5

REPARENTING YOUR AUTHENTIC, TRUE SELF

Be yourself; everyone else is already taken.
OSCAR WILDE, ATTRIBUTED

LITTLE WISH

In my home growing up, there was plenty of unidentified family dysfunction. For years I carried a lot of emotional and neurological baggage because of my wounded inner child and the programming I created due to family dynamics. As a child in a big family that never—and I mean *never*—talked about our feelings, I quickly learned to become self-sufficient through knowledge. Like Will Smith, who pacified his family's dysfunction by acting funny, being smart got me noticed among the crowd of siblings. Using knowledge to distract myself from the pain of my emotional needs and the lack of being seen became programmed into my system: Seek more knowledge to feel good. Be smart to get attention.

I got put on the family map by not only achieving A grades in school but also constantly learning and knowing more than others. Early on, "smartness" became an identifying factor. Acquiring more and more knowledge to distinguish and satisfy myself became a pattern of survival and safety. I worked hard in school. I was staying in my head instead of enjoying my life. I got more degrees than any of my five brothers and sisters. I loved being in school. It made me feel safe. That is likely why I became a university professor. So I could stay safe in school forever. Or so I thought.

Knowledge seemed to provide safety, but I still felt a relenting emptiness inside, the feeling of not genuinely being my true Self. It left me searching. The entire time I went to school and taught at the university, I had this empty, aching feeling. It led me to move houses over and over, searching for a home that felt good to me.

A turning point came when, at the age of thirty-nine, with five small children of my own, I applied to medical school to achieve another degree and a ton more knowledge. I was still looking for safety. After being accepted, I dared to look inward and get honest with myself. Subconsciously, I think I knew that this time the personal costs would outweigh the reward of perceived safety for my wounded inner child. Not only did I discover that I didn't need to keep going to school, but I also realized it would be detrimental to my beautiful family. More schooling could never produce what I was looking for. So I called the medical school back and told them I wasn't coming. Simultaneously, I left the university for a fresh start on a purposeful journey as my authentic, true Self. Real Trish, here I came. Ever since then, I haven't had the urge to move houses. I had arrived at the home within, so the searching could cease.

My father used to call me "Little Wish" when I was young. I love this term of endearment, and it makes me think of a picture of us in the backyard walking hand in hand. Little Wish is my inner child. She needed to study when others were playing. In 2015, just before I empowered myself to end the madness of degree-seeking, I would crank up a song by Imagine Dragons. If you know me, you know I love music—empowering music, especially. The song was "Warriors," and the lyrics begin, "As a child, you would wait and watch from far away, but you always knew that you'd be the one to work while they all play."[1] It resonated with me. Why was I working so hard? Little Wish was clawing to come out for all those years; I just didn't know it. Thankfully, she made her way out at forty years old to join me in creating my life of balanced purpose from here on out.

YOU ARE SAFE; YOU ARE ENOUGH AS YOU ARE.

That is what I want for you. No matter your age, you can let Little You out so you can create the life you want for yourself and have fun doing it.

In my moment of revelation, I reparented myself by returning, in my mind, to the lost moments of excessive knowledge-seeking in my childhood. I calmly and coolly, using emotional intelligence, told Little Wish to put the books down and go outside and play. I told her, "You are safe, you are enough as you are, you don't need to know more than others to be great, you are great just the way you are . . . Now go play and have fun." Not only have I freed Little Wish, but I have also freed my kids from studying too much and too hard, from feeling the pressure to over-achieve. They have learned to work hard and play hard, enjoying the balance of a healthy lifestyle. The fruits of my emotional work are the gifts that keep giving to future generations.

It is essential to take the time to connect with your childhood and to hear your wounded inner child's voice. You must get to know the Hijacker. Who is he? What does she want? What does he need from you now to release him from his patterns? What is her driving force, the motivator for her actions? Help him resolve the pain and learn to be enough as he is so you can get back on the superhighway of your dreams.

Brain Hack Number 8
Historical Dig: Think of Difficult Childhood Events or Patterned Behaviors

Dig back through your history from today to when you were young. Think of your harrowing childhood experiences or a patterned behavior you have used in the past. Now write about all of it in your journal. I find it beneficial to rewind in five- or ten-year increments, evaluating stages of life. Describe the details of what happened over time. Uncover those difficulties that keep you stuck. Did you have anyone to help you with healthy emotional support? Replay the event or events while giving your young self the needed support. Tell Little You what you needed to hear back then.

Brain Hack Number 9
Purify the Past—Reliving the Joys of Childhood

"Time travel" back to your childhood. Not all of it was painful. Make a list in your journal of things that brought you joy when you were young. Spend some time daydreaming and reliving these memories as though they are happening today. This way, you can bring back love from the past and use the happy memories to propel you forward.

NEGLECT AND FAMILY DYSFUNCTION

"Little t trauma" can add up like small paper cuts over time. One paper cut is a nuisance, but hundreds are distressing. The emotional wounds can compound and fester over time, continually distressing the wounded child within. One such source is parental neglect. You might have had a parent who was emotionally distant or always occupied, as Sam did. As a child, you were used to not having your needs met or having to meet them yourself. If a parent neglected you, it could create shame in you over time due to the maladaptive behavior patterns you developed. The shame can linger. As the fifth of six children, I had to get used to the fact that I would not get much of my parents' time or attention, and I would try not to take it personally. That took me a long time to do. I became known as the strong one in my family. My emotions weren't considered much because I was tough. I could deal with them. My sensitive siblings' needs were taken care of over mine. I learned to reduce my needs to almost nil; that way, I wouldn't be disappointed if nobody noticed I had them. Paper cuts, over and over.

Dysfunctional family patterns can also contribute to past trauma. We all have dysfunctional family dynamics somehow; it's just a matter of degree and flavor. Sometimes they stem from your parents' addiction issues or behavioral compulsions. Sometimes it is just a matter of their attitudes or emotional maturity. Your parents' interaction styles influence you and stay with you your entire life, whether that means toxic partner dynamics or fear of commitment and intimacy. A parent's attitude toward sex can also play a significant role in their child's sex addiction. Children are often ashamed when they become sexual beings. Did your parents explain sex to you? What was their attitude toward it?

Family roles and identities are also impactful. Did you have your own identity in your family? Or were you playing a role that

was not authentic for you, like being a parent to a younger sibling? Birth order can significantly define who we are and how we see ourselves in our families—like the proverbial neglected middle child. The more rigid your family identity, the more trouble you will likely have when attempting to figure out who you truly are.

Now that you have connected with your inner child, it is time to fortify that connection even further by allowing him to reach out to you for support. You can uncover much about yourself writing from your wounded inner child's perspective. Have her share her thoughts and feelings with you as the compassionate adult you are becoming. Have him get out all the hurt he could never express before. Let her tell you—a trusted, loving adult—her needs. Writing from your inner child might take a little practice. It's coming from a different part of your inner being—the subconscious.

Brain Hack Number 10
Write a Letter from Your Inner Child

Write a letter from Little You to your compassionate adult self in your journal. An excellent way to proceed in this exercise is not to overthink it. Try writing the letter with your nondominant hand to tap into other parts of your brain and differentiate your inner child's voice from your own. So if you are right-handed, write this letter with your left hand, and vice versa. See if you can get into automatic writing mode and let it flow.

Once your writing starts flowing, the thoughts of your inner child will come through you and to you. You'll be surprised at what comes out. But remember, you need to be honest with the

process. You can't self-censor. It all needs to come out. Little You is sensitive and vulnerable. Pay attention to the fears, insecurities, joys, and feelings of wonder that often arise when connecting with your inner child. Throughout the day, check in with yourself and ask, *How am I feeling right now?*

Also, be mindful of your inner critic. One of the biggest challenges I faced in spending time with my inner child was feeling like a fool for doing so. I'm an adult, and it felt silly to try to connect with the feelings I had as a child. This was my inner critic speaking. It's essential to listen to this voice simultaneously with the voice of your inner child. Your inner critic may dominate your thoughts. She may have overlooked your ideas for a long time. Most times, the inner critic is the voice of someone else from your past or the voice you have taken on as an adult. Honor that voice by listening, but don't always believe it.

Your inner child may or may not decide to reveal himself to you today. Remember to be patient, loving, and accepting of him. If he doesn't want to tell you much, embrace that. It's important that your inner child feels safe, secure, and ready. When she is prepared, you will be too. You can come back to the exercise over and over as necessary or desired. You can learn to take her by the hand and walk with her side by side, giving her and yourself everything you need to be strong and confident to live life to the fullest.

PATTERNS OF THE WOUNDED INNER CHILD

I will now outline four main types of wounded-inner-child patterns that emerge from childhood trauma and dysfunction. Healing the contamination of the wounded inner child can help you improve your quality of life.[2]

- **The Abandoned Child:** This inner child often emerges due to not getting enough attention from parents. It can be relatively innocent, such as parents being too busy, or it can be more severe, coming from abuse or neglect.
  - ☐ **Characteristics:** feels left out, fears being left, dislikes being alone, codependent, threatens to leave their home or partner, attracts emotionally unavailable people
- **The Guilted Child:** This child often grew up with enmeshed family dynamics of highly reacting to each other's emotions with limited boundaries. This child may have grown up with neglect or a parent dealing with trauma. Guilt over others' emotions created pain and anxiety.
  - ☐ **Characteristics:** feels sorry or wrong, doesn't like to ask for things, uses guilt to manipulate, is afraid to set boundaries, attracts people who make them feel guilty
- **The Neglected Child:** This child received a lot of criticism and regularly experienced anxiety when he or she did not get enough affirmation.
  - ☐ **Characteristics:** struggles to let things go, has low self-worth, gets angry quickly, has difficulty saying no, represses emotions, fears being vulnerable, attracts people who do not appreciate them or make them feel seen
- **The Untrusting Child:** This inner child grew up unable to trust the adults in their life and learned not to trust their own instincts, creating fear and anxiety.
  - ☐ **Characteristics:** is afraid to be hurt, doesn't trust themself, finds ways not to trust people, feels insecure, needs lots of external validation, doesn't feel safe, attracts people who don't feel safe

In adulthood, your inner child may use old programming to deal with difficulties. Inner child wounds show up in different

ways depending upon the type of inner child at the core of your Hijacker. These descriptors show the behaviors you might be dealing with due to your inner child.

Brain Hack Number 11
Identify Your Specific Inner Child

There are patterns of childhood that are common to most people. Note which patterns resonate with you to see what is coming up in your life today. Use the guidelines on the four inner child patterns to direct you. What type of inner child do you most relate to? In what ways does your inner child behave today? Take notes in your journal.

PRAGMATIC HOPE
VS. TOXIC OPTIMISM

This discussion of childhood trauma, family dysfunction, and the negative impact it may still have on you might have you a bit down at this point. But hold out hope. And by "hope," I don't mean toxic optimism, which is the notion that everything will always be great, no matter what. That's not true. Toxic optimism is harmful in all situations, as it is a maladaptive, survival-mode defense mechanism along the lines that everything will always work out. For instance, if you stay in a detrimental situation and continue to believe, without putting in the effort, that it will eventually get better, it might actually get worse.

Instead, I proclaim the merits of pragmatic hope, which means doing what you need to do while believing it will work.

Instead of "seeing is believing," you shift to a mindset of "believing is seeing." Your life improves because you faithfully believe it will, while putting in the effort to achieve the improvement.

The mental change in perspective is essential to succeeding.

SHIFT YOUR PERSPECTIVE TO ONE OF HOPE AND PRAGMATIC OPTIMISM. IT CAN HELP YOU.

This isn't just a cheerleading session either. It is supported by science. The Mayo Clinic published a book on the nocebo effect in comparison to the placebo effect that powerfully summarized these ideas.[3] Let me explain these two concepts.

The *placebo effect* refers to benefits produced by a treatment that cannot be attributed directly to the treatment. The treatment works even if it doesn't physically change anything. It may be a drug test where half the people receive the actual pill, the other half receive a sugar pill (the placebo), and both groups get better. There have even been sham surgeries where some participants got surface incisions, no actual surgery, and got better.[4]

In fact, research suggests that the placebo effect can be just as powerful as traditional treatments under the right circumstances.[5] Being told the treatment will work is an important aspect of this effect's success and has been shown to condition the brain to respond to the therapy, as evidenced on brain scans.[6] The placebo effect requires faith, and it can help you. It is mind over matter. Believing is seeing.

The *nocebo effect* is the opposite. It is when a treatment doesn't help a person or even makes them worse just because they think it will. The nocebo effect (faithlessness) can keep people stuck and struggling because they think nothing can help them.

Shift your perspective to one of faith, hope, and pragmatic optimism. Do what you need to do to succeed, believing it will

work, reminding yourself that you are on the road to the life of your dreams. You will be so glad you did.

HEALING YOUR INNER CHILD

You may already have a clear picture of your inner child and the role he is playing in your life right now. On the other hand, she may still be eluding you. If you create time and space in your life, you can learn to know your inner child extremely well moving forward. You will feel him when he tries to take control or hijack your brain. Next time you have a *mantrum*—my word for the adult-male version of a tantrum—you can identify him, Little You, being unable to deal with his present reality. You can help him regulate and respond. If you engage in *sister stewing*—my version of the female suppression of emotions—by leaving the room quietly to run scenarios while ruminating in your head, you can help the little version of you process instead of replay events. You will learn to listen to her.

And don't worry; I say this without judgment, because we all lose it sometimes. I call my tantrums *momtrums* because they usually have to do with my inability to deal with the constant co-regulation that I need to provide for my children in a delicate dance of modeled behavior and nurturing responses as they develop emotionally. Due to my personal growth, my momtrums are few and far between. Adult tantrums happen to the best of us. The key is to identify them early to avoid them, reduce them as much as possible when they happen, repair the damage afterward, and learn from them. Now, let's turn to supporting your inner child so you can get better acquainted as his nurturing role model.

Brain Hack Number 12
Write a Letter to Your Inner Child

In your journal, write a letter to Little You. Write it from the perspective of the loving adult you want to be. If you are not sure whether you have the emotional skills yet to be this loving adult, think of a mentor or a role model for the kind of responses you needed when you were young. You can have some fun with this exercise, but it must come from a place of loving empathy. The first letter might be one of encouragement so your inner child can release the grip he has on your mind. When you honor the inner child within you and guide her in better ways, you can alleviate the strife in your life.

If you are frustrated or upset by how much your inner child has held you back or sabotaged your growth, don't be afraid to get mad when you write. Don't hide anything. You must experience that grief and anger to gain courage, willingness, and acceptance. This will heal your brain, positively impacting your mind and body. Get a pillow and hit it if you feel compelled. Scream into it. Go for a run if that helps. Let it all out. Purge your system and free your mind. You can work these lingering traumas out and get them to leave your nervous system through your writing, voice, and movement.

NEO-FAMILY SUPPORT

Trusting others and relying on their support plays a critical role in handling the challenges involved in recovery and healing from your

trauma. Reconnecting with your inner child, processing dysfunction, reparenting yourself, and rebuilding healthy family dynamics can't be done in isolation. This is why I strongly encourage you to create a new family, or *neo-family*. This can be made up of actual family members or brothers and sisters in arms—friends you trust and with whom you enjoy healthy relationships.

My best friend, Chanel, a longtime trusted confidant, is part of my neo-family. I asked Chanel once, "Which version of me do you like best—the usual happy, full-of-life version, or the one who shows up with my wretched heart on my sleeve, needing your support?"

Her spontaneous answer was the best: "I love both."

This is neo-family at its finest. You may have grown up with emotionally immature parents who were not able to provide love and nurturing when you needed and desired it. But that doesn't mean you must go without that support forever. During recovery, many people meet a mentor who can play an aspect of the father or mother who wasn't there for them. This is an opportunity to have someone in your life who can give you the attention and intimacy that was missing when you were growing up, and they can benefit from the closeness too.

Brain Hack Number 13
Identify Your Neo-Family

In your journal, list those you'd like to be members of your neo-family and plan how to become more intimate with those people. What did you miss growing up? Were you lacking a responsive father, a nurturing mother, or friends who would support you unconditionally? Create what you need for yourself now.

REPARENTING ACROSS YOUR LIFETIME

Learning to reparent the inner child within you can be one of life's greatest gifts. It can become a skill you employ for continual growth across the rest of your lifetime. In times of increased stress, Little You might try to take over.

After learning to reparent Little Wish, I now know how to parent her anytime she tries to act out with emotional immaturity. I can sense her trying to grab the wheel of my life, and I can take evasive action before she has the chance to take hold. With increased practice I have had increased success. For the most part, she wants to be smart and right. So, when I am in a conversation with someone, and they speak incorrectly or on a topic that I know more about, I can feel her want to speak up to correct and intellectually overshadow the other person. In those times, I've taught myself to ask questions of the other person so as not to outshine their understanding with mine. This allows me to connect with people and share experiences instead of overpowering them to be right, an old defense mechanism to feel safe.

In times of disagreement with my husband, I can feel my feet begin to take me out the door. The flight stress response is ingrained deep in my nervous system and tries to activate. During those discussions, I anchor myself to the ground and focus on clearly and lovingly communicating my point with compassion and empathy. It is not always perfect, but I have learned to show up as an evolving version of my true Self through my reparenting practice. You can too.

CHAPTER 6

UNDERSTANDING
YOUR PORN HABIT

Fear is the memory of pain. Addiction is the
memory of pleasure. Freedom is beyond both.
DEEPAK CHOPRA

THE SEEDS OF ADDICTION

Sam's story shows how a porn habit can start early and slowly take over one's brain and life. It may sound eerily familiar to you. When Sam was twelve, his older brother showed him a porn magazine. Immediately he felt the intense rush of pleasure jolting through his body as he viewed the images. His brain felt like it would explode, and his body tingled everywhere. It was like nothing he had ever experienced before. Later, he took that magazine and masturbated while looking at it. The pleasure he felt when he first glanced at the magazine was heightened even more now that there was physical

MIND OVER EXPLICIT MATTER

stimulation. In that moment, Sam's porn habit was born. The seeds of addiction were planted without Sam even knowing it. He continued to water those seeds for decades.

Flash forward to the early 2000s and the dawn of the Internet Age. Sam began to search for images on his computer, and with the click of a button, he could find photos and videos of all kinds depicting sexual acts and scenes. The grainy videos took forever to load, but to Sam, it was worth the wait. As high-speed internet continued to flourish, and ever-increasing amounts of erotic material with it, so did Sam's growing dependency on it. He still didn't recognize it as dependency, though. He would stay up late to watch porn to relax before bed. It became his bedtime routine for over a decade. As his need for porn grew, without him consciously realizing it, he began to watch porn more and more during the day. He thought it was just a way to chill out on his days off. It would continue for years.

Sam's porn habit didn't stop there. Once the seeds of his addiction had taken root, they continued to grow and spread to other aspects of his life, altering how he perceived the world and acted within it. This distorted way of thinking and acting generated unexpected (and often unseen) side effects within his relationships and work.

In the previous chapter, we went over some of the sources of early trauma, pain, and discomfort that can lead to hypersexuality and porn addiction. Now it is time to learn more about the seeds of porn addiction and the types of behavior it increases and influences. In addition, you will gain tools to start weeding out those bad habits to create the space for the seeds of your authentic self, the Real You, to grow.

TYPES OF PORN ADDICTION

Everyone's tale is different. But when it comes to porn addiction, your story will typically follow one of three progressions, often depending on your age, gender, and circumstances.

Classic

Trauma and family dysfunction are the impetuses for classic pornography addiction. The push of dysfunction coupled with the pull of early exposure led you first into magazines and then possibly later into discovering internet porn to continue the habit.[1] This habit was developed before high-speed internet and easily accessible online pornography and sexual media. As a result, I have found this type occurs primarily in men over sixty who never really got into the variety and intensity of video consumption from an early age. The trademarks of this type of habit are early exposure at lower levels, with frequent, consistent, and continual use over a much more extended time. Think twenty-, thirty-, or forty-plus years of print and video porn.

Contemporary

First exposure to high-speed internet porn, with its multitude of much-higher-level eroticism of all sexual kinds, pulled you into the screen during childhood or adolescence. Porn in your pocket, as such, impacts men and women in modern society. Dopamine hits can be accessed quickly, easily, and anonymously all day and all night, and they are. Contemporary problems come with a higher incidence of early-onset, porn-induced erectile dysfunction (PIED), a type of SAD (sexual arousal dysfunction), because of the negative changes in baseline brain arousal.[2] It has an earlier onset of symptoms and occurs primarily in men and women in their teens, twenties, and thirties.[3]

Mixed

This hybrid addiction primarily affects middle-aged men, like Sam, who were exposed to pornography in magazines during adolescence but began watching internet porn during their late thirties and early forties. Habit initialization with print but becoming hooked on videos is characteristic of this classification type. Men between the ages of forty and sixty primarily succumb to the sneakiness of this mixed type, with its imperceptible hold taking over with the passing of time.

THE EASY-BUTTON LIFESTYLE

The need to escape discomfort through pleasure is the driving force underlying all three types of porn addiction. And all grow out of similar mechanistic dynamics playing out in your brain. At any age, your brain seeks homeostasis—the baseline where everything is balanced and healthy. It tries to create stability. When you started watching porn, the excessive dopamine rush disrupted homeostasis and threw you off-kilter. But then your brain's stabilizing mechanisms kicked in and tried to balance those levels. Once changed, your brain needs increasingly higher doses of dopamine to balance itself in this new mode, called *neo-homeostasis*—"new" baseline. It becomes your new operating mode. But your brain is now unstable, always seeking balance, as it needs more and more dopamine to feel the same or increasing levels of goodness.

This creates many problems, especially in younger people suffering from contemporary porn addiction. Your brain becomes bonded to the screen. The more you return to the screen, the more you desensitize the reward center in your brain. That makes it harder to enjoy pleasures in the real world in the same way. You can no longer get the same dopamine release and pleasure response from hanging out with friends and doing other activities you might have loved without the influence of porn. You can no longer get aroused by a human partner because they cannot possibly stimulate you at the high levels your brain has become accustomed to through porn and masturbation. *Habituation*, the diminished response with continual use, also means you will need more intense pornography to satisfy your craving. The pendulum in your brain swings even more wildly. Porn becomes the ultimate quick fix. You turn on porn to feel good, fast.

If you remember the commercial of the man with a problem stepping up to a desk for help, the clerk offers the Easy button to solve it for him with no effort at all. "That was easy!" proclaims the now problem-free man. Porn is like hitting the Easy button for pleasure and escape without working for it. Unfortunately, this establishes an "Easy-button lifestyle" that soon spreads and invades other aspects of your life. You start relying on fast food, video games, social media, your phone, and other quick fixes for dopamine, with porn being at the top.[4] It is hard to get motivated. Your sex life becomes lackluster. You can't even enjoy just relaxing with family and friends. You are stuck in the loop of constant pleasure-seeking to offset internal pain.

YOU ARE WHAT YOU SEARCH

When you seek out sex online, it hunts you down too. This is because websites, including porn sites and social media, use special algorithms to present to you more of what you have previously searched. In this way, the websites serve you images, ads, emails,

WHEN YOU SEEK OUT SEX ON THE INTERNET, THE WEB WILL SERVE IT BACK TO YOU.

and even texts seemingly from real women, who many times are bots, to keep pulling you back into the screen. Similarly, social media platforms employ sophisticated eye-tracking technology so that the longer you visually linger on an image or a portion of an image (such as a body part), the more of the same the artificial intelligence software serves you.

But this does not mean you are helpless. Here is the reality: When I open my phone, I am exposed to zero sexual media. *Zero.* Even though I am constantly searching topics related to porn use, I don't visit any sites or accounts that would show me explicit content; thus, I am not served any. I don't search for sex, so it doesn't look for me. It will rarely come to you if you don't search for it. If you search for sex on the internet, the web will serve it back to you.

As you change how you use the internet, forgoing sexual media, it can help provide positive content that inspires and motivates you to be more intentional about attaining your goals. When you search for things you love, they will be provided to you instead, helping you stay on track toward your full potential instead of derailing you.

Brain Hack Number 14
What Can You Search for Instead?

In your journal, contemplate the following ideas. Where do you find hypersexualized material? How is it served to you? What could you do instead?

NOT JUST A BAD HABIT BUT
DISORDERED BEHAVIOR

Compulsive sexual behavior is not just a bad habit; it is recognized as a behavioral disorder.[5] I don't want you to feel "disordered," but I want you to realize the magnitude of the issue with hypersexuality. Disorder is the disruption of the systematic functioning of your nervous system. The criteria for compulsive sexual behavior disorder are listed below. Meeting the criteria indicates that a person has developed high-level needs for physical and mental sexual-activity engagement. This means you think about sex and try to have sex often, even most of the time.

Compulsive Sexual Behavioral Disorder Criteria

1. Repetitive sexual activity becomes central focus with neglect of other interests
2. Diminished control with unsuccessful efforts to reduce sexual behavior
3. Continued sexual activity despite negative consequences
4. Little to no satisfaction derived from sexual behavior but continued engagement
5. Significant distress across important life domains[6]

BEAUTIFUL BUTTERFLIES

Pornography addiction is the primary way this behavioral disorder manifests itself. What your brain is struggling with is a very real thing, and in many ways, it is biologically predisposed to be vulnerable to such pleasure-seeking behavior. The compulsively sexual brain is not just driven by habituation and cycling, there are also some other neurobiological processes at work, some driven by millions of years of evolution.

One such process is called the *cardboard butterfly effect*. Scientists interested in explaining behavioral instincts painted oversized cardboard butterflies with exaggerated colors. The male butterflies swarmed the visually enhanced cardboard butterflies, preferring them and ignoring the genuine female cohort altogether. Their brains, like ours, were enticed by a supernormal stimulus.[7]

Porn, like the artificially ornate cardboard butterflies, presents the brain with a heightened sexual experience that is difficult for the brain to resist.[8] Once you become accustomed to the bedazzlement of porn performers, acts, scenes, and accoutrement, it can be almost impossible to be satisfied by your partner, and life as you know it pales in comparison. Continual exposure to the "cardboard butter-fly" of porn distorts your ability to find pleasure and happiness in the world around you. But we must remember that butterflies, so to speak, are inherently beautiful in and of themselves.

PORN AS PAINKILLER

Most people understand the idea of drug addiction. Consume the drug, feel good, and keep going back for more. Just like drug addiction, porn takes advantage of a biological process in your brain. Endogenous opioid peptides are small molecules that emerge in the brain, producing the same effects as morphine and heroin. As a result, they can decrease pain and even induce euphoria.[9] Changes in the natural reward pathways in the brain occur by increases in these peptides during sexual experiences.[10] This is why porn use appeals to so many people, especially high-performers who are not interested in mind-altering substances. No drugs are necessary to feel the high. The peptides not only douse the pain of the human

experience but also reinforce addictive and compulsive behaviors, such as the use of drugs, alcohol, gambling, and porn.

THE ONLY THING YOU NEED TO GET YOUR DRUG OF CHOICE IS YOUR MIND.

One of the most distressing aspects of porn use is that these mechanisms are likened to an internalized drug addiction and can be accessed through the recall of porn fantasy, called *euphoric recall*. The only thing you need to get your drug of choice is your mind. One of my clients aptly put it like this: "If you put a drug addict and an alcoholic in a padded room for a month, they come out clean. If you put me in the same room for a month, I come out the same."

DISTORTION OF BIOLOGICAL NEEDS

Most people have heard of Darwin's survival of the fittest theory, postulated on how the strong survive and procreate to secure their lineage. The driving forces behind male-female mating essentially boil down to this. Higher-quality females were ready to mate with eager, higher-quality males earlier, leaving lower-quality males and females to mate with each other.[11]

Modern day "high-quality" features have been evaluated such that women prefer men who demonstrate ambition, intelligence, and prospective financial security while men desire younger, attractive, modest partners with a high likelihood of reproduction.[12] The takeaway is that innately speaking, men preferred young, attractive, sexually reproductive women. It is a priority in healthy mating. However, this natural preference can be distorted by pornography with the endless novelty of young, beautiful women performing sexual acts. These women are not, in reality, viable sexual partners, but instead they are only fantasy.

Evolutionarily, though, many nonmonogamous animals are instinctually driven to procreate with many partners to continue their species. Known as the Coolidge effect, it has been shown to be enhanced by high levels of dopamine, associated with novelty, even in these animals.[13] Male rats that were sexually fulfilled, when presented with a new female, would copulate again, a behavior shown to be driven by a 44 percent increase in dopamine flow upon exposure.[14]

Novelty drives increased sexual desire and behavior. Porn serves the viewer continual, novel "high-quality" females, increasing dopamine flow in the viewer's brain and keeping them stuck in perpetual novelty-seeking mode.

Pornography satisfies, yet heightens, the urge for sexual novelty; it gives you the novel stimulus your brain wants but keeps you seeking more. Now, watching porn does not, of course, satisfy the evolutionary need for paternity and lineage, as was presented by Darwin. Instead, it detracts from the natural, healthy mating and bonding behavior of innately monogamous beings. Viewing strangers in an artificially composed scene, on a screen, by yourself while masturbating does not serve survival, reproduction, or evolution.

In the animal kingdom, superior-level males and females seek out first-rate mates for procreation. In addition, the human need for love, connection, and pair bonding supersedes the biological underpinnings of seeking out multiple sex partners.[15] Human brains are more developed than animal brains; thus, we desire offspring and the happiness and joy of having a partner.

Women and men want fidelity and loyalty in their relationships.[16] A high-quality way to keep a top-level partner, in the evolutionary sense, is to be a top-notch partner yourself. If you want to have an awesome mate, be one. When you and your partner are top tier, you can have a first-class relationship. Porn does not fit into that equation. How can you get the sexual novelty that your ancestral brain is looking for? Create it within your relationship. Get inventive and design healthy sexual novelty with your partner. This is a win for you, your partner, and your family.

Brain Hack Number 15
Are You a Top-Tier Partner?

Top-tier females want to mate with top-tier males. Is distorted sexual-novelty seeking taking you away from a healthy partnership? What can you do to become a top-notch partner and be more attractive to a top-level mate?

DEVELOPING YOUR SEXUALLY STUNTED FULL POTENTIAL

Let's consider a helpful model of self-actualization. Maslow's famous hierarchy of needs, one of the best-known theories of motivation, proposes that our actions are motivated by certain physiological and psychological needs that progress from basic to more complex.

When you experience trauma in childhood, your brain can get stuck in an unhealthy way at the lowest level of the pyramid: seeking basic physiological needs, including procreative sex, for survival. The introduction of porn at an early age, often before healthy sexual development, distorts sexuality with a hyperfocus on porn due to neurological changes. You stay stuck at the lowest level of self-actualization with your brain seeking porn out of seeming survival.

Maslow's Hierarchy of Needs

MASLOW'S HIERARCHY OF NEEDS

Some people might consider self-actualization, becoming your most sought-after self, as a luxury. It is a "thrive" mechanism, the realization or fulfillment of one's talents and potentialities. However, it is considered an innate drive within humans, one I believe every person has the right—nay, the duty—to achieve. Okay, that might seem over the top, but hear me out. If we all self-actualized, becoming the most purposeful and peaceful version of ourselves, the pain and discomfort of the human condition would decrease significantly because we would all be living on purpose, loving life and all it has to offer. Less pain for everyone results in less acting out of that pain via physical and emotional violence and less need for self-soothing. Porn use would diminish as the silent tsunami receded. Society, and the individuals that constitute it, would be thriving, not surviving.

I recently read a definition of *hell* presented as this: "The last day you have on earth, the person you became will meet the person you could have become."[17] I hope I look in the mirror that day with absolutely no regrets. Far beyond only taking care of my basic physiological needs, I hope to have experienced true intimacy through acceptance of myself and others, to have achieved my big goals while enjoying every minute of it; and I hope to be filled with peace, a sense of accomplishment, and gratitude for the life I have lived. I want this for you too. That is why I am here. That reason alone motivates me to show up here for you. Now is the time for you to show up for yourself.

Brain Hack Number 16
What Does the Self-Actualized Real You Look Like?

Maslow said, "What a man can be, he must be."[18] Dare to dream what the best version of yourself looks like, the one you will meet on that last day. What has he accomplished? How does she spend her time? What does a life filled with your most extraordinary creativity look like? What are your unique gifts, and how can you express them? How could you spend your time engaged in purposeful activities to close the gap of who you are now and who you want to be? Write about the authentic you and what he or she will be doing once you rise.

BREAKING THE VICIOUS
PUSH-PULL CYCLE OF PORN

The push of past and present pain and the pull of porn's high-level stimuli create a vicious pain-pleasure paradox cycle that is difficult to escape. As a result, the steady push (dopamine deficit) and constant pull (supernormal stimulus) becomes a vicious cycle of porn use that many people are unaware has taken over their lives. Anxious feelings of stress and despair are experienced, then short-term relief sets in. Then, the process starts over again. Sometimes it takes days for the relief to dissipate; sometimes it's only a matter of moments.

The solution? Breaking you out of this push-and-pull cycle permanently. There is a moment in time when this is most easily accomplished: just after you've enjoyed watching porn but before you feel shame and anxiety again. This fleeting glimpse, when you acknowledge that porn is holding you back—what I call the *change point*—is the time in the dopamine cycle to commit to transformation and begin to implement the success strategies that can get you there.

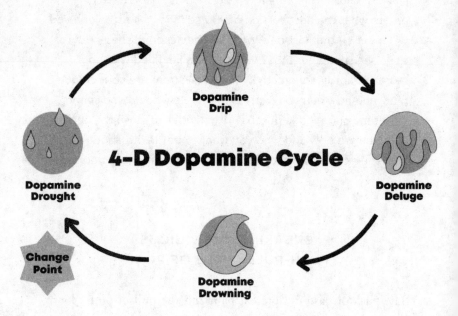

Dopamine Drip

4-D Dopamine Cycle

Dopamine Drought

Dopamine Deluge

Change Point

Dopamine Drowning

Brain Hack Number 17
Charting Your Porn Cycle

Figure out your porn cycle. Record in your journal the days and times you watch porn, including how long your sessions typically are and the length of the time between sessions. Does a pattern emerge? Have you felt that moment of regret before anxiety and shame creep in? What did it feel like for you? How can you use it to break free?

SIDE EFFECTS OF PORN USE

Porn contributes to mental and physical health issues in men and women now more than ever. Constantly watching the performers' physiques may leave people deflated and feeling bad about themselves.[19] When people leave porn behind, they see their partners with renewed arousal and beauty and feel stronger and better about themselves.

Judgment may also suffer as increased risk-taking to consume pornography takes over, often watching at home when others are around or at work. Like Sam's wife, your partner likely knows something is up even if he or she doesn't know about the pornography.

Side Effects of Porn Use

- General malaise
- Guilt and shame
- Secretiveness
- Brain fog
- Memory and concentration issues
- Difficulty focusing

- Anxiety
- Depression
- Moodiness
- Irritability
- Distorted view of reality
- Self- and body-image issues
- Need higher levels of stimulation to become aroused
- More frequent, longer porn sessions, increased intensity, and multiple genres
- Erectile dysfunction
- Delayed ejaculation
- Lowered libido
- Impaired judgment
- Fixations on certain body parts
- Fetishes
- Less attracted to a partner
- Relationship problems
- Sexual arousal template confusion: aroused by violent, morally incongruent, or non-sexual stimuli
- Premature ejaculation
- Sexual anxiety
- Social anxiety
- Feelings of guilt

Brain Hack Number 18
Side Effects of Your Porn Use

Review the side effects of porn listed in the chart and write the ones you are experiencing in your journal. How often do you experience them? How do they impact your life?

ACTING-OUT BEHAVIORS

The impact of porn use does not stop with the side effects experienced by the viewer. The more entrenched Sam's porn cycle became, the more it impacted his relationship with Krissy. He would try to choke and gag her during sex. He continually wished to, and would inadvertently try to, slap her and pull her hair. As his porn use increased, he could feel the desire to do the acts he saw in real life. He didn't want to view them anymore; he wanted to experience them. Sam started to follow a porn-informed script in the bedroom in terms of how he wanted his and Krissy's sex life to unfold, primarily things he wanted her to do to him. He would fantasize about how sex could be, and he would resent her for not wanting to follow the script he had in his mind, the one in which she was an object to fulfill his desires. As Sam's porn habit escalated, his wife told him it was like having sex with an eighteen-year-old teenager. Childishly, he would try to engage in as many pleasure-inducing acts for himself as he could at any given time. It was like a three-ring circus.

At the time, Sam did not realize he was one of the lucky few: he escaped before his porn habit could escalate to the next level of compulsive sexualized acting out. It is imperative that I not give you any ideas you don't already know about because the Hijacker may want you to realize those ideas. So please be advised.

In the following vignettes I will share stories of others who were not as lucky as Sam, those whose porn habits escalated beyond their control into dire behaviors they were otherwise appalled by but could not stop engaging in. You may recognize yourself in some of these stories of acting-out behaviors.

Constant Sexual Media Use (Norman)

Norman told me he enjoyed social media.

"Who are you following on these sites?" I asked.

Not surprisingly, he was following young women, and lots of them. He was not actually using social media but partaking in sexual media for dopamine hits. He wasn't fully aware of his behavior until we dissected it together.

Lost in the Dark-Porn Web (Tyrese)

Tyrese found himself plunging into dark-porn genres that sickened him after he finished watching. A teaser had popped up one day in the corner of his screen, and he wondered what it would be like. He often wished he had never clicked on the link. It would have saved him from future brutality.

The link led to darkness and violence coupled with kinky sex acts that made him squeamish initially but aroused overall. These barbaric videos made him anxious and excited and kept him returning ever increasingly over the years. And they changed him. His thoughts became as dark as the scenes he watched. He found it difficult to go out in public because every woman he saw made him think of the savagery on the screen and desire it for himself. He found it incredibly difficult to stop.

Penis Size Praise (Michael)

Michael began watching porn when he was thirteen years old. From watching years of porn, he always thought his penis was small. Porn instills and worsens this idea in men with its porn performers, enhanced technology, and camera angles. When he was twenty-one, Mike began to pay for webcam sex in which he would have the girls tell him how big his penis was. He persisted in this behavior for years, and he is not an exceptional case.

OK with Violent Sex (Chandra)

As a young girl, Chandra never thought she would find herself in relationship after relationship with sexually violent men. She never stayed within any of them very long, but the next sexual relationship was the same as the last. She told me that at first, she thought it was the men, but then she realized she was perpetuating the same scenario by convincing herself she liked rough sex and that it was what she deserved.

After working with a sex addiction recovery coach, she realized that she could find a healthier partner and a loving sexual relationship by becoming emotionally intelligent first.

Married on Dating Apps (Max)

Max, a fifty-year-old man, loved using dating apps to look at younger women like he would watch in porn. The fact that he was happily married didn't come to the forefront of his mind when he was scrolling through the app. He was just checking girls out, he would tell himself. One crucial day, however, he swiped right.

Studies show that 65 percent of dating app users are married.[20] Research suggests these apps decrease self-esteem, lower satisfaction with the appearance of one's face and body, and increase psychological distress in users, with equal effects for men and women.[21]

Max would spend time on and off all day long looking at profiles on the app. Each time he accessed the app, his brain would get a dopamine drip. Sometimes he would interact with women for even more stimulation. He would chat back and forth, which made him feel great and validated. He paid some women to send him sexual images—until his wife found them on his computer. The Hijacker led Max into personal interactions with real young women but couldn't bring him back to his previous relationships with his wife and family.

One-Night Stand (Alex)

Although Alex had watched porn for years and fantasized about what it would be like to engage in some of the acts he saw, he never thought it would impact his life in a drastic way. But his guys' weekend in Las Vegas turned into a one-night stand with an exotic dancer after a night of gambling, drinking, and strip clubs. When he awoke, he couldn't believe what he had done. He wanted to turn back time and take it back. But it wasn't that simple. His fiancée was at home waiting for him. When Alex told me his story, I could tell he thought I would be shocked. I wasn't. I had heard the same tale from many men caught in the downward spiral of compulsive sexuality escalation.

Escorts and Prostitutes (Jeff)

After years of watching porn, Jeff was restless. He found the scenes and acts boring. He wanted to experience the roughness and brutishness of the scenes, but he could never get his wife to participate. So he began visiting escorts and prostitutes. The first time the Hijacker convinced him to meet one of these women, Jeff told himself it would only be once, just to see what it was like. But once didn't suffice, and his habit of paying for porn-influenced sexual experiences continued for over a decade.

These are just a few of the many stories I have heard, but the underlying ideas are the same: pleasure-seeking and escalation. Famous musician Billie Eilish publicly shared her story of porn addiction, stating, "I used to watch a lot of porn, to be honest. I started watching it when I was like 11. I think it really destroyed my brain and I feel incredibly devastated that I was exposed to so much porn." She indicated that she felt traumatized by the violent porn scenes that she watched and believes they contributed to the sleep paralysis and night terrors that she experienced. She said that during her first sexual encounters, she allowed her partners to treat her poorly, and she didn't say no to acts that she really didn't want to participate in because she thought she was supposed to be attracted to them. Porn's popularity and her own past thinking that porn was OK now anger her.[22]

Staying with one or a variety of hypersexual acting-out behaviors and then needing more dopamine due to increased tolerance is very common. All these porn users didn't realize their brains were driving their behaviors until it was too late. Habituation in the brain made it so they could no longer feel that high-level rush from the same sex acts and scenes. They needed something new. For some, it was dopamine hits all day long from sexual media; and for others, it was darker and more violent porn; and for others still, talking about or reenacting porn scenes with real people.

If you have felt the pull of escalation, know it is a downward spiral until you heal your brain. Before long, the screen will no longer satisfy your hypersexuality. A few acting-out behaviors like those just described can grow out of this insatiable need for more pleasure. Like Sam, you might try to get your partner engaged in new sex acts, many of which they do not find pleasurable. In fact, if she is emotionally healthy, she likely will consider them demeaning and demoralizing. You may also start to pursue other sexual experiences outside of your relationship. This might be online dating apps or chat rooms with cam girls. Sometimes this leads to cheating, hookups, and even the use of prostitution.

Acting-out behaviors drain your brain and make you less confident and desirable to yourself and others. Here are some more examples:

- Ritually watching porn (after wife leaves, before bed, every morning, etc.)
- Staring at people or specific body parts often or all the time (dopamine hits)

- Compulsive masturbation
- Wanting a partner to perform sex acts you view in porn
- "Emotional" affairs (emailing, talking, etc.)
- Social media misuse
- Sexualizing everything
- Wanting to watch yourself having sex instead of experiencing it
- Voyeurism, exhibitionism, fetishes, etc.
- Live sex webcams
- Dating apps (browsing eventually becoming using)
- Hookups
- Prostitutes
- Affairs

Brain Hack Number 19
Your Acting-Out Behaviors

Review the acting-out behaviors and write down in your journal those you engage in. Start tracking how often sex pops into your mind, including in environments that shouldn't be sexualized. Many people use the "rubber band on the wrist" trick here. Wear a rubber band on your wrist and snap it whenever you have a sexual thought. It is not to punish yourself. Instead, it is to break the positive-feedback loop you have established in your mind and brain associated with sexual thoughts. Instead of dopamine, the stress hormone cortisol is delivered, and instead of pleasure you experience pain. When you snap the rubber band, it delivers a negative-feedback signal, helping to break the pattern while increasing your self-awareness.

Self-awareness is only the first step in increasing your emotional intelligence to assist in quitting porn. With your new understanding of how your porn habit started and what sparks cravings for hypersexual novelty, you will have increased understanding of your porn cycle. By recognizing how the side effects of porn are impacting how you feel and act, you can move forward to regulate your mood more healthily. In doing so, you will exercise the second step in emotional intelligence: self-regulation. The roots of addiction can run deep and may have been growing for years, but when you act, think, and feel in a new way, they can be disrupted and uprooted.

CHAPTER 7

HOW TO STOP WATCHING PORN

Wisdom consists of the anticipation
of consequences.
NORMAN COUSINS

A LOST CAUSE

Sam visited two therapists before he came back to me. According to Sam, the first, a certified sex addiction therapist, became instantly chummy with him. Sam is bright, and because he is highly intelligent, so is the Hijacker who lives within him. He was a master of disguise. Sam told the therapist precisely what she wanted to hear, befriending her and giving her the impression that he was making progress. Sam didn't like going to therapy, but he kept returning despite the lack of measurable changes in his behavior because it made him *feel* like he was trying.

Krissy, like many wives, was more discerning than her husband assumed. She knew his efforts were a smoke screen. And yet, she was so stuck in her own codependency, paralyzed by the fear she might destroy her family, that she pretended everything was fine. She told me later that she was engaged in "planned ignoring." So Krissy turned a blind eye to Sam's continued habit. And over time, a pattern emerged: Krissy would find Sam in sexually compromising situations, Sam would swear that nothing was happening, and Krissy would let it go because she couldn't bear the thought of the alternative.

Many partners have engaged in "planned ignoring" when they feel overwhelmed by their partner's porn habits. They ignore the clear signs, participate in their partner's charade, and hope that the situation will resolve itself somehow. It is a sign of sexual-betrayal trauma experienced by partners that is thought to lead to psychological, physiological, and behavioral harm. It's been reported that 84 percent of partners stay in their relationships, with 87 percent of partners blaming themselves for their partner's betrayal.[1] Since the cycle continues in private, hidden from the view of the couple's family and friends, everything seems fine—even though it isn't. But like many spouses, Krissy couldn't ignore it forever.

As Sam embarked on his slow recovery process, he would constantly vacillate among his three personas—Dr. Jekyll, Mr. Hyde, and the Real Sam (who was beginning to shine through occasionally)—with dire consequences. Once, during a party Sam was hosting in his Dr. Jekyll persona, a sexy text from a woman came through on his phone while Krissy was standing nearby. (Remember, when you seek porn on the internet, it is usually served back up to you in the form of websites, emails, and even texts.) Sam quickly tried to hide the text from her, but she glimpsed it anyway. Krissy never thought Sam would actually cheat on her, but the text was devastating all the same. Later, when she asked Sam about it, he denied receiving the text. He, now engaging his Mr. Hyde persona, told her she was "seeing things" and insisted she not look at his phone again. Suddenly, Krissy was framed as the offender for snooping and invading his privacy.

Two days later, Sam was no longer acting out of the wounded child within him, and Real Sam appeared again. He admitted the existence of the text that was sent by a spam bot from a porn site, not a live woman. Sam had never cheated on Krissy and would later prove it to her via a polygraph test, which is customary in many sex addiction recovery programs. He felt shame and disgust at himself for the text and for defensively lying about it, but he didn't know what to do. After that, he always kept his phone close by to avoid another slipup. Rather than get better, Sam was merely getting better at hiding it. And so the vacillation between personas continued, undermining his relationship with his wife in the process.

Like many people trying to recover from porn addiction, Sam tried not to watch porn but would instead consume lower-level sexual media on various non-porn websites and social media. Although it wasn't porn, the intent and the effect were the same—dopamine hits from looking at sexual and suggestive content. One day, after Sam's family left for school, Krissy unexpectedly returned to the house to retrieve an item she had forgotten and caught Sam masturbating. Embarrassed and frustrated, Sam erupted and yelled at her for walking in. As the words came out of his mouth, he realized that his need for masturbation superseded his need to get to work on time, as it was 7:34 a.m. and he was supposed to be at work across town at 8:00 a.m.

Still trying to quit on his own but not able to achieve a sexual release that day, he was beginning to unravel with the need for dopamine. He called Krissy later to schedule a lunchtime sexual rendezvous, but she was so utterly distraught over Sam's behavior toward her that she was totally uninterested in sex with him. Sam grew angrier and more argumentative, filled with shame and driven to find some form of sexual release from the increasing stress. He'd lost touch with reality at that point, sinking further into his Mr. Hyde persona.

Before finally working with me using the program I had created, Sam met twice with another therapist in a group setting to appease his wife. Recognizing the fraudulent intent behind Sam's presence, this therapist determined that Sam was never really "in the room." His body attended the meetings, but he wasn't actively engaged in recovery. When this professional deemed Sam "a lost cause to porn addiction," something snapped inside him. He did not believe he was beyond hope and help, and he determined right there that he could—no, he *would*—overcome porn use. At this point, our work together commenced.

You may have experienced a roller-coaster ride like Sam's, in which case this is probably not your first attempt at recovery. Maybe, like Sam, you've reached the end of your rope and are determined to win the battle once and for all. This is the point on your journey where you must disrupt the cycle and rewire your brain to start healing at last.

BREAKING THE CYCLE OF SHAME

Shame is at the core of a porn habit. It can impact you over years, even decades. Sam's original shame felt like inadequacy and social anxiety. He compared himself to idealized versions of others and then never felt he could live up to the comparison. Porn contributes to this way of living. Porn makes men feel they aren't manly enough, strong enough, big enough, or confident enough; that their woman isn't hot enough, sexy enough, or enthusiastic enough. Women, too, are made to feel deeply lacking in self-worth by pornography consumption. Shame from "not enough-ness" is a central and recurring theme of porn addiction.

During recovery, shame may increase as the porn-adjacent sexual media increases in strangeness. This could manifest as perusing lingerie sites, watching yoga videos, or repeatedly watching sex scenes in movies. These kinds of actions are merely expressions of the brain searching for a dopamine hit. Many clients of mine, during their recovery, say something like, "Things are getting weird." I encourage them to use this feeling to increase self-awareness and take new action. In some cases, like Sam's, shame also comes from acting-out behaviors during everyday life, such as lusting after young women while out with your spouse, giving in to urges to masturbate frequently and at inconvenient times, or behaving in flirtatious ways with coworkers, friends, and strangers.

Shame is also often paired with defensiveness. When others become aware of, or confront us about, our behaviors, we will often lash out and become highly defensive because of our shame. Often the implementation of the defense mechanisms that we've already explored becomes a primary way that shame is offset internally. Sam often felt, due to shame, that others were attacking him, even when they weren't. He would snap at friends, family, and frequently at his wife.

Here is a list of some of the most common defensive behaviors that arise due to porn use. Do any of these behaviors sound familiar?

Denial: You claim you weren't actually looking at sex-related content. (You were.)

Minimization: You believe it's no big deal. Everyone does it. (Remember, normal does not equal healthy.)

Rationalization: You claim this content can help you become a better lover or keep things interesting. (You don't need porn to achieve either of these things.)

Justification: You assert that you have sexual needs, and porn is just helping you meet those needs. (Your high-level "needs" may actually be the result of your porn habit.)

Blaming: You say that porn is a stress reliever, and, well, if your partner weren't so demanding/nosy/prudish, then you wouldn't be so stressed out. (No one else is responsible for your actions.)

Gaslighting: You begin to spin a story of half-truths that shield and deflect, intended to make your partner doubt the truth. (Trying to hide the truth is a pretty good sign that you need to deal with it.)

All these behaviors contribute to the problem they are trying to solve, perpetuating the sense of shame you feel. The lying, hiding, and double life of porn forces you into a shame spiral as you vacillate between Dr. Jekyll and Mr. Hyde.

In order to break the shame cycle, you need to take this big first step: *tell someone about your porn habit.* Tell someone who makes you feel safe, who will understand, and who will offer no judgment. This might be a parent, mentor, close friend, or a brain-health porn-addiction-recovery coach. He or she can guide you through the first and subsequent action steps toward success. If you can tell your partner and have them stand beside you, that's even better. They don't have to offer you advice or solve the issue for you; they just need to support you in your journey.

Brain Hack Number 20
Release the Shame; Tell Someone About Your Porn Habit

How is shame showing up in your life? Have you engaged in any of the shame-based strategies I listed? Tell a trusted, emotionally mature friend or coach about your struggles—it breaks the shame cycle and frees up your nervous system, making it more neuroplastic for change.

Shame lives in secretiveness. The cycle can only be stopped after the windows are thrown open and the light is let in. So tell someone that your brain has been hijacked. Tell them that you don't want the Hijacker to remain in control any longer. Take the first step toward reclaiming your power. Addiction breeds in isolation; it is stifled by connection.

As Sam and I began to work closely together, he opened up with me, becoming more vulnerable by sharing his feelings of inadequacy and disgust toward himself for the explicit content he had come to depend on. He reflected on the realization that he did not recognize his nagging feelings of shame until long after they had passed. It's often difficult to discover the dark, repressed feelings at one's core after burying them and faking happiness for so long.

Once Sam started to investigate the trauma in his past, how he was living his life in the present, and how he hadn't set many future goals, he saw how shame had driven him to ignore the impact of his past experiences, escape from his present reality through short-term pleasure, and ultimately disengage from long-term consequences or goals. This is when he started to change, and it can be the beginning of your transformation too.

PUTTING UP FENCES

The Hijacker in you will try to keep a pinky finger on the wheel if you let him. He will convince you to save one last outlet for your urges. This could be a bookmarked website, a dedicated device, a social media account, or anything that is sexual in nature, including sensual photos of exes or past partners. This is how the Hijacker sucks you back into the shame cycle.

It's time for a clean break, which means preventing regression. If this sounds like hard work, that's because it is. It takes discipline to give up pornography and not to yield to temptation. But through my work over the years, I've discovered some proven tools and strategies that help make this process easier.

For starters, many people find it's helpful to initiate their new lifestyle by performing a ritual to say goodbye to old habits and patterns that no longer serve them. I often ask clients to sit down and write a farewell letter to pornography. I know, I know. Talking to porn like a person may sound a little silly. But I've seen this ritual be very effective. Tell porn that you now realize it has taken more than it has given you and provide some specifics. You might even thank porn for helping you cope in the past while reassuring your true Self that porn will no longer be needed in the future.

Brain Hack Number 21
Farewell-to-Porn Letter

Draw two columns in your journal. At the top of the first column, write "Thank You" in bold letters. Underneath, list all the temporary benefits that porn has given you in the past. For example, it made you feel good, reduced your anxiety, offset your boredom, and was there for you every time you needed it. Pornography has been a close friend to you in the past, and there's no harm in acknowledging it.

Now, in the next column, write "Goodbye" in bold letters and list all the things that porn has taken from you. For example: time; money; energy; dignity; integrity; income; opportunities; a healthy sex life; relationships with your kids, girlfriend/boyfriend, or spouse; and so on. List everything you have forsaken due to porn. Don't leave anything out.

Read over this list, and realize that porn has taken more from you than it has given to you.

Now put these lists into sentence form as a letter and bid porn farewell. "Thank you, porn, for serving me and helping me through hard times. But I don't need you anymore. I am healing the wounds of the past. Goodbye." Many find it helpful and symbolic to burn their lists and/or letters as they commit to the future.

Once you've told someone about your habit and you've said goodbye, you'll need to stay out of the shame cycle so that the Hijacker has no grip on your life. You can do this by building some physical and mental boundaries to keep you out of porn and masturbation. I refer to this type of boundary setting as "putting up fences" because they are the fortifications you set up for yourself so you do not accidentally slip back into destructive habits. Pop culture is so sexually explicit, and the internet is so pervasive that it can be difficult to avoid triggers because they seem to be everywhere. Putting up fences will help to keep you safe.

MAKE EYE CONTACT

The first fence is to stop objectifying others. Your brain has been wired to look at specific body parts and imagine certain sex acts to get a dopamine hit. But you can unwire and rewire that part of your brain through a simple hack: make eye contact. They say that the eyes are the window to the soul, and practicing direct eye contact will help you recognize and acknowledge the other person's true Self. It can help instill dignity and integrity in the people you interact with and help rewire your brain accordingly. If you are not in a position for eye contact, then redirect your eyes to art or nature. Both are dopamine-producing and relink your brain into associating the dopamine already dripping with your real-world experiences.[2]

Brain Hack Number 22
Make Eye Contact

In your journal, list the most important people you should make eye contact with. Then practice this when you're next out to dinner or with friends in a social setting. If you are in a crowd and are checking people out from afar, redirect your eyes to art or nature. This way, you will associate the dopamine drip that has already been initiated with your life and environment rather than something sexual. You can find works of art in just about any public place through pictures, vases, statues, and flowers. While outside, look at the beauty of nature all around. Redirect and take it in.

FENCE IN TECHNOLOGY

Given the ease and ubiquity of cell phones and computers, you'll need to build some fences with your technology. Delete any apps on your phone, tablet, or computer that have encouraged hyper-sexual behavior in the past. This will help you stop consuming pornographic material or sexually explicit videos, images, or movies on your electronic devices. If you need an extra layer of help, download a password-protected porn-blocking app or software and/or a monitoring service. Covenant Eyes's blocking software uses advanced AI technology and accountability settings to prevent porn usage and has been highly rated for many years.

Next, create a list of best practices to prevent you from using your phone in ways, circumstances, or places that might trigger your habit. For example:

- No phone use in the bathroom (leave it in a public space)
- No phone use in bed (leave it across the room)
- No phone use in your car or other trigger locations

Brain Hack Number 23
Cell Phone and Computer Management

In your journal, list the steps you have taken to fence off your cell phone and computer use. Be sure not to leave any critical pieces out. Don't give the Hijacker an opening.

SOCIAL MEDIA FAST

The next fence is one that a lot of people want to skip, but I strongly encourage you not to: forego social media for at least ninety days. This is not an indefinite absence, but you must learn to live without social media for a longer period of time. Clean up your feeds and accounts before you begin your washout period. Remove or unfollow any and all sexual media accounts that give you dopamine drips. For every account you remove, replace it with a motivational and empowerment feed connected to your authentic purpose—hobbies, interests, and positive influencers who spark a passion to live your best life.

Don't be surprised if this ninety-day period is a struggle. Feel the resistance and recognize this as a signal that you're addressing a deeper need. Once you return to social media after this cleanse, your brain will have established new patterns with your social media networks. You will already have unfollowed any triggering people or feeds and will be poised for inspiration through your new ones.

A lot of my clients have decided not to reengage with social media, so don't be surprised if you prefer your life without it. But, if and when you do choose to reengage, consider scheduling specific times in your day to use social media in a limited capacity, perhaps twenty minutes at a time. In this way, you can turn a harmful activity into a healthy one by using social media intentionally.

Brain Hack Number 24
Social Media Management

Go into your social media accounts and unfollow all feeds that are sexual or sensual in nature. Follow and subscribe to accounts that inspire you to get on purpose with your work and hobbies. Now delete the apps for ninety days. In your journal, list the additional steps you will take to fence off your use of social media. Well done, my friend.

FENCE OFF SEXUALIZED SHOWS AND FILM

You must also retrain your brain's dependence on sexualized television shows and films. This will also require a period of abstinence. As with social media, I recommend no sexualized television shows or movies for the first ninety days of your intentional recovery program. This can be difficult to accomplish with the level of sexualization that happens within most streaming services; however, there are shows and services that are rated PG (parental guidance) with no sexual content within them. If you can reduce your show and movie watching to nonsexualized forms, it can be a healthier habit-replacement activity, especially if you watch with family or loved ones.

If you continue to expose yourself to sex scenes within shows or movies, I recommend you completely avoid them. Again, this may sound stringent, but it has worked for countless people. Following this ninety-day period, when you return to watching media, put some new guidelines in place that will help your brain remain healthy. For example, you might:

- watch preselected shows only—those without sexually explicit content,
- check IMDb (Internet Movie Database) for sexual-content warnings to be prepared ahead of time,
- watch shows only with your partner or family present, and/or
- decide on no media-viewing past 10:00 p.m.

Brain Hack Number 25
TV Show and Movie Management

In your journal, list the steps you have taken to fence off your use of television and movies.

WHAT ABOUT MASTURBATION?

Let's talk about masturbation. I know this may be a difficult subject, but we can't avoid the topic just because it's difficult to discuss.

The program outlined in this book aims to reestablish a pattern of healthy sexuality with another human being. Thus, I encourage you to create boundaries around any materials or objects that are used on or by yourself for sexual gratification. You can integrate these materials, including sex toys, into healthy sexual intimacy between you and your partner so long as both of you are comfortable and they are not detrimental to either of you.

So, am I asking you to avoid sexual behaviors that are objectifying or fantasizing, including masturbation? Yes, I am. Eventually, masturbation may be an area of healthy sexuality. But for now, it must be managed or even abandoned to rewire your brain from compulsion toward healthy physical intimacy. Sex is best experienced between two people, and the goal is to rewire your brain for relational sex.

You might think this is too much to ask. Maybe you're willing to take the other steps I suggest in this book, but not this one. Many people tell me that abstaining from masturbation is just too challenging. The problem is that secretive masturbation creates the shame of deception for many people, and therefore it has a negative neurological impact, impeding progress. This step is essential, and it will accelerate changes in your brain patterns.

If you are absolutely not willing or able to create relational sex right now or perhaps ever, then I would suggest considering *masturbation meditation*. For most people, self-pleasure is purely mechanical and leads to objectification and fantasy, but this meditation strategy incorporates the intentional use of masturbation to reconnect to yourself mentally and physically. It can help you learn to feel the sensations in your body in the present moment, just like a meditation experience. It requires you to stay alert in your body and not dissociate into fantasy. In this way, masturbation meditation will help you limit masturbation and can help you be present in sexual experiences with your partner too. Here is a strategy for masturbation meditation that has worked for my clients:

- Choose one day per week or per month to be sexual with yourself. Schedule it.
- Do not use porn or sexual materials.
- Rather than fantasizing (yes, I know this is a new experience, but this is the point), stay with the feelings and sensations in your body. No disconnecting.
- If you feel shame or guilt, stop immediately.

Brain Hack Number 26
Masturbation Management

In your journal, list your steps to fence off masturbation. Create a clear masturbation plan and reward yourself for following it. When you feel the urge to masturbate, try waiting at least forty-eight hours. If you give in to your urges, discuss this with your therapist or recovery coach.

ACCOUNTABILITY IS A MUST

Who will hold you accountable for checking in about your fences? Having an accountability partner, safe friend, sex-addiction-recovery coach, or group to help provide accountability is critical for long-term success. If you don't know anyone in your life who can serve in this role, no worries. Finding a supportive mentor, coach, or group is easier than ever with online forums. Preferably, this should not be someone who is currently battling porn use too, but rather someone who is ahead of you in the process.

Artificial intelligence within porn-blocking software has improved accountability more than ever through captured screenshots of sites you have visited that are blurred and sent to your accountability person for review. This way the Hijacker knows that someone else can see what you are seeing. It is highly effective for maintaining abstinence from porn.

Brain Hack Number 27
Accountability Systems

Make a note in your journal about how you will hold yourself accountable. Who will support you in learning from the challenges along the road to success? Keep a record of what you have told your accountability group, mentor, or partner.

THREE-SECOND PIVOT PLAN FOR EARLY SUCCESS

The best way to enforce the fences you have created and ensure your continued progress is to have a good plan—the more thorough, the better. Remember that when an urge strikes, it creates a dopamine drip in your brain that will make it difficult for you to ignore until you give it the dopamine deluge it is used to. And, neurobiologically, three seconds is all you have to pivot effectively in the early days of leaving porn behind.[3] Thus, drafting your *three-second pivot plan* is imperative and will help you avoid relapse—falling back into porn—in the early days of your brain rewiring.

Try this: Set a timer for three seconds and feel how very short it is. It is an instant. Repeat this several times. Each time you do, recognize that you must know precisely what you will do to pivot so you can do it successfully when you need to. Whenever the Hijacker tries to convince you to watch porn and masturbate, that is your cue to activate your plan, with the goal of shifting you into a new physical and mental space so you can move beyond the urge. In three seconds, there is no time to think and consider what you will do. There is only time to pivot into that predetermined something else, changing your space and retraining your brain into associating the new location and activity with the dopamine that has already begun to flow in your brain. Each urge is a call for mood regulation to offset stress, boredom, or overwhelm. When you see it as such, it is much easier to shift. But a plan is essential in order to succeed.

Let's go through an ideal three-second pivot plan step-by-step to make sure yours is ready to go. First, consider what, precisely, you will do instead of watching porn and masturbating. Be sure to create a pivot plan for daytime hours and one for the middle of the night if you are at risk of being awakened with unhealthy thoughts. Be very specific about what you will do, and remember, it should be enjoyable to produce dopamine and serotonin and have an element of connection to produce oxytocin. This way, your alternative activity will serve your brain's needs while healing. Having a plan for the daytime and one for late at night can help you succeed even further.

During the day, the best thing is to leave the house. Call someone or get connected in some way. Do something with others, whether an activity or just chatting. Change your physical and mental environment.

During the times in the day Sam would typically watch porn, he began to play basketball, his favorite sport. If he felt an urge while at work, he would search for gardening tips and recipes online because he loved growing and cooking farm-to-table food.

If he struggled to pivot, he would watch fifteen minutes of one of his favorite TV shows on his phone. This filled his need to go to the screen for dopamine, and it also gave him healthy projects to think about.

At night, instead of watching porn, connect yourself to music, a book, or a favorite hobby or activity (but make sure it avoids driving you back toward porn). A movie can be soothing if you must turn toward the screen.

If Sam awoke at night, he created a music playlist to soothe him back to sleep. He also followed a progressive-relaxation app to learn how to relax his muscles while focusing on his breath to help him drift back to sleep.

Brain Hack Number 28
Your Three-Second Pivot Plan

To outline your personal pivot plan, start by jotting down the areas in your life where you might need to pivot. Now create a very specific and personalized pivot plan for the daytime. Write in your journal three things you could do when triggered during the day. Something to do for thirty seconds to one minute so that you can choose to go in the other direction when you are entertaining the thought of watching porn.

Personalize it so it works for you: "If I get an urge during the day, instead of watching porn, I will

_____."

Now repeat this process, creating a pivot plan for nighttime.

YOUR PIVOT-PLAN TOOL KIT

Changing your physical and mental situation is vital, but the brain responds well to tactile engagement. So take this plan a step further by creating a physical pivot-plan tool kit you can feel in your hands. This will make sure you are one step ahead of the Hijacker.

Get a toiletry bag and fill it with dopamine-producing items and activities that bring your brain into the calm-focused brain pattern. Make sure the items in your bag are things that are helpful to you. Try to incorporate all five senses (sight, smell, hearing, taste, touch) to produce dopamine in various ways. You can use this tool kit to pivot when necessary and then celebrate the small wins when you have successfully pivoted. Having your favorite objects and other positive materials nearby can be beneficial in this process.

Here are some suggestions for items you can include in your tool kit:

- Favorite magazine
- Favorite songs (have them in a playlist ready to go)
- Essential-oil roller (lavender or something calming)
- Hydration packet
- Herbal tea
- Favorite snack or treat (Food produces dopamine, and chocolate even more so. Many of my clients choose dark chocolate.)
- Worry stone (This is a small object to rub within your hands. I call my hematite stone a "thinking stone" because it helps me *not* to worry.)
- Written affirmations
- Personal mantra
- Inspirational quote
- Story about one of the best times in your life

- Goals list
- Photograph of your partner or family or your purpose
- Replacement dopamine-inducing thought (Write three to five pages about your favorite things in life. Next, summarize these pages into a single paragraph. Then, consolidate that paragraph into a single sentence.)

Organize your tool kit materials ahead of time and have them ready at the time and place you are most likely to need them. If you plan on going for a run in the morning instead of staying in bed, which might trigger you, place your running gear on the floor next to your bed. Now, make your plan for success. And when the Hijacker tries to take the wheel, tell him, "Not today!" and go get your tool kit instead.

Now you're armed with a slew of healthy boundaries, an accountability structure to support you, and a three-second pivot plan and tool kit for when you are beset by urges and cravings. Each of these are confidence-boosting reminders that you're not alone or unequipped for this journey. Remember, the more strategies you implement, the easier it will be for you to offset withdrawal and begin to build the liberated life you've dreamed of.

Dig in, because there is more to come. Now you're ready to rewire your brain to overcome the desire for porn itself.

CHAPTER 8

OVERCOMING OBSTACLES
IN YOUR PATH

I don't like to lose—at anything—yet I've grown
most not from victories, but setbacks.
SERENA WILLIAMS

WITHDRAWAL IS REAL, VERY REAL

Sam had read online about men struggling with withdrawal symptoms after they'd quit porn. He was under the false impression that he wouldn't have the same experience because he didn't have an "addiction." It was just a habit he had developed. Yes, it was challenging to stay away during his half-hearted attempts, but it was because he was not trying. Now that he was ready to give it up for good, it would be no problem. Or so he thought.

Sam started by drafting a defensive plan. He avoided porn entirely. Days one and two were no sweat. *This is going to be easy,* he thought. Then day three began. At this point, Sam's brain was used to getting big hits of dopamine, if not every day, then at least every other day. Now that he'd hit three days without porn, he began to feel it. But he still didn't recognize it as withdrawal. He felt anxious, angry, and uncomfortable. He was restless and snapped at everybody all the time. Krissy was upset and couldn't stand to be in the same room as him. Although he was staying away from porn, he started checking out women even more in public. He couldn't help himself. It was like he *needed* to look at them. Sam was slowly losing control of himself, unable to regulate his mood and behaviors—so much so that he thought it best to be away from his family. He moved into the spare room in his basement for a while until he felt better and more stable.

IT IS DARKEST BEFORE DAWN, BUT THE PLAN PROVIDES THE LIGHT TO MOVE FORWARD.

Sam would tell me later that he thought my pivot-plan tool kit was unnecessary, even silly. But that was before those intense withdrawal moments set in. He ordered himself a leather toiletry bag and stocked it with all the dopamine-producing goodies he could think of: chocolate, herbal tea, hard candies, a gardening magazine, a printed screenshot of a funny text from his best friend to remind him to reach out, a picture of his family, a token from his work to inspire him, a playlist of songs that empowered him, and a list of his favorite movies so he could watch them instead of porn. He planned to do push-ups every time an urge hit. One Friday night, he plowed through the entire kit while doing many push-ups, almost through tears, until he successfully made it to Saturday morning. That afternoon, he took a trip to the store to refill it.

Sam figured out early on that withdrawal is real, very real. He also figured out that the more defensive and offensive strategies he employed, the less he suffered from withdrawal symptoms and the more he avoided relapse. This motivated Sam to follow the plan

I had created for him—the very strategy you have before you. He was about to transform his life in ways he couldn't imagine. It is darkest before dawn, but the plan provides the light to move forward. It was getting dark for Sam, and the plan I created enabled him to change his behaviors incrementally with ever-increasing momentum. The massive transformation in Sam's life would happen through small action steps that he learned to put into place in the seemingly meaningless moments of his day. Each action created new outcomes and added up to big success for Sam. This plan can do that for you too.

Committing to recovery was a big step for Sam. But just committing wasn't enough; there were plenty of other hurdles. You will also encounter some stumbling blocks early on in your journey. Now is the time to learn to cope, persevere, and lay the groundwork for permanently rewiring your brain and removing the Hijacker from your life once and for all.

RELAPSE: THERE IS NO LOSE, ONLY WIN OR LEARN

There is no such thing as a loss when it comes to relapse; there is only win or learn. If an urge strikes and you know exactly what to do to dampen it, extinguish it, and get back to living your best life, it is a win. If you are challenged by an urge to watch porn and masturbate, then it is time to learn. If you are genuinely on the road to recovery, you will learn to treat every relapse situation as a vital learning opportunity on the road to success.

Relapse is not inevitable. I want you to know that. You can move into a porn-brain rewire and never relapse. However, if you do relapse, that is understandable too. The most important aspect is learning from early relapses and avoiding them long-term.

RELAPSES SEEM TO COME OUT OF THE BLUE, BUT THEY DON'T.

Relapses are like rocks on the new neural pathways of recovery. If you trip over a rock early in your venture on this new path, that is entirely understandable. It is new territory, and you are still learning the terrain.

There are two types of relapses: early and late. Early relapse occurs within the first ninety days of your porn-brain rewire journey. It has to do with unwiring and rewiring your brain and implementing your defensive plan while establishing your offensive strategies for an amazing, purpose-filled life. Sometimes early relapse is all but unavoidable. Early on, you do not have the brain regulation, knowledge, and skills you need to succeed. In this case, relapse teaches you along the way.

Late relapse is different. Suppose you have implemented all the strategies and established an authentic life of integrity while creating healthy mood regulation, healthy sexuality, and a lifestyle that suits you. In that case, there should be no reason to use porn as an escape. If you do, it means something has broken down.

Relapses seem to come out of the blue, but they don't. They are minutes, hours, days, and even weeks in the making. When relapses are evaluated in hindsight, people usually can see how stressors and events from the weeks and days before led to the increased need for self-soothing and the stimulation of porn. It could be work stress, relationship difficulties, or financial pressure building over time. Thus, it takes time and attention to learn from them. It is essential to understand which parts of the foundation have broken down over time. When you find the gap, it is critical to fill it and secure it. This way, you are less likely to relapse again.

Potential relapses can be so powerful that their worth should not be underestimated. Every time you feel urges, cravings, stress, boredom, and other emotions that threaten to drive you back to the screen, learn to listen to them instead of giving in to them. With each circumstance, you gain vital information about the motivating forces behind your porn habit. Then you can use new skills to overcome cravings each day until they disappear. In the meantime, it is essential to consider the causes behind the triggers as you build the necessary skills to overcome your urges and cravings. What cues are spiking the need for porn in your brain? Why?

Brain Hack Number 29
There Is No Lose, Only Win or Learn

What will you do if you relapse during your porn-brain rewire? Remember not to beat yourself up if you relapse early in your recovery. Instead, take the time to journal. This will help you to learn from what happened so it does not happen again.

What led you to the screen? How can you avoid it next time? Remember to continue to learn so you can win.

TRIGGERS INSIDE AND OUT

There are two main types of activating events, called *triggers*, that cause you to act out sexually: internal and external. Within each primary type are four subcategories of triggers.

Internal triggers come from within and are typically associated with feelings and states of being. We know that emotional regulation is a core challenge for those who escape into porn, which means it is essential to learn about these feelings and how to deal with them.

Conversely, over time, external triggers have been wired into your brain through your responsive behaviors. They have to do with your environment. Driving forces in your life and world push you back to the screen through habit and conditioning.

Let's explore these main types and the subcategories within them.

INTERNAL TRIGGERS

Internal triggers can be more challenging to control than external triggers. They include anxiety, and various other feelings, whether negative, positive, or even typical. Learning to ascertain your internal state on any given day can help you act accordingly to stay the course of authentic living.

Anxiety and Worry

External stress and the internal anxiety that it causes can threaten to derail your progress at all stages of recovery. With one untamed stressor, you may find yourself fleeing to the screen for dopamine as fast as you can get it. Recognizing stress and having a plan to reduce anxiety can ensure your ultimate success over time. The leading stressors that cause anxiety and worry include:

- work,
- finances,
- divorce,
- relationship issues,
- kids,

- family,
- school,
- social status, and
- traumatic events.

Of course, there are a wide variety of stressors, yet eliminating and reducing them can help tremendously in your recovery. The first step is to become aware of the role stress plays in your life and your subsequent anxiety levels, then mitigate and manage it with as much precision as possible. Learning to offset external pressure and internal anxiety in healthy ways is critical for long-term success and is the central aspect of your offensive plan.

Negative Feelings

Negative feelings are dangerous and can send you down the slippery slope of porn use. Master Yoda, from *Star Wars*, once wisely proclaimed, "Fear is the path to the dark side. Fear leads to anger. Anger leads to hate. Hate leads to suffering."[1] Negative feelings begin with fear, and several different ones are associated with relapse, including:

- fear,
- guilt,
- irritation,
- overconfidence,
- anger,
- hate,
- jealousy,
- shame,
- depression,
- loneliness, and
- feeling criticized.

Negative feelings can throw you to the screen, seeking reprieve from their aftermath. Instead, you can learn to feel them, live with the discomfort, and resolve them through emotionally intelligent strategies.

Positive Feelings

Party time! Positive feelings may spark excitement to watch porn, especially if you have previously used it to celebrate. Emotions that make you feel good, like happiness, can also be a risk factor for relapse because you may subconsciously want to intensify those feelings by using porn. As you increase self-awareness, you might discern that even optimistic feelings can be triggering for you. Positive feelings related to relapse include:

- celebratory feelings,
- confidence,
- happiness,
- passion,
- strength,
- exhaustion from exertion,
- healthy sexual arousal, and
- plain ol' feeling "good."

Learning new, healthy ways to celebrate that include happiness and connection, not just pleasure, can rewire your brain to stay present in your real life without the need for artificially high levels of dopamine to get a celebratory rush that leaves you depleted and alone.

Normal Feelings

Even "normal" feelings can be uncomfortable if you have not practiced feeling them and responding to them healthily. Porn use is associated with reduction of uncomfortable feelings, albeit sometimes common ones. Remember, increasing emotional intelligence is critical to success in this journey. This means you must pay attention to your emotions, moving toward them instead of away from them. Recognize that you can handle experiencing them without the need to dim or remove them.

Typical feelings that are associated with relapse include:

- nervousness,
- insecurity,
- boredom,
- sadness,
- embarrassment,
- loneliness,
- pressure,
- fatigue,
- frustration, and
- neglect.

We are all exposed to these feelings at different times. They make up the spectrum of human emotion. With improved emotional maturity you can learn to allow your feelings to inform your experiences for growth toward your full potential. Many peak performers believe the most difficult, but not necessarily the most extraordinary, experiences forge them into the highest versions of themselves through adversity. No pain, no gain, if you will. You may have heard that diamonds are formed at high pressure and high temperature. All our typical, yet challenging, experiences can help us become diamonds. The solution—moving toward, not away from, feelings—can do the same for you, but now with lasting positive effects instead of negative ones.

Brain Hack Number 30
What Triggers You from the Inside?

Think of your porn habit and evaluate the internal triggers
just discussed. First, list the triggers that impact you. Then
write about how these triggers creep up on you. Identify
situations that frequently or commonly bring on stress or
various emotions. Prepare yourself for the next time an
urge might sneak up on you because of these internal
states.

EXTERNAL TRIGGERS

External triggers come from outside of you, but they have been
created by a neurobiological association—usually of arousal, anxiety, or boredom—as a conditioned response you feel within that
is initiated from an external factor. Basically, something outside
of you is associated with the need to use porn. For example, many
people experience increased stress when visiting their in-laws. In
those times, they feel the need to escape into the bathroom and
self-soothe with porn. External triggers include people, places, situations, and objects.

People
People can invoke the desire for porn or sexual acting out.
They can include:

- your partner,
- parents,

- family members,
- coworkers,
- employees/employers,
- porn performers,
- acquaintances,
- former sexual partners, and
- your sexual arousal avatar.

Perhaps you follow a porn actress online or have a coworker who sent you pictures in the past but is now at the desk beside you. They are triggers because your brain associates porn or sex—and thus the dopamine deluge—with them. Or maybe you encounter someone who fits the description of an avatar of the "type" of person who arouses you most, such as someone with a certain body type or personality. Or perhaps it is simply a person who induces stress and negative feelings, which then pushes you toward porn, like a parent constantly disappointed in you or even a spouse questioning you about your porn use.

Places
Places can be equally as off-putting as people and include things like:

- a man cave,
- she shed,
- office,
- hotel room,
- bedroom,
- bathroom,
- shower,
- massage parlor,
- strip club,

- nightclub,
- bar,
- mall,
- restaurant, and
- gym.

Some of these might seem obvious, such as strip clubs or nightclubs. Some less apparent places might be the mall, bars, restaurants, or places your ideal avatar might be, such as at sporting events or the gym. A compulsively sexual brain will be aroused regardless of whether the people there are acting in an overtly sexualized manner. Knowing the places that might trigger you to return to the screen is essential.

Situations

Situations trigger the habitual dopamine drip that your brain is looking for. If you usually watch porn on Friday night, then your brain will look for it at that time. In the early days of recovery, using your three-second pivot plan is vital during these routinized, habitual times.

Some examples of situations often associated with relapse include:

- evenings or mornings,
- weekends,
- holidays,
- days off from work,
- workdays,
- the death of a loved one,
- an argument with your partner,
- a promotion at work,

- drinking,
- showering,
- intimacy, and
- parties.

Situations might also include a reprimand from your boss, parenting your children, unresolved conflict with a friend, or even vacationing with your family. Masturbation, for instance, is often performed in the shower. Thus, showering can become a triggering situation. Although enjoyable, traveling can be exhausting with little down time. Watch out for situations that catch you off guard. Be prepared.

Objects

Objects, as we have already discussed, can have an unassuming effect on you also, such as devices (your phone, iPad, computer, etc.), furniture, or personal belongings. Other objects associated with relapse include:

- a bed,
- car,
- sex toys,
- magazines, and
- TV.

Become aware of any triggering things and remove them if they are not healthy for you (such as self-pleasuring sex toys). Replace them with new versions that are not associated purely with sex (such as your phone). Or ideally, decondition your brain by using new, healthy patterns with the objects you currently own (like your computer).

> **Brain Hack Number 31**
> *Identify Your External Triggers*
>
> In your journal, list your external triggers and then write about them in detail to better understand how your environment affects your porn and masturbation habits.

THREE CIRCLES OF SUCCESS

Sam had an established evening routine at the height of his porn addiction. He would pour himself a drink and watch his favorite show. This would help him to relax. Once relaxed, and after his wife went to bed, Sam would play video games. He could feel the intensity in his brain increasing as he played. After an hour or two of games, he would feel the full thrust of the pendulum effect in his brain, even though he couldn't articulate it in this way. Feeling the internal shift, he would switch from games to porn. This was his nightly habit for over a decade. He would stay up late and watch porn alone in the darkness of his man cave.

Sam's behavior, and the prevention thereof, has been noted in sex addiction recovery for many years and is called *the three circles.*[2] The three circles are like the bull's-eye on a dartboard.

As you enter your recovery, you need to know how close you are to moving from the outer circle of safety toward the inner circle of relapse. This involves continually monitoring your behavior regarding the three safety circles: the innermost circle indicates danger, the middle tier indicates caution, and the outermost circle indicates safety. When you are acting in accordance with behaviors in the outermost circle, it means that you are on track with recovery, and

Three Circles of Porn Addiction Recovery

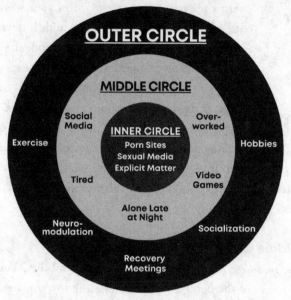

you are not in danger of sliding back into your porn habit. You are safe. Sliding toward the middle circle behaviors means you can get into trouble if you let your guard down and are not careful. Moving toward the inner circle indicates you are about to cross the line and breach one of your protective fences, falling into your porn addiction.

The Outer Circle

The *outer circle* is where I want you to stay, and it will help you to feel and perform at your best. It will be easier to create and maintain your new, authentic identity to live as the highest-quality version of yourself. You can do this through new actions, habits, and routines that keep you in integrity and on track for your best

WATCH FOR THE HIJACKER. HE WILL TRY TO CONVINCE YOU THAT DANGEROUS IDEAS ARE BRILLIANT ONES.

life. You will be in the outer circle in your life when you are enjoying your favorite hobby, hanging out with your friends, or engrossed in your work. You are safe from sliding through the middle toward the inner circle when you get proper food, sleep, and exercise and are engaged in activities that serve you, and you're not getting any artificially high dopamine dumps and your brain is working optimally. These are times when you are in no danger of consuming porn and have few temptations to lead you toward porn. When Sam was happy with his work and life, relaxing and watching TV with his family in the evening, he was safely in his outer circle.

The Middle Circle

The *middle circle* involves a level of vulnerability. You have left the safety of the outer level and are sliding toward the danger zone. You are at risk of engaging in porn if something pushes you, like all the triggers we have already discussed. Like Sam, you may be alone watching sports, playing video games, or drinking. Then something kicks off an urge in your brain that pushes you into porn: it could be something on your phone, an image, some financial situation to deal with, your partner seemingly nagging you, or some other stressor. In these cases, you are in a dopamine-drought state, looking desperately for a drip to make you feel less anxious and overwhelmed. Your brain is used to feeling better through porn.

Sometimes the middle circle is a ritual or a place: for example, when you go to your man cave, or she shed, to be alone like Sam. The thought of it can set off a dopamine drip. You are in the middle circle when a sex scene occurs in a movie you watch. The dopamine starts to flow, threatening to push you into the dangerous inner layer. Online browsing for lingerie or sex toys, even if you vow to yourself that they are to use with your partner, is just an excuse to view those items with models. Or when you are tempted to look at some files you "forgot to delete" on your computer. In these situations, watch for the Hijacker. He will try to convince you that dangerous ideas are brilliant. He will plant seductive thoughts in your head to get his dopamine fix. You are likely in trouble.

The Inner Circle

When you enter the *inner circle*, you already have engaged the 4-D Dopamine Cycle that pulls you into relapse. Perhaps you have been playing late-night video games in isolation, like Sam, starting the pendulum swinging in your brain. Maybe you have clicked on a "soft porn" video to test your fortitude in recovery and to see if it still arouses you. The dopamine has already started flowing in your brain, and stopping the pull toward the deluge will be difficult.

On your recovery journey, you must stay in the outer circle. If you find yourself in the middle circle, tell yourself, *I'm not going into the danger zone today.* Ask yourself, *What am I doing here, and how can I get back to safety? I don't want to regret this tomorrow.* Use the knowledge and skills you have gained to move back out to the safety of the outer circle.

SURF URGES TO LEARN FROM THEM

The cravings and urges that tempt you back toward porn can be a crucial aspect of recovery if you engage them intentionally. You will need to become comfortable with being uncomfortable to gain traction in this journey. You first need to implement your three-second pivot plan to avoid urges. Getting past them is step one, but step two is learning from them.

EMOTIONS LAST NINETY SECONDS. THAT'S IT. THE REST IS A REPLAY.

As you gain strength and learn to identify and overcome these urges, you can engage directly with the cravings using your newfound power to feel them. This is called *urge surfing*. Like coasting on a surfboard, ride the wave of the urge to interpret what it means for you. Feel it. Listen to it. What is it telling you? Learn from it. Most times, there is an emotional trigger buried below the surface. Ride out the emotion and realize it's not going to kill you. Emotions last ninety seconds. That's it. The rest is a replay. After the initial minute and a half, you are replaying an emotion, and your brain does not know the difference. Thus, when you pause and feel the emotion in real time, you can learn to realize what you are feeling and what needs to be done to alleviate it in a healthy way. Don't run. Approach and engage. If you stay with an uncomfortable emotion, you can learn to identify the root of the problem. This, in turn, will help you figure out how to solve it.

Suppose you work at your computer and are overcome by an urge to watch porn. Stop and feel it. Go down a layer under the sexual feelings masking the genuine emotion. What is going on deep down? Perhaps you are behind in your sales quota and the day is zipping by with no new prospects on the horizon. The feeling of overwhelming, impending doom is unbearable, and you look for escape. Porn provides it, but only for a short time. So, instead of using porn as an escape, which inevitably only makes everything worse, take a break. Get outside for fifteen minutes. Then come back and take out a list of potential new clients and email them all. Call the top five and tell them about your product update. Action toward a solution breeds more action. With each step in the right direction, where you seek to resolve the problems that push you into porn, you will build and traverse new neural pathways that will keep you out of porn for good. With each reinforcement, your brain becomes stronger, not needing porn. Neurons that fire together, wire together. Neuroplasticity at its finest.

By now, you have started to realize that the Hijacker is behind the urges tempting you back into the pain-pleasure paradox to pull you toward the inner circle of brain dysregulation that perpetuates your porn habit. But those desires will fade as you rewire your brain toward the healthy, optimal pattern—slowly at first, but with increasing acumen as you continue to work the program. When you're ready, you can confront them head-on and learn from them to dissipate them. A bison on the prairie doesn't run away from the storm. If it did, it would be stuck in the downpour for twice as long. Instead, it turns and stares into the storm with trepidation and then growing confidence. Mustering courage in fear, it charges ahead directly into the oncoming challenge, effectively decreasing the storm's impact. You, too, can move toward your pain and then through it toward peace.

HANDLING WITHDRAWAL SYMPTOMS

Ups and downs will come during early recovery. It is perfectly natural. If you stop watching porn, you will receive less dopamine, and you will likely feel more stress from increased cortisol. It may also produce anxiety. But this is the first sign you are starting to recalibrate; you are beginning to unwire the brain pattern you have used for so long. This is great news! Withdrawal symptoms are a good sign. Your brain is changing, improving, and healing. Keep following your pivot plan. The more tools you use, the easier the process will become. You can help the unwiring happen quickly by pivoting and redirecting yourself in many new ways. As you accumulate more days

YOU ARE STRONGER THAN YOU KNOW. REMEMBER THAT!

free from porn, your brain will continue to unwire, and you will feel better.

As you go through this process, you may also encounter sexual challenges or difficulties, including low libido, erectile dysfunction, or delayed ejaculation. Taking a thirty-day sex break—no sex and no masturbation—can help you reboot your system. Withdrawal can sometimes seem unbearable. But you can do it. You're stronger than you know. Remember that! If things get complicated, reach out to your accountability partner, group, or members of your neo-family. They can talk you down from heightened anxiety and away from porn.

TAKE A MOMENT TO CELEBRATE

As you battle the cravings and urges, you must continue rewarding yourself. Celebrating small wins can be very powerful, like when you experience a stressor but don't resort to porn. Keep track of your progress and reward yourself in a way that is meaningful to you. Michael, a longtime client, continues to keep track of the number of days he has abstained from porn and masturbation. His streak is up to 437 days. Susan prefers to denote the passing of major life events. She is proud of her "sober celebrations"—such as Christmas, a struggling professional time, and her birthday—without porn. You, too, can celebrate critical milestones like one week or month of sobriety. If you like counting days, then count days!

Brain Hack Number 32
Celebrate Milestones

In your journal, determine how you can benefit from keeping track of progress. Perhaps note the following dates of porn sobriety and record other key milestones as they happen.

- First week
- First month
- The first fight with your partner without resorting to porn
- The first financial crisis averted without porn
- Mind Over Explicit Matter annual anniversary

Sam thought that quitting pornography would be easy once he committed to doing so. But he soon found himself in limbo, tempted again and again out of his zone of safety toward the danger zone of relapse. He knew he had to make fundamental changes to his lifestyle to succeed. You may decide you need to change your lifestyle entirely. Move into that spare bedroom to instill new personal habits and routines for yourself for a while—whatever it takes to keep your brain healthy and your behaviors in the outer circle and away from porn. A *defensive* plan can get you only part of the way forward on this path. Sam made his defensive plan like the one you have created. Then he drafted an even more crucial *offensive* plan to reconnect to the authentic version of himself—the Real Sam. He was shocked by what he found waiting there.

PART 3

REWIRE:

TRAINING YOUR BRAIN

CHAPTER 9

DRAFTING YOUR
OFFENSIVE PLAN

If you change the way you look at things,
the things you look at change.
DR. WAYNE DYER

A CHANGE OF PERSPECTIVE

Sam had become motivated like never before. He was still in the basement, but everything else had changed. His perspective had shifted. Instead of feeling shame about being stuck in the porn cycle, he could sense, for the first time, that there was relief and excitement on the other side, even though he wasn't there yet. But Krissy became nervous. Why was he spending all his time down there?

As it turns out, Sam liked being in the basement because it gave him quiet time to recognize his thoughts, genuinely feel his emotions, and learn how to take new actions toward his goals. Being away from his regular routine and family dynamics provided the time and space for him to do this. He had bought a leather journal and got up early every morning to plan each day. He set action steps to help him stay in his authentic identity, balancing work, play, and relationships in a way that made him feel good. He learned to identify when he was getting off track so he could quickly get back on. And even better? He couldn't wait to share that feeling with everyone in his life.

WITH EACH STONE HE LAID TO CONSTRUCT THE PERIMETER, HE FELT A SMALL SENSE OF SATISFACTION.

Porn used to consume so much of Sam's thought life. Now, as he moved away from porn, I helped him identify some healthy things he could focus on instead. This not only served as a redirect, but also as a project to heal the areas of Sam's brain that had grown accustomed to hitting the Easy button. Sam built a garden. He had always loved piddling around the yard, but now he decided to build something beautiful he could tend daily. With each stone he laid to construct the perimeter, he felt a small sense of satisfaction. With each wooden board assembled, the reward center in his brain continued to heal. With each seed sown, he gained greater satisfaction. It wasn't easy to build the garden, but it was fulfilling at new and different levels.

Sam and Krissy started having date nights. At first, the dates revolved around the idea of building intimacy in new and exciting ways via new experiences. Sam purposely stayed away from sex during this time because he found it difficult to turn off his compulsive sexuality. It was mentally and physically draining, so he followed a ninety-day sex-washout period. That was rough for Sam, but he was glad he did it. Eventually, when he started to be intimate with his wife again, it was a new experience with ups and downs. As it turns out, healthy sex was not something Sam was very familiar with, and so, in some ways, he was exploring uncharted territory.

You may have heard the expression "The best offense is a good defense." It's something sports fans love to say, and it has merit. But now, we are going on the offensive. You have worked hard to confront trauma and unwire your brain from porn, and now it is time to build your decisive offensive plan. Your plan will be designed to resensitize the reward center and activate the frontal lobe in your brain. This will help you think, make good decisions, and reap the neurobiological rewards.

NOW IT IS TIME TO BUILD YOUR DECISIVE OFFENSIVE PLAN.

I will help you shift your perspective, just as Sam did, and change your behavioral habits. When you have a good or bad habit, a habit loop occurs. The first part is a cue that sparks a particular behavior, giving you a result, or reward, that reinforces that behavior. Right now, when your brain receives a cue—one of the stressors or triggers we've discussed—you're prompted to watch porn and masturbate, which gives you the reward of the dopamine rush that makes you feel relaxed. This leads to a negative habit loop, which is the porn cycle we discussed earlier.

Your offensive plan will help to reduce the cue, first by helping your brain perform better and then by instilling a new, healthier behavior in the middle that still produces dopamine without consuming porn. The dopamine hits will not be at the same damaging, artificially high levels, but you won't need them to be; they will be healthy for you. As the days go by, you will learn to give your brain what it needs to feel motivated and engaged, and in the process, you will create lots of new, positive habit loops that add up to a fantastic lifestyle. As a result, you won't need excessive dopamine for your brain to feel calm and relaxed. Instead, you will *be* calm and focused, enjoying the authentic life you have always wanted. You will become the Real You. Does this sound too good to be true? It's not. Ask Sam and the many others who have succeeded using this formula.

NEUROMODULATION WITH AND WITHOUT TECHNOLOGY

Neuromodulation, or brain-adjusting, techniques can unwire and rewire your brain without you having to think about it. In this way neuroscientific technologies can be used to train your brain to use the healthy performance pattern consistently. In turn, this establishes the neurological foundation you need to move forward with the self-regulation techniques you will use with your mind and body to begin to recede the tsunami of porn addiction we talked about in chapter 2.

Meditation

Meditation, a technology-free type of neuromodulation, even when used for just thirteen minutes a day, has been shown to shift the brain into an improved temporary state that is known to enhance creativity, attention, mood, memory, and overall ability to think.[1] In this way, meditation can strengthen the underlying brain pattern to improve emotional regulation. It has been shown to decrease depression, anxiety, pain, psychological stress, substance abuse, and sex and porn addiction.[2] Meditation can be done with no technological assistance or through guided meditations using apps, online videos, or audio recordings.

To engage in meditation without guidance, you can use a technique that I frequently incorporate called *getting in the gap*.[3] Starting with three minutes and working up to thirteen, repeat an inspiring phrase in your mind. Pause in the middle of it or between repetitions. This creates a "gap" of silence that helps to regulate your brain and calm your mind. It can be a verse, passage, affirmation, or mantra that helps you to feel peaceful and present.

I like to use a mantra that was chanted by a character in a *Star Wars* movie. It goes like this: "I am one with the force, [gap] the force is with me."[4] I place the gap between the phrases, and with each repetition I hold the silent gap longer and longer in duration. I start with a one-second gap and work up until I can hold the longest silent, thought-free gap that I can attain. You can try this strategy yourself.

Neurofeedback

Neuromodulation-using technology has been scientifically proclaimed to "hold promise for the . . . remodelling of circuit dysfunctions in addiction."[5] Neurofeedback, the technological neuromodulation method that I introduced you to earlier, does not put anything into your brain; it uses electroencephalography (EEG) to simply read how your brain is performing and then teaches it to use more of the speeds associated with calm, focused feelings and less of those that instill anxiety, overwhelm, and compulsion. The technology determines the gap between your brain's performance and the optimal brain mode and then gently guides you toward optimization naturally through positive reinforcement. Sessions are enjoyable as you sit quietly watching videos and listening to audio that changes with fluctuations in brain functioning. You can even watch your favorite show while your brain does all the work. When your brain improves its performance, the show you are watching plays brighter and louder. If you default back to a dysregulated brain pattern, your show turns dim and low. The neurofeedback system reinforces the use of the optimal brain pattern over time, while the old brain pattern is extinguished. With improvement in brain performance, the software increases difficulty to continually challenge your brain toward the most regulated state. Over time, as your brain enhances its performance using neuroplasticity, you can feel more relaxed, present, and focused with less need for porn. Neurofeedback can be done in professional offices around the world and at home using advanced, app-based software. As a global neurofeedback provider, I work with people in all corners of the world from the comfort of their homes.

You can think of it as a workout for your brain because it provides the proper amount of reinforcement so that the muscle of your brain becomes stronger.[6] This is like exercising any other part of your body. If you want stronger biceps, you can use twenty-pound weights each day until lifting is easy, then increase the weights to thirty pounds. When your arms get stronger, increase the weight even more, and so on. In this way you keep working your bicep muscles, improving their strength until you reach your goal. There is no need to think about your biceps, nor do you have to consult many people to tell you how to get your biceps stronger. It is simple; you just must do the training.

Neurofeedback works in the same way, and an added benefit is that it provides a plethora of concrete data that can show you exactly how your brain is performing. Charts and graphs can link porn urges that are experienced to the brain activation marker that sparked the craving.[7] This helps to connect brain performance with behaviors. Visualizing progress through diagrams can show you that your brain is getting stronger, using the healthier brain performance pattern each day and over time. The seen results help you to stay motivated.

Sam was originally a neurofeedback client, and honestly not a very committed one due to what I later learned to be his addiction to porn. He originally came to see me for symptoms of anxiety and brain fog, or a wired-and-tired brain. When Sam learned that his brain had been damaged by porn and that it was the root of most of his challenges, he committed to using neurofeedback with frequency and consistency. This allowed him to engage in a new, healthy mood regulation activity at the outset of his recovery program that uniquely addressed his specific brain dysregulation. He could read the data for himself. With every session, he knew that his brain was getting stronger and healthier. He felt it too.

Studies show that neurofeedback can robustly modulate the dopamine reward pathways in the midbrain and the prefrontal cortex, where complex thinking occurs, for improved brain performance.[8] Moreover, these brain improvements translate to improved self-regulation skills and cognitive control.[9] In this way advanced technology can shorten and simplify your recovery journey.

Engage in a neuromodulation session each day, with or without technology, and as you do, your brain can adjust itself away from the strained brain or drained brain of porn addiction toward the optimal brain pattern of healthy arousal. As your brain shifts from dysregulated to regulated, you will feel and perform better. This is key to successfully leaving porn behind for good.

We saw in the silent tsunami of porn addiction the first disruptive factor is the neurological dysregulation deep below the surface in your brain. Thus, it is imperative to train your brain toward a healthier performance pattern for you to achieve your goals of long-term success without relapse. With a more regulated brain, you are much better able to regulate your emotions and behaviors.

Brain Hack Number 33
Neuromodulation for Improved Brain Performance

Give your brain a daily workout with neuromodulation techniques. You can start with "getting in the gap," and eventually explore guided meditations or neurofeedback if you are inspired. Remote neurofeedback is highly effective and makes it easy to do frequent sessions in your own home with ease. You can search for a reputable provider online. Decide which technique you will start with and schedule it into your routine.

By addressing the underlying brain dysregulation, you'll go directly to the source of your challenges, just like the disruption caused by the earthquake preceding the tsunami. Even though it is far below the surface, neurological dysregulation is the primary cause of hypersexuality, and healing it increases recovery success significantly.

THE THREE MAIN BRAIN STATES OF BEING

As we start rewiring your brain and learning new habits and routines, I want to draw your attention to the types of activities you may encounter across your day and their effect on your brain. There are three broad categories of activity: brain draining, brain boosting, and brain neutral.

Brain-draining activities include drinking, taking drugs, procrastinating, arguing, shaming, blaming, justifying, objectifying, fantasizing, and isolating. These activities involve anxiety, stress, conflict, or escapism. Brain-draining activities stem from fear, which can take you off purpose, disrupt your mood, and drain your energy. You lash out at yourself and others. Porn, as we've discussed, is a *massively* draining activity.

Brain-boosting activities stem from peace and purpose. They involve optimism, hope, calm, and focused joy. Love is the energy for creating the life you want—your best reality. Love-based activities include creating, sharing, collaborating, giving, laughing, praising, supporting, touching, connecting, and having healthy, intimate sex with a partner.

When you are doing activities you love, you boost the energy in your brain. You give your brain the perfect amount of dopamine, serotonin, and oxytocin, creating that optimal neurochemical mix. In this state, you're glad to be doing what you're doing. It's the ideal state. You feel refreshed and alive. You find ways to engage with your work within a schedule that serves you. You find time for hobbies that enrich you and for people who allow you to relax. You won't *try* to be in a state of joy; you can just *be* in that state of joy.

Brain-neutral activities are about energy recovery and include napping, reading, walking in nature, jogging, doodling, hanging out with friends, and showering. So many people consider brain-neutral activities a waste of time. But that's not true. They are investments in your health and wellness. Our brains need time to recover within the day, and we must make time for these activities. For me, the ideal brain-neutral activity is sitting on the porch. I can

The Three Main Brain States

Brain Draining

decreases energy in your brain, leaving it wanting self-soothing and stimulation

Brain Boosting

increases energy in your brain, helping it feel motivated and engaged

Brain Neutral

recovers energy in your brain, giving it time to refresh and renew

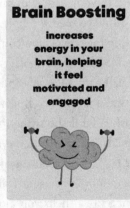

sit on the back porch at sunrise and have a private place to relax and be alone with my thoughts. And I can sit on my front porch at sunset and chat with my neighbors. In both instances, my brain downshifts and revitalizes itself.

The goal is to have as many varied brain-boosting activities and as few brain-draining ones as possible, with enough brain-neutral activities to allow your brain to recover. This can be more challenging than it seems. Survival mode keeps us stuck doing things we don't necessarily want to do, but that validate Dr. Jekyll and Mr. Hyde. This is classic self-sabotage. Reframing your life toward thriving is essential. Knowing that you deserve to thrive, not just survive, is fundamental to the shift that allows you to find peace and stay there.

Allowing yourself to enjoy brain-neutral activities might be new for you. That was my experience when I started incorporating them into my life. Before, I had always prided myself on being a human *doing*—rather than a human *being*—always busy accomplishing something. When I realized I was exhausting myself and harming my brain, I began to allow myself the necessary time and space for recovery. It was a game changer.

Figure out which activities boost your brain and increase its energy, which drain and leave it depleted, and which allow it to shift into neutral for a while to recover. This is an individualized list; what is brain boosting for one person could be brain draining for another. My husband loves golf. He golfs three times a week. If I had to hit a tiny golf ball across fairways multiple times a week, it would leave me frustrated and tired. But not him. He loves it. It helps his brain downshift while boosting itself into the healthy mode he needs to achieve balance. I work out and take an evening walk each day without fail. My husband watches me go out the door without any desire to join in—just as I prefer it.

Here's a neuroscience tip to help you along the way: do the

activities you enjoy less or find more challenging earlier in the day, and reward your brain with more enjoyable tasks when you feel more fatigued and need a lift. It's the same philosophy as if you are a student: if math is the most challenging subject for you, study math first and reward yourself by studying for your favorite topic—let's say, history—later.

Brain Hack Number 34
Your Activities

In your journal, write down the following:

- **Your work:** List the aspects you like about your work and those you don't. If there are more aspects you loathe than love, you might consider a career change. Many times, you can make subtle changes to your job to make it more enjoyable by collaborating with or delegating undesirable tasks to others. Most people spend a lot of time at work. Get creative to make that time as pleasurable as possible.
- **Your relationships:** Think about your relationships: Are they brain boosting or brain draining? What can change in them? Who can you just "be" around? Who must you watch yourself with, or can't relax with? Spending time with people who enhance your well-being can be essential for success in recovery. Can you find regular times to be alone? Alone time is very important.
- **Your daily activities:** List your daily activities according to the three categories: brain boosting, brain draining, and brain neutral. The goal is to reduce brain drain as much as possible.

CREATE A LIFE YOU LOVE

When I talk about creating "a life you love," it can seem like a big, intangible concept, but it isn't. It can be achieved through the choices you make about where you live, the work you do, who you spend your life with, or whether you'll watch TV, drink alcohol, or consume porn every night. If you are stuck in brain-draining survival mode, it may not seem like you have a choice. But you do have options. They are just difficult to recognize and even more difficult to actuate, and so they produce fear of the unknown. That fear can keep you stuck in the freeze stress response, making it difficult to climb Maslow's pyramid to self-actualization. I use the following exercise to help me continually review my progress toward personal transformation. This way I can maintain momentum toward my ideal life filled with love and not fear.

Brain Hack Number 35
Your Ideal Day

I love this brain hack; it is one of my favorites. Write down what your ideal day would be like from dawn to dusk. What would it include, and who would it be spent with? What about your ideal week? What would that look like? Flesh it out on paper. Contemplate it. Once you've drafted it, be bold and make it happen.

BRAIN-BOOSTING REWIRE PROJECT

Sam's garden was pivotal to his recovery. It gave him a project to focus on, which he found both absorbing and incredibly rewarding.

You, too, can embark on an executive function brain-boosting rewire project. This passion project will help resensitize the reward center in your midbrain and boost activity in the prefrontal cortex. Your brain *needs* both to feel better and perform better if your reboot is to be successful. This brain-hack activity is *essential*. It will help you think better and enjoy life more, and even help to heal erectile dysfunction, if needed (more on that later).

Pick a project that will take you at least one month to complete. It should be something you are interested in and want to return to each day. Your project should involve your mind, body, and authentic, true Self. Choose something that has small steps you can take every day. Try to get your body involved. Perhaps this is a home-improvement task like putting solar panels on the roof or building a patio. Maybe it is improving an existing hobby or skill, like becoming a better cook. Or it could involve learning a new skill entirely, like playing chess. Make it something you *want* to do, not *have* to do. Think thriving, not surviving.

Brain Hack Number 36
Childhood Passions

If you are having trouble thinking of a passion project, pick up your journal and write a long list of things you used to like when you were a kid, before you discovered porn, such as soccer, learning to ride a bike, playing a musical instrument, drawing or painting—the list is endless. Your items should be highly personal to you. Keep writing for at least three minutes. Allow the ideas to flow freely. Now choose the top five. Circle them. Start there.

Once you have a potential project in mind, think of a multi-sensory way to engage with it. For example, suppose you are building a garden. In that case, you might buy some gardening books and magazines, find a gardening channel on YouTube, visit your local gardening shop, buy some gardening tools, or visit a beautiful garden in your town. This involves your senses and different ways of thinking about your project. Next, it is time to create a schedule for your project.

Brain Hack Number 37
Scheduling Your Offensive Plan

Plan to implement your project over the next thirty to ninety days. Create time each day for different aspects of your project. Schedule it. If it is not scheduled, it is not real.

By this point, you should have a straightforward project in mind that outlines the steps involved to complete it. Most importantly, don't forget to enjoy your project time and celebrate small wins at each stage. This will give your brain dopamine and begin associating its production with the project, not porn. It will create a brain-neutral time for recovery and brain boosting to increase your motivation, pleasure, and happiness. When you get absorbed in a task that you highly enjoy and is meaningful, you enter the peak-performance mode of *flow state*.[10] Here are some steps to take to get your brain-boosting rewire project off the ground.

Brain-Boosting Project Summary Checklist

- ☐ Identify your project.
- ☐ Research your project.
- ☐ Get materials for your project.
- ☐ Schedule your project into your life (fill the holes where porn used to be).
- ☐ Celebrate small wins around each step toward the larger goal.
- ☐ Stay consistent and enjoy your project.
- ☐ Reward yourself for accomplishing the goal.

This project will start to run in your mind instead of porn. It will help your mind triumph over explicit matter. It will create a healthy brain state grounded in the enjoyable reality of your authentic life. You can turn to the project in times of need, when urges strike. Feel an urge? Instead of turning to porn, you can look up some information about your project using the screen or, better yet, work on it for a while. With every choice you make to engage in your life, you will reinforce your brain toward seeking dopamine from real-world events, not porn.

SCHEDULE YOUR LIFE WITH FLEXIBILITY TO BOOST YOUR BRAIN POWER

You can begin to chart out a whole new life with your offensive plan, filling it with brain-boosting projects that help you live with purpose. When you live authentically on purpose, you do not need porn. Living on purpose like this is as easy as LIVE—your plan to live. The acronym stands for Logical, Intentional, Vital, and Experienced. I like to use the acronym to remember that life should be lived, not just endured. When you create your new life schedule, add a level of flexibility to it so it feels self-disciplined yet free. This will help you thrive.[11] Porn use can instill cognitive rigidity, which can make it more difficult to switch from task to task with ease.[12] By scheduling your days and weeks but still allowing room for life to happen within that schedule, you reinforce the neural pathways of cognitive flexibility that facilitate authentic peak-performance living.

Life Should Be Lived, Not Just Endured

The LIVE plan is *logical* in that you create the plan and schedule it into your life. Remember, if it is not scheduled, then it is not real. *Intention* must be built into the activities and tasks you perform. Know why you are doing everything you do and believe in its contribution to your well-being. Live on purpose, and you will never regret it. *Vitality* is about making you feel alive. Many people who have a porn habit report feeling dead inside. This project is designed to reignite the spark inside you: your hobbies, people you love to be with, and work that jazzes you up. Life can, and should, be fun and wonderful. Life should be lived, not just endured. Finally, this plan is *experienced* because nowadays so many people are sucked into the passive consumption of online content. You are watching instead of enjoying. This plan gets you being and doing rather than consuming. It starts using new neural pathways and helps the old ones to unwire.

Purpose Helps You Flourish in the Present and into the Future

Use your planner or phone (or both) to keep your life engaged with just the right amount of busy. Not overly busy but ideally engaged. Start filling your calendar with brain-boosting activities. Fill those holes in your schedule—where porn used to be—with a new, healthy habit. Perhaps you might read a good book or take a relaxing bath at night when you used to masturbate. Be careful to avoid too much downtime or getting overly busy. Both put your brain at risk for wanting to watch porn. Create balance and choose a lifestyle that will help you stay there.

EASE IN AND OUT OF YOUR DAY TO BOOST YOUR BRAIN

To stay strong on this journey, you must get your offensive plan up and running as the sun rises and wrap it up as the sun sets, reinforcing healthy circadian rhythms. Developing a healthy morning and evening routine is one of the most critical aspects of your new life. Spending quiet time in solitude each morning can forge stronger commitment, discipline, and resilience, which you will need throughout the day. Relaxing and being with loved ones in the evening can feed your need for connection. This will be a game changer and a lifesaver.

Each morning, start your day in quiet reflection to set yourself up for success with intentional action. This routine will keep your brain healthy and strong all day. Get up early, if needed, to create more time. Dedicate, if possible, a quiet space for yourself. Keep the light low. *Don't* touch your phone or computer for at least thirty minutes. Hopefully, you can go for an hour without a screen. *Don't* start checking your emails. Ease into your day.

Brain Hack Number 38
Your Brain-Boosting Morning Routine

Determine how you will start your morning with inspiration. For fifteen to thirty minutes, try to take the time to enjoy and focus on the following:

Movement: Move your body intentionally to stimulate your metabolism. The Five Tibetan Rites are powerful movement exercises that can be done in just a few minutes to get the electrical energy flowing in your brain and body in a positive, calm, and focused way.[13] You can also establish your own movement practice first thing in the morning.

Drink: Drink a glass of water. This is a fantastic boost for your brain first thing in the morning. Drinking plain water has been associated with reduced risk for anxiety and depression.[14] Even mild dehydration can be a stressor, and we know that stressors can be triggers back to porn, so drink early and often throughout the day.[15] Get your nervous system going. If you love coffee, like me, pour yourself some after you have moved and had water.

Spiritual or positive-psychology practice: Reflect, pray, or use positive affirmations while practicing deep breathing and mindfulness. This can be anywhere from three minutes to thirty minutes or more. Work your way up. Repeat a mantra or affirmation that compels you. You could focus on your breath, rehearse your favorite verse or passage, or even tell yourself, *I am strong and healthy.* When engaged in this way, your brain can facilitate some of your best, most creative thoughts. Keep your journal handy to capture them.

Read nonfiction: My sister once asked me how I escaped the thought patterns of our family. I told her, "I read every day." Read something positive and thought-provoking for at least five minutes daily. Authors can help to usher you into new ways of thinking, feeling, and acting. Think of it as contributing to a healthy mind-diet. Feeding your mind positive, intentional content, instead of mindlessly consuming passive content, is crucial to having a joyous day. Something inspiring will help offset any negative feelings you have later in the day.

Journal: Celebrating small successes is crucial. Tapping into gratitude each day by remembering and writing down three joys from yesterday and three things you wish to accomplish today can help you stay grateful for your opportunities and accomplishments. You are grounding yourself in gratitude each morning while setting your sights on the day ahead, which can have a powerful effect on your motivation.

Eat breakfast: Eat something healthy and not too heavy. Green smoothies are relatively delicious and super nutritious. Start your day with healthy fuel for sustained energy.

As evening approaches, develop a signaling routine that it is time to wrap up business for the day to transition to a time of relaxation. I always tidy my desk before I leave my office for the day. This allows me to release myself from the pressures of productivity and ease into the presence of personal time. Wrap up screen time on your computer and phone at least an hour before bed. I make dinner, eat with my family, pour organic tea, and chill with my children.

Brain Hack Number 39
Your Brain-Boosting Evening Routine

Each evening, take time to bring down the stress activation from the day. For fifteen to thirty minutes, try to take the time to enjoy and focus on the following:

Evening walks: Daily walks to release the tension from the day, even just for eleven minutes, have been shown to improve health and reduce cravings for dopamine.[16]

Socialize: Evenings can be used for going out into your community to build connections and socialize. If you can't venture into the world, you can call a friend to stay close. Socializing has many physical and health benefits, including improving mood, which can help you stay away from porn.[17]

Read fiction: Healthy fantasy, like that found in nonsexual fiction, can help you escape at the end of a long day. Not only that, but reading fiction has been associated with boosting your brain performance and improving social cognition and empathy.[18] Science fiction, mystery, historical fiction (a personal favorite), and thrillers can all be exciting additions to your evening routine.

Someone once asked me how habits affect recovery and an overall happy life. My response was that it is all about routines. Your routines inform your habits. You can use positive habits with an optimistic mindset to enjoy a joyous life filled with what you want. Or you can default to negative patterns with a survivalist attitude to suffer through a life you can complain about. The choice is yours. Figure out your ideal life. Then plan your routine to move toward that life, not away from it.

CHAPTER 10

HEALING YOUR BRAIN USING YOUR MIND AND BODY

The only true voyage . . . would not be to
visit new lands but to have other eyes.
MARCEL PROUST

ALL ALONE WITH EVERYONE

Before his porn habit escalated and sent him on his recovery journey, Sam went out with friends a fair amount. Most weekends he was either in party mode or in isolation mode. Sometimes he would swing back and forth, depending on his porn use. But, as the saying goes, "you can be lonely in a crowded room." Sam had many people in his life, but he felt lonely. He just didn't realize it at the time. Porn kept him from creating deep and meaningful relationships because it kept his brain in the hypervigilant state of the pendulum effect. It is challenging to relax and be vulnerable if you are constantly in survival mode, scanning for threats. He hid the true, authentic version of himself from his wife, kids, and friends. He was plugged into the screen alone or went out into the world with his party-face mask—Dr. Jekyll and Mr. Hyde personas in play. If he couldn't access his mask, the anger and irritability of his wounded inner child would seep through. His friends never saw this side of Sam, but his family certainly did. It created even more disconnect.

Sixty days into working together, as he healed his brain from porn use, Sam put the mask away and dared to be himself. He shared his struggles with porn with his best friend, who reciprocated by sharing a significant battle in his own life. It was an instant connection that would not have been possible without the vulnerability allowed by Sam's new, better brain pattern. He shared his true feelings with Krissy. He broke down and sobbed. He divulged the hurts that had led him to porn and his shame about his habit. Krissy showed grace, love, and deeper commitment because of that conversation. Sam would be lonely no more.

To facilitate brain healing, you must remain as strong as possible by staying fed, hydrated, connected, relaxed, and rested. And there's no better way to keep your brain at its best than exercising, eating well, sleeping, and deepening your spirituality. These will help you improve your personality, thoughts, and interactions and allow your brain to create a new pathway.

REWIRING YOUR BRAIN
WITH EXERCISE

Exercise has been shown to contribute to improved neuroplasticity, which is imperative for your recovery journey.[1] Sam dug into exercise as his primary way of staying sane during the early days of his porn-brain rewire. His system was hit hard, and he needed something to anchor him, something to help him offset both withdrawal and urges while establishing a new lifestyle. Sam had always worked out, but now he enjoyed his workouts more than ever. "Lift heavy things" became an early maxim for him. Sam found that if he lifted heavy things during the day—which was a necessary part of his garden-building project—he could also offset urges and feel better in the evening. Sometimes it would keep him from yelling or acting out in other ways. It really worked.

You may not enjoy lifting heavy things, but you can still accomplish what Sam's exercise regimen did. The key to success is to work out to the point of exhaustion. That's where the magic happens. Exhaustion doesn't mean you collapse at the end. It means that you push yourself beyond the perceived limits of your body and, more importantly, your mind. Pushing your body a little harder when it feels like it can't go any longer gives your brain the chemicals it wants. Be sure to include body-weight and cardio training for maximal results and, for your well-being, consult your doctor or fitness professional before implementing a new workout regime.

The beauty of body-weight training is that you do not need any equipment to engage in it, just your body and its weight. You don't need to go to the gym. Push-ups, sit-ups, tricep dips, squats, and planks are highly effective ways to work out your arms, core, and abs. Start with push-ups. They are simple and you can do them anywhere, even next to your desk, when an urge strikes. Push-ups are the go-to brain booster in my house. Next, work in some cardio. Get your body moving and flowing. Go for a jog and crank out some sprints. Mix it up. Jumping jacks, running in place, and skipping imaginary rope can all be done anywhere, anytime, with no equipment. Do some interval training. Put together the workout that suits you to enhance your brain rewiring journey.

Find a fitness activity that you love. Make it fun to move your body. Most importantly, find a fitness activity that you *love*. Make it fun to move your body. It will improve your brain performance and your mental and physical health.[2] Personally, I love to box. I had been planning to go to the boxing gym to learn how to box for years—always talking about it, never doing it. Then one day, a boxing dummy that looked like a cynical ex-marine drill sergeant showed up at my door. My husband had bought him for me. I quickly ordered myself pink boxing gloves and made short work of him. This equipment motivates me to crush a boxing workout, and having it at home is essential for me in my current season of life. The ability to box when I want to ensures that I actually make time for it.

"Lift heavy things." It can be as simple as that. Can't motivate yourself to do any of the above? Make your motto for the time being "lift heavy things." It can be as simple as that. One of my clients would "lift heavy things," including furniture, logs, and anything else that was close by, every Friday afternoon to get himself through the weekend with no porn. He gained greater success with every Friday afternoon heavy-lifting session.

Brain Hack Number 40
Off-Loading Everyday Stress

It's beneficial to off-load stress from your brain daily to stay neurologically healthy and keep your discipline and resilience levels high throughout the day. This helps prevent stress from building up and your brain from swinging into the pendulum effect. Here are four powerful ways to avoid burnout and off-load stress:

- **Punch and kick:** I love kickboxing the General, my boxing dummy.
- **Expressive arts:** Use art to express your emotions. It has been shown to improve mental health.[3]
- **Lift heavy things:** Use your muscles to eliminate the excess energy; let the stress out using your body.
- **Cry:** Crying releases excess energy and relieves stress. If you don't want to cry in public, do it in the shower.

Just do something to get all the high, fast energy in your system out.

FUELING YOUR PORN-BRAIN REWIRE WITH PROPER NUTRITION

With all this exercise and brain rewiring, you will get hungry. And you'll be tempted to eat things that could undermine your recovery. Porn and junk food, neither of which are found in nature, capitalize on the insatiability of dopamine in a dysregulated brain.[4] Sex and food, on the other hand, are natural reinforcers and, when used in a healthy way, contribute to our survival and thrival.

Junk food and porn are "super stimulating synthetic versions of food and sex."[5] With junk food easier and cheaper to find than healthy food and porn easier to access than creating healthy, engaging sex within a fulfilling relationship, it is no wonder people are hitting the Easy button with both. Sugar, salt, fat, and refined carbs in all varieties keep consumers returning for more junk food with the ease and satisfaction of a full belly, adding to their waistlines and dysregulating their brains. These

THE EASY BUTTON EVENTUALLY HURTS.

foods have been found to change the reward-system functioning in adolescents' brains, derailing overall brain development due to craving dopamine.[6] But neither junk food nor porn is natural; they harmfully desensitize the reward center in your brain and decrease frontal lobe function to keep you returning for more. The Easy button eventually hurts.

Although Sam was healthy and relatively fit, when he was stressed and watching a lot of porn, he would more often hit the Easy button with fast food, desserts, and unhealthy snacks. Many people succumb to this without realizing that their brain has switched into Easy-button mode in many aspects of their life. Getting quick satisfaction in this way is the opposite of healthy executive functioning.

Eating properly throughout the entire day is important as you recover. And preparing healthy foods takes time. While you prepare that food, you are building brain-neutral recovery time to avoid the pendulum effect in your brain. It is a two-for-one, if you will. And if you have never paid much attention to nutrition, this is a good time to start. Healthy food sustains healthy neurological regulation, which enables easier self-regulation and avoidance of porn.

What foods should you avoid? Put simply, you should stay away from anything that has a long list of artificial ingredients. And if you do partake, only have a little. Pour it into a small bowl and indulge, knowing it likely has preservatives and other neuro-toxic chemicals your nervous system will have to deal with. This can have a short-term fulfilling effect but ultimately dysregulates your brain. Sugary foods stimulate your nervous system. Have you ever seen a child eating candy filled with sugar and red dye? Kids buzz around like bees until they crash. If you've ever felt the high and low of a sugar rush and subsequent crash, you know how it feels. These foods make you want to return to your porn habit to stimulate a brain that has slowed down and sped up—the pendulum effect. Staying away from sugar is important. Sugar addiction can take the place of a pornography habit. With the continued consumption of Easy-button foods, your brain is falling into the Easy-button lifestyle. So, when you eat a big piece of pizza, know it represents more than just a slice.

We are trying to keep your nervous system and brain running clean. The standard American diet is filled with what are sometimes called "gray foods": white bread, rice, pasta, and other bland, gray-colored food items that are composed of simple carbohydrates that break down into sugar in your body. Instead, follow this easy motto: "Eat the rainbow." Make sure your plate is filled with colorful foods from nature, not a factory. Be sure to have a healthy combination of protein (chicken and tofu), healthy fats (like fish, nuts, or avocados), and carbohydrates (fruits and vegetables). For example, I like to make homemade minestrone. Filled with tomatoes (red), celery (green), carrots (orange), and squash (yellow), in addition to nutritious bone broth (healthy fat) and navy beans (protein), it represents a mini rainbow of goodness in my bowl. Challenge yourself to create a colorful meal that feeds your brain and body. Food is fuel and has been shown to contribute to healthy cognition and emotional regulation.[7]

EAT THE RAINBOW.

Eating well protects you from strained brain and drained brain. A combination of protein, fats, and complex carbohydrates is most desirable. Try to eat as many vegetables as possible. Add fruits more sparingly, as they are higher in natural sugars, which makes them taste sweet. Organic vegetables and fruit are preferable because they do not contain toxins, chemicals, and other additives that can harm your brain and nervous system.[8] Learning about nutrition and healthy eating could be part of your executive function brain-boosting project so you can learn optimal nutrition for even greater gains along your way to authentic living at high levels.

VITAMINS AND MINERALS: WHY
SUPPLEMENTATION IS IMPORTANT

Now more than ever, our food is less nutritious.[9] Thus, it is important to take a high-quality nutritional supplement to boost your system with the vitamins and minerals that might be depleted, especially from exhausting and overwhelming your brain through porn use. Studies show that taking a high-quality multivitamin can help you feel and perform better in thinking and physical activities.[10] Additionally, it can stave off mental and physical fatigue. When your brain has been stuck for a while in the pendulum effect, it can add to depletion through its impact on neurotransmitter release, hormones, and even cellular function. Specific nutritional supplements can even boost your nervous system and help you heal both strained brain and drained brain. Remember, working with a professional for your specific needs is always best.

SLEEP WELL TO REWIRE YOUR BRAIN

Sleep had always eluded Sam. Falling asleep was no problem. He crashed hard as soon as he got into bed. But, of course, this was largely due to his nightly porn use, which became a type of sleep medication. The flood of dopamine would temporarily relieve the stressors of the day. But Sam also woke up at 3:30 a.m. almost every night. Some nights he couldn't get back to sleep. He would get out of bed, watch some TV, and get back in bed around five, waking for the day at six. Other times he would just stay up until the day began. This routine left him depleted, irritable, and never fully refreshed. He thought he was just a guy who didn't need much sleep. When he stopped watching porn, it took longer to fall asleep as he developed a new healthy sleep routine, but surprisingly, he could sleep for eight hours straight every night. He felt great the next day. He was no longer irritable and restless. He had no idea how much porn use impacted his sleep.

———————

Sleep is neuroprotective and is essential for neuro-integration and recovery. At least seven hours of sleep is necessary for your brain to move optimally through the sleep cycle, which requires your brain to slow down and speed back up multiple times a night. It is essential for healthy thinking, behavior, and judgment. Getting good sleep helps you continue developing the discipline and resilience you need to succeed.

Compulsive porn use has been shown to cause insomnia due to the neurochemical changes in the brain that disrupt circadian rhythms.[11] The psychological stress and emotional dysregulation that result can make it difficult to sleep. Even one night of insufficient sleep can impair executive function skills that allow you to use working memory, flexible thinking, and self-control.[12] Sleep deprivation can lead to longer-term negative effects, such as attention issues, poor decision-making, and trouble with long-term memory skills.[13] More than that, the negative impact of sleep deprivation on overall health and well-being is well documented. Lack of sleep degrades your daytime brain-based functions, which is just about everything, impeding your ability to think, act, and feel well emotionally and physically.

Studies also show a high association between internet addiction—including pornography—and insomnia, stress, anxiety, depression, and self-esteem.[14] These issues are born from the pendulum effect that contributes to strained brain. When your brain increases the use of the extra-fast brain speed throughout the day, it is inevitably left strung out, overworked, and unable to recover.

Restorative sleep is a crucial factor for warding off anxiety and depression. I figured this out a long time ago. There was a time when I had four babies—all just one year apart in age. *Four* small children who needed me to keep them alive every single second of every single day. (My fifth child is four years younger than the older ones.) Difficult times. Sleep-depriving times. Someone was up during the night most nights, and the days were filled with chaos.

During this time, I realized how much the lack of sleep impacted my physical health and, more importantly, my mental health. I began a habit that would continue for decades that smoothed itself into a healthy sleep routine I still follow.

I started using a sleep timer. Now, as soon as my sleep timer goes off, I stop what I am doing and begin my nightly wind-down routine. We spend our days winding ourselves up; we need *healthy* wind-down time in the evening. The sleep timer allows me to have enough time to bring the fast energy in my system down as I lower the lights, sip some organic tea while chatting with my kids, then engage in my hygiene routine. I also like to listen to relaxing music, read for few minutes, and gently coax my brain and body toward sleep through enhancing positive circadian rhythms.

Many people recovering from porn addiction have trouble getting to sleep at night. Perhaps you used to masturbate before bed, and your body is used to the calming effects of viewing porn. Without that release, you may find it hard to relax and fall asleep. If you don't let your brain calm down, it will stay hyperaroused and you will have trouble sleeping. If you let your brain recover, however, it will latch onto a slower speed, and you will get to sleep faster and easier. Here are some tips for helping bring the energy in your brain down before bed:

Build a new bedtime routine and establish a new habit.
Cheat in the right direction, at least to start, if that is easier: play video games for thirty minutes, but no more than

an hour; hang out with your family; watch TV; take a bath; or read a book.

Leave electronics behind at least one hour before bed. No television, video games, phone, iPad, smartwatch—nothing with a screen beyond this point.

Keep your phone out of reach during the night. Try putting it in a different room entirely. Use an alarm clock instead of your phone if you need an alarm.

Use low-level lighting or mood lighting. Try turning on lamps instead of overhead lights.

Play calming music. Create a spa playlist to listen to while lying in bed or relaxing in the bath. I love soothing classical music like Pachelbel's "Canon."

Make a multisensory effort to bring down your system. Try drinking a soothing beverage before bed. For me, it is a kombucha spritzer with fresh lime. If you wake up during the night and have trouble getting back to sleep, try focusing on your breath. Say or think "in" and "out" as you breathe in and out.

Brain Hack Number 41
Build Your Bedtime Routine

Now that you have crafted a morning and evening routine, build a similar menu of options for your nighttime routine. List in your journal the activities you will engage in and the tools you will use to bring your brain down before bed.

HEALING YOUR BRAIN THROUGH
SPIRITUAL PRACTICES

Spiritual practices, such as prayer, intentional breathing, connecting with nature, and reflection, help you rewire your brain to a calmer, more peaceful state.[15] This works to get your brain out of the extreme states of extra-fast and slow and toward the medium speeds of healthy baseline arousal. Spiritual practice should be an essential component of your morning routine, but it doesn't have to be done only in the morning.

Start by sitting in a chair with your feet on the ground and palms up. Going outdoors and placing your bare feet in the grass is even better. Focus on connecting your feet to the ground. This is called *grounding*. Now focus on feeling your entire body. Listen to the world around you. You spend most of your time in your head, thinking about the past and future. Ground yourself in the present and listen. This is a type of embodiment exercise that can help you offset the stress and fatigue of being in your head a great deal of the time. Embodiment is an important aspect of recovery that teaches you to connect with your body to enjoy present-moment experiences without defaulting to worry about the past or future or escaping into fantasy. Try focusing on your breath or even repeating your favorite mantra, quote, verse, or song lyric—something powerful that brings you back to what you are trying to accomplish: reducing anxiety. This helps reset your nervous system.[16]

You can ease into quiet time alone with your thoughts if this is a new habit for you. Start with three minutes and set a timer if it's helpful. Three-minute mindfulness breathing space, where you focus on your breath and relax, has been shown to help improve mood and decision-making.[17] In fact, this technique helped people make decisions that allowed them to approach a solution quicker and with less difficulty. Increases in self-reflection and value identification can allow you to overcome uncertainty to commit to a beneficial course of action. This can be incredibly helpful for you on your road to quitting porn. It can be the difference between the worst decision and a better one, and it will be challenging at first. Stop before you feel your mind getting squirrely. Just a few minutes helps to improve your blood chemistry and circulation. It also changes your electromagnetic energy. Make sure you feel peaceful and calm for three minutes, then move to longer sessions from there.

You can also practice spiritual mindfulness in motion by walking or doing yoga, especially outside. Get outside, experience some green space, listen to the sounds around you, smell the aromas, and feel your body in space. Focus on your breathing. Be present.

Brain Hack Number 42
Daily Spiritual Practice

Set aside time for spiritual practices that might include prayer and reading Scripture verses or passages that inspire you. Engage in positive reflection of your life every day, perhaps as part of your morning routine. Each day this will set the tone for superconscious living guided by divine purpose.

PERSONALITY TYPE—HOW IT IMPACTS YOUR THOUGHTS AND BEHAVIORS

Most people love a good personality test. Knowing more about your personality can help you better understand how you tend to cope with stress and trauma. It can also give you a road map for releasing that negative energy. Each of us has a unique personality, but you might not know that your personality can usually be grouped into several broad types. Your primary personality type was developed early in your life in response to dynamics and stressors in your family of origin. It is interesting to explore, but it can also be helpful to identify your type to learn how stress impacts your thoughts and behaviors. For example, it's important to figure out your basic fears and core desires.

When acting from a place of fear, your personality colors your identity to be more like the Dr. Jekyll mask you wear. As you heal your brain and create an authentic identity, it might require you to guide your personality closer toward your true Self, that of self-actualization, not survival. This version of your personality can be at its healthiest, most confident, self-assured, and self-restrained with intentional purpose. You are acting out of your purposeful self, the Real You, in a meaningful way. You engage in brain-boosting and recovery activities and avoid brain-draining activities like porn. You thrive at top-tier levels that reflect a healthy brain pattern and healthy emotional regulation.

Your personality can be shaped by what you fear and what makes you feel safe and secure in the chaos of your world. It is often shaped by your response to your parents' parenting style and situation.

There are a variety of personality-typing frameworks, such as StrengthsFinder, Myers-Briggs, and the Enneagram, that can provide insight into your strengths, desires, fears, and defense mechanisms. This information can provide insight into some of the subconscious motivating factors of how you navigate the world and especially your relationships. I prefer to use the Enneagram typology system because of its power to help you see your behaviors in terms of how they relate to your ability to self-regulate while considering your stress levels. The Enneagram recognizes that individuals have behaviors defined by their personality that can be improved with learned skills.[18] It also has been suggested to have usefulness in developing improved interaction and communication abilities.[19]

Brain Hack Number 43
Personality Type

Learn more about your personality to become aware of the subconscious driving forces of your behavior. You can search online for sites that offer free personality testing and receive results that provide insight into new ways of thinking and acting. Knowing your personality type can help you put down the mask and embrace your authentic, true Self.

Sam's personality had been designed by his wounded inner child to protect himself through strength and staying closed off from intimacy with others. It is also one of excessive lust, which makes him more susceptible to porn addiction. This is not just a lust for sex but for sensual stimulation and satisfaction of other physical desires, including video games, food, and alcohol. Sam's basic desire to protect himself and the fear of being controlled by others at times led him toward isolation as a flight, then freeze, response. During times of heightened stress, Sam retreated into his head to solve his problems by himself, often taking on too much and exacerbating his feelings of anxiety and overwhelm. Stress disintegrated his personality into self-protection mode, which pushed him toward the screen, making him feel better for a while, but ultimately making his brain, and therefore his life, much worse. As he allowed himself to be vulnerable with his wife and best friend, he moved toward his virtue of innocence, which led him away from guilt and allowed him to solve problems with the support of his neo-family. This kept him, and continues to keep him, healthy, happy, integrated, and at peace.

This is exactly what you deserve and what I want for you. With the knowledge of your personality type and the understanding that you may have been operating in a default mode of survival due to your childhood pain, you can make new choices to live a new life free from porn and full of love and happiness.

CHAPTER 11

CREATING HEALTHY SEXUALITY

Success is liking yourself, liking what
you do, and liking how you do it.
MAYA ANGELOU

A LOST CONNECTION

Sam's preference for performing high-dopamine-producing sexual acts changed the way he interacted with Krissy in the bedroom. His sexual arousal template had changed from a relational, intimate experience to performing highly stimulating acts.

A sexual arousal template is made up of the constellation of thoughts, images, behaviors, sounds, smells, sights, fantasies, and objects that arouse a person sexually.[1] Before internet pornography, this template was thought to be fairly consistent within a healthy range of stimuli for an individual, but now with reinforcement for the high-level intensity of supernormal levels of dopamine coupled with sex acts that might not be inherently sexually stimulating, many people's templates have changed.[2] This can include sexual attraction to children, violence, and dangerous and unhealthy sexual acts.[3]

As the changes ensued in Sam's arousal template, his sex life diminished. Eventually, it dwindled mostly to porn and masturbation. Sam blamed it on Krissy. As we have already discussed, this is typical of many men with porn addiction. Sam watched intense, violent porn scenarios and sex acts that Krissy had no interest in partaking in. The women in the scenes were also much younger. This left him wanting what he had been watching instead of the healthy sex life he had before the uptick in porn use.

SEX IS SUPPOSED TO BE RELATIONAL—BETWEEN, FOR, AND ENJOYED BY BOTH PARTIES.

Distorted arousal templates can be tricky to reverse.[4] Recall the neuroscience behind this phenomenon: if a neural pathway of pleasure associated with a particular type of person, act, or scene is traversed repeatedly over time, then the frequency of use strongly wires that arousal template into the neural pathways. So, it was important for Sam to stay off screens and block any fantasies involving these highly arousing templates.

At the same time, Krissy had become sensitive to the fact that Sam had begun to use her as a sex object for his pleasure. The mutuality of their sex life had waned, and it had become one that now primarily served Sam's increasing and insatiable sexual needs. Sex is supposed to be relational—between, for, and enjoyed by both parties. Some consider sex with the right person to be the most spiritual and intimate experience a person can have. Relational sex includes connection, joy, and pleasure. Sam would have to learn to create a new version of healthy sexuality. Yet again, this would be more difficult than he realized.

———

The goal of sex must change for your brain to change. Your porn-influenced goal for sex—maximal pleasure with high-intensity levels through a strong dopamine flood—should yield to a healthier goal: happiness, pleasure, and connection at optimal levels, yet still highly enjoyable (possibly even more so), through serotonin, dopamine, and oxytocin. Oxytocin is the bonding neurotransmitter—important for experiencing pleasure and happiness within an interwoven sexual experience with a partner. This also means a shift is required—from seeking intense gratification to sustained, lower-level dopamine boosts. This builds connection and leads to intimacy and vitality—a zest for life itself.

HUNGRY VS. SENSUAL TOUCH

Sam had watched intense porn for so long that his brain was conditioned to want incredibly high levels of intensity all the time. This played out as *hungry touch*. Hungry touch stems from hungry, lustful thoughts driven by an insatiable craving for dopamine. This is a "touch that takes." Anytime you touch yourself or your partner solely for pleasure, the driving force is actually hunger for dopamine. It is animalistic and rooted in a distorted need to mate, not bond. It motivates your brain toward the highest dopamine-producing activities,

IT IS BETTER TO GIVE THAN RECEIVE.

which generally include more violent, taboo, or self-pleasuring acts, as witnessed in porn. Hungry touch might include acts like grabbing, choking, slapping, forceful touch, and intense thrusting. Hungry touch is ultimately selfish.

Sensual touch, on the other hand, is selfless. It is shared. It is comforting and connected. It seeks love, not just pleasure. The catalyst of sensual touch is entirely different from hungry touch. Its neurobiological intensity is lower, at healthier levels that create more balance, and is sustained longer.

I know what you are thinking. *Lower levels of pleasure? No thank you.* But you know what they say: it is better to give than receive. Neuroscience research has shown that when you give support to others, the stress in your brain is reduced more than when you receive it. Thus, when you give sensual touch, you also receive. Dopamine, serotonin, and oxytocin are produced by giving to your partner, and you both get to benefit from the happiness trifecta. The frequency of affectionate touch, approximately one time per hour for kissing, hugging, and gentle touching, was shown to be important in loving relationships worldwide.[5]

Sensual touch enhances the bonds of love between two partners. It involves reciprocity and shared pleasure and helps both people access the truest versions of themselves simultaneously. Sensual-touch acts include:

- Smiling with eye contact
- Skin-to-skin contact
- Providing a service or treat, like a massage or champagne
- Gazing into each other's eyes for several minutes
- Listening intently and restating what you hear
- Laughing together
- Sharing a meal or walking with your attention on each other

- Kissing with lips and tongue
- Stroking or hugging with intent to comfort
- Holding or spooning with stillness for at least twenty minutes
- Gentle touch all over with the intent to soothe and comfort
- Gentle intercourse
- Making time together at bedtime a priority (even if one partner gets back up to finish working on something afterward)

These acts can be used in and outside the bedroom to increase affection. They are intimate, comforting, and connection-building.

Brain Hack Number 44
Hungry vs. Sensual Touching

List the ways you use hungry touch and any hungry thoughts stemming from that touch.

List the ways you can include sensual touch with your partner. Identify sensual thoughts and how they are different from hungry ones.

Reduce or eliminate the hungry touch and increase the sensual touch in your sex life for more balanced dopamine production and increased serotonin and oxytocin production. This will help you in and outside the bedroom as your brain heals itself and gets accustomed to healthy, balanced levels of dopamine all day long.

———

Sam had to take out some of the hungry-touch acts he had been subconsciously including in his sex life for a long time. The hungry touch was driven by the narcissistic bubble he had found himself in. As he engaged in the brain hack on the two types of touch, he discovered how often he used hungry touch and how infrequently he used sensual touch. He worked diligently to get back to the fun, engaging sex life that made him feel genuinely happy. Sam began by practicing self-awareness. He became aware of the hungry thoughts that led to hungry touch in the bedroom. At first, he struggled to reduce them, but through practice and gentle guidance from Krissy, he began to embark on a journey of sensual sexuality instead of constant pleasure-seeking. His sex life improved to levels that he never thought possible.

Sam had heard, from me, that his sex life could be better than ever through his porn addiction recovery. But he did not believe me. You might not believe me either. And yet his experience of sex changed dramatically. It was difficult for him to explain, as it is for many men. While using porn, it is hard to fathom how lower levels of intensity will still feel good. But once you experience the happiness trifecta, everything changes. Sensuality combined with affection from another can be stimulating to your brain and thus your mind and body in a more complete way. You are aroused by being with someone who genuinely wants to be with you sexually and intimately. The difference is like devouring a big piece of chocolate cake by yourself that can make you sick afterward, versus a gourmet, six-course meal shared with friends. The first provides a quick bout of pleasure, often followed by pain, but the joy of the second provides lingering happy memories that last a lifetime. This shift was transformative for Sam—and not just for his sex life but for his whole life.

THE PENDULUM EFFECT, DOPAMINE, AND YOUR RELATIONSHIP

To create a healthy relationship and healthy sexuality, it is important to rewire and recalibrate your brain back to healthy, sustained, balanced levels of dopamine—what I think of as getting away from the pendulum effect and into the "dopamine dream." The dopamine dream creates flow in your life and will allow you to heal your brain and relationship, providing longevity of health and well-being. In this balanced state, you can bond in a soul-filling way with your partner; your libido will be perfectly charged up (not overcharged); and you can feel strong, confident, filled with energy, excited by life, and able to derive pleasure from it. Doesn't it sound like a dream? Well, it can be yours.

Dopamine Levels' Impact on Your State of Being

Dopamine Drowning	Dopamine Dream	Dopamine Drought
Excessive levels	Balanced levels	Deficient levels
More wanting, less satisfaction	Healthy bonding	Anhedonia
Hypersexuality	Healthy libido	Low libido
Distorted arousal template and compulsions	Feelings of well-being	Erectile dysfunction
Addictions	Pleasure in accomplishing tasks and activities in life	Addictions
Impulsive sensation-seeking	Energy and vitality	Depression
Dangerous risks	Healthy risk-taking	Lack of ambition
Narcissistic bubble	Good feelings toward others	Low affect

THERE'S NO GOING BACK: SEXUAL AROUSAL

In this recovery journey, especially when it comes to relationships, there is no going back to what was before; there is simply moving forward into what will be. The future is not a repeat of the past. Instead, you can create a life you love so much that porn becomes unnecessary. At the precipice of change, but still caught in the porn cycle, you probably have yet to experience that life. Remember, porn was part of your *past* sex life. There's no going back, only forward, charting new territory into the unknown. For Sam, that involved figuring out what his healthy arousal template should look like in the future.

FINESSING THE DISTORTED SEXUAL AROUSAL TEMPLATE CAN ORCHESTRATE PLEASURE IN NEW WAYS.

Sam had been watching two specific sexual acts in porn for a very long time. Consequently, he found them highly arousing—that is, the source of a dopamine deluge. He watched those acts thousands of times, probably tens of thousands of times, and they were wired into his brain. One of those acts, due to its violent nature, could not be incorporated into a healthy sex life with Krissy. It had to go.

The other act, however, could be shifted from the unhealthy version he had been consuming to a healthier, less intense version that he and Krissy could experience together. I helped Sam figure out how to shift this act into a pleasurable experience. Finessing the distorted sexual arousal template can orchestrate pleasure in new ways. The act was highly arousing for Sam, which helped to arouse Krissy so that she began to enjoy it too.

Brain Hack Number 45
Your Arousal Template

List the acts, positions, and scenarios that have become highly arousing. List them in two columns. The first column contains those that are unhealthy and cannot be incorporated into a healthy sex life. You can refer back to our comparison of addictive versus healthy sexuality (see chapter 3) to help you discern which behaviors fall into this category for you. The second column includes acts, positions, or scenarios that, if modified, could be included in a healthy sex life with your partner. This might be difficult for you to figure out independently, and you may want to consult a coach or professional for assistance.

If you have difficulty letting go of acts that do not make the healthy arousal template list, you can revisit some of the techniques we explored in previous chapters. You can make a cost-benefit list that demonstrates how the costs significantly outweigh the benefits of continuing to fantasize about a particular scenario, or you can write a goodbye letter to those scenes, thanking them for their comfort in the past but telling them they are no longer necessary in the future. It's time to create healthy sexuality.

HEALTHY SEXUALITY: WHAT IS IT AND HOW DO YOU CREATE IT?

Healthy sexuality is not shameful or secretive. And to truly free your nervous system, you need to eliminate any behaviors that bring you shame. The goal is to create an experience of timelessness in which your body, mind, and spirit unify with your partner. When you share connected, vulnerable intimacy with a partner whom you love, you can feel safe enough to let down your guard. You let another person see the Real You. Being seen and accepted at this level can be incredibly freeing and healing. You may even discover aspects of yourself that you hadn't gotten in touch with before.

When shared transcendentally with someone you care about and revere, sex can take you to a place you have never been before with porn. You can be the Real You in its raw, naked, and exposed version, the one that is free to have fun and be accepted wholeheartedly by a chosen other. Certainly, porn does not bring you this shame-free elation and joy, but the Hijacker may trick you into believing it does because there is less risk of rejection from a stranger or screen.

LUST FADES.

There are three main stages of love you need to understand as you transition from compulsive sexuality to a healthy, connected sex life—each with its own unique brain patterning.[6] First, the initial lust, which is the sexual craving that prepares you for mating. Lust is exciting and feels good. You can't get enough of each other. There is a ton of sex. For most people with compulsive sexuality, there is excitement during this phase that almost competes with porn. Unfortunately, or fortunately—depending upon how you look at it—lust fades. It doesn't disappear entirely, of course, but continues at healthier, sustainable levels.

Next is romantic love, which involves bonding with a partner and creating intimacy. After you have been together for a little while, you no longer feel the need to be the shiniest version of yourself. You feel free to open yourself up and be more authentic.

Finally, there is long-term bonded love, which means committing to a single partner for a long time. It is not as glamorous, but it is more rewarding. It includes your first fight that doesn't result in hours of make-up sex but ends in a smile and a hug. It might include children, a house, bills, and the many life situations you figure out together. Although all this stuff feels like minutiae, it is what makes you a team. It makes you a family. A family and a tribe are incredibly important for both survival and thrival. You are no longer alone. You have your honey, who accepts and loves you for who you are. The Real You is home.

If you fall into the porn trap, you are most likely struggling with unhealthy courtship and shortchanging yourself out of the deep satisfaction of bonded love. Porn stunts your emotional capacity and keeps you stuck in the lust phase of mating, never fully allowing you to become vulnerable and able to bond with another person deeply. Love can be tricky in the third phase of courtship, but that is where the true payoff is. You can be fully seen, accepted, appreciated, and loved at this level.

The hubs and I have been together for over twenty-three years. The intimacy we share allows us to enjoy a big family and all its challenges together. We run businesses side by side, we work out together, we text each other dumb stuff, and we often weirdly dance together in the kitchen to our kids' dismay. We laugh together; we cry together. He has seen the Real Trish repeatedly, and he keeps coming back. I've seen him in all his glory too. It's not always pretty, but it is always authentic. What we appreciate the most is that we *get* to see these sides of each other. It is the greatest gift of a healthy relationship.

HEALTHY SEXUALITY INCLUDES THE INTENSITY OF PLEASURE WITH CONNECTION.

So how do you create healthy sexuality and move beyond lust alone? Healthy sexuality includes the intensity of pleasure with connection. This means agreeing with your partner about what acts and positions are enjoyable when you have sex. It is imperative that you accept your body and your partner's body without shame. Self and partner body image have been shown to suffer due to compulsive porn use. As your brain heals from porn, it will be easier for you to enjoy your body and your partner's. Make your bedroom a safe place to explore your sexuality without objectification. You can cautiously integrate masturbation and fantasy into the mix. But this must be done together, such as when including masturbation as a foreplay activity. Healthy sexuality integrates the intensity of a partnered experience that includes eroticism, engagement, and connection.

WHAT'S IN YOUR GARDEN?

One of my mentors refers to sexual acts, positions, and scenarios that stay within a couple's sexual relationship as their "sexual garden." I have never been a fan of the cheesy reference, but it perfectly articulates what needs to happen moving forward in your healthy sex life. It goes like this: you figure out what arouses you, your partner determines what arouses them, then you decide which acts stay in the mix of your sex life and which need to go.

Remember that porn use has distorted your vision of what healthy sex looks like. If you have been watching porn for most of your life, you may not know how to have a healthy sex life. You may only know porn-informed sex, which is the opposite of healthy sex.

Research has shown men tend to be more visual regarding sexual arousal, whereas women enjoy sensual touch.[7] These two modalities might be incorporated for a multisensory experience. Creating an intimate mood with candles, scents, lighting, and music can foster connection and intimacy. Don't get me wrong; as the parent of five kids, I know this can't always happen, but you can go out of your way to try.

Brain Hack Number 46
Grow Your Sexual Garden Together

Spice up your sex life with your partner. Identify which acts, positions, and scenarios you enjoy and find arousing. A client recently told me that he and his wife have been working on their garden, and it is exponentially easier to stay away from porn when they enjoy a spicy sex life together. So grow your garden together in order to thrive.

THE ELEPHANT IN THE ROOM

Before we move on, I must address the elephant in the room. You may already have thought, *All this sounds great, Trish, but my partner doesn't want to have sex with me.* Or perhaps you are thinking, *My partner has always been prudish; what do I do to turn up the heat in the bedroom?* If you do not have a partner, we will discuss that shortly. But if you want to help your partner increase their sexual intimacy, the solution is twofold.

First, it will take time for your partner to heal from the rupture in your relationship. Sexual betrayal can lead to *reactive intimacy anorexia*, the active withholding of sexual intimacy, because your partner does not feel safe in your sexual relationship anymore. If they don't want to have sex with you for a time, give them space and show compassion for their situation. Discuss your shared sexual garden and help your partner feel secure to explore her own sexuality with you in new, healthier ways. If

EMOTIONALLY HEALTHY PEOPLE WANT THE LOVE AND PLEASURE OF INTIMATE SEX.

they have always been guarded around sexuality, they may need to address this with a coach or therapist. Many women are taught that sex is bad—that they should not talk about sex, think about sex, or even consider enjoying sex. This can lead to *hyposexuality*: low levels of sexual desire, the opposite of hypersexuality. Your partner, with your support, can learn to become confident and enjoy your sexual relationship in new and fulfilling ways.

Unfortunately, violence against women is rampant, and many women (and men) suffer sexual assault. Sexual violence has been related to more impersonal, casual sex, such as that found in "hookup culture," which has been increasing over the past decade.[8] Coercion and force tactics are used more often in these scenarios, and men report feeling better about themselves emotionally following casual sex whereas women regret the experience and have more negative emotions, such as depression and loneliness.[9] Healing from the hurt, pain, and trauma is critical for these survivors to live free and enjoy healthy sexuality with a loving partner. Emotionally healthy people want the love and pleasure of intimate sex with their relationship partners. Support your partner as they heal from their past so you can create the future you envisioned for yourselves.

Second, many women are learning to be objectified and engage in hypersexual behaviors and acts that serve primarily the pleasure of their male partner. Sex becomes a partner-pleasing activity rather than an experience of connected pleasure and enjoyment. We explored this in chapter 1, as related to many women being conditioned to play into male fantasy ideals and rape culture through sexual media. If your partner is caught up in this role, she may be on a similar journey of appreciating the deeper connection of healthy sex. Some of your partner's programming may need to be updated for the two of you to have a healthy sex life. Women's sexual satisfaction has been shown to be related to:

- feeling attracted to their sexual partner,
- not feeling obliged to do something they do not want to,
- having confidence in their sexual partner,
- experiencing sexuality as something healthy,
- desiring to have a sexual relationship with their partner, and
- feeling comfortable with their own body.[10]

ERECTILE DYSFUNCTION AND AROUSAL ISSUES

Erectile dysfunction (ED) and sexual arousal issues can go hand in hand with porn use. Porn-induced erectile dysfunction (PIED) has been recognized as a persistent issue for many men who engage in frequent and intense porn use. Its underlying mechanisms have been shown to be neuro-bio-psycho-social in nature.[11]

Nervous system dysfunction is at the root of many men's erectile dysfunction issues.

ED is occurring at "alarming rates" in young men and is highly associated with compulsive porn use.[12] There is a direct relationship between the duration of porn use and erectile dysfunction. Men who watch porn and masturbate more frequently have higher levels of ED and anxiety due to poor erectile function.

As we have discussed, the neurological dysregulation caused by habitual porn use can lead to desensitization of the reward center in the brain, directly impacting the level of sexual arousal needed to reach the threshold for erection.[13] When the brain is stuck in a stressed and overwhelmed operating mode, it changes the cascade of neurochemicals and hormones, inherently altering the way nerves and blood flow to your sex organ during times of sexual arousal.

Essentially, porn use changes the baseline arousal state of a

IF YOUR BRAIN IS USED TO EXTREME LEVELS OF AROUSAL FROM PORN, YOUR PARTNER CAN'T COMPETE.

healthy circadian rhythm. Your brain is not able to reach a calm, focused state because it is flooded with dopamine at times and is dopamine deficient at others. Baseline arousal is impaired, making sexual arousal difficult or impossible.

What I have learned from working with thousands of men who suffer from erectile dysfunction is, the more frequent and intense the porn consumption, the worse the dysfunction. If your brain has been supporting the onset of erection with high levels of dopamine from porn—a supernormal stimulus to reach and sustain an erection—it cannot reach that same level of arousal without porn, such as when you are with your partner. Even if your partner is gorgeous and adventurous in the bedroom, she still cannot compete with that supernormal arousal your brain is used to.

What's the solution? As your brain heals, arousal improves, which means erectile dysfunction can be resolved too. It sounds fairly straightforward; however, it may not be as easy as that for some. This goes back to the concept of unwire versus rewire. Unwiring the brain pattern that causes porn-induced erectile dysfunction may not be enough. For some men, higher levels of intentional rewiring are required. But it can be done. You can heal your brain and body. Rewiring the brain to heal erectile dysfunction requires you to do the following:

1. Stop desensitizing your brain: stay far away from porn, fantasy, and masturbation.
2. Extinguish the Easy-button lifestyle.
3. Start resensitizing your brain using neuromodulation techniques consistently.
4. Develop healthy sexual arousal and sexuality with a partner.

The first item on this list—staying away from porn, fantasy, and masturbation—is critical to rewiring the brain for healthy baseline arousal and sexuality with a partner. In this way, you stop desensitizing your brain. Your brain is used to heightened arousal levels from all three. The fantasy-provoking supernormal stimulus of porn, coupled with the heightened sensations of masturbation, which can often be much more intense than intercourse with your partner, leaves your brain wanting more dopamine. Thus, it is essential to practice enjoying lower, healthier arousal levels with your partner. Practice. With your partner. Not alone. It will help to resensitize your brain.

THERE IS NO GOING BACK, ONLY FORWARD INTO THE NEW, UNKNOWN, FABULOUSLY REWARDING TERRITORY.

The shift in baseline arousal throughout your day and sexual arousal in a healthy sexual experience will not happen overnight, but it will shift as you continue to practice a healthy lifestyle and healthy sex with your partner. Stay connected, don't go for fantasy, and don't count on masturbation within sex to get you where you need to go. Enjoy being *with* your partner—the experience of loving, connected, erotic, pleasurable sex *together*. Practice makes perfect. It is essential to exercise the muscle of your brain in a healthy way without the support of fantasy. This is likely different from what you have been doing. That is why you must remember that you are establishing a new relationship with your partner—creating new ways of interacting. There is no going back, only forward into the new, unknown, fabulously rewarding territory.

"WHAT ABOUT THE LITTLE BLUE PILL?"

"What about the little blue pill?" I have been asked this question thousands of times. If you give pharmaceuticals the edge over your brain, it does not have the opportunity to get itself to the level of arousal needed to rewire the system. Of course, if you feel a strong need to use the pill as a Band-Aid in the meantime, I understand. Band-Aids are meant to be used temporarily to stop the bleeding. Stitches are designed to bring the skin together to promote healing. Similarly, the little blue pill should be a temporary aid, not permanent.

Your brain and body are designed to heal by themselves when pushed in the right direction. Neurofeedback brain-training provides the stitches to heal the wound of erectile dysfunction. Dysregulation in the brain is the primary problem that impacts neurotransmitters, hormones, nerve impulses, blood vessel function, and ultimately the perpetuation of sexual-performance anxiety. Healing your brain is the key. A healthy brain means a healthy flow of your body's physical and mental systems working together for a healthy sex life. Through neurological regulation you can become sexually aroused in those special moments and not need to depend on anything from outside yourself for artificial arousal.

Two roads can converge for better sex with your partner. As she heals from reactive intimacy anorexia, hyposexuality, or objectification orientation, you can provide the support for her to feel safe. While she learns to embrace healthy sexuality in a new way, healing the resultant sexual arousal dysfunction from porn use can be a priority for you. In this way, as you build a new sexual relationship, it will be one in which both partners can be aroused in a healthy way, stay present, and enjoy sexual intimacy with each other.

CHAPTER 12

BUILDING INTIMACY
IN YOUR LIFE

We accept the love we think we deserve.
STEPHEN CHBOSKY

ADVENTURE AWAITS

Sam always had a strong, intimate connection with Krissy, but over the years—before she discovered him watching porn in the basement, when his porn habit really ramped up and got away from him—the intimacy declined, and the pleasure-seeking increased. Sam would have to work his way back from this extreme. It would be a more difficult challenge than he initially thought, like much of his porn recovery.

As his brain began to heal, and with my encouragement, Sam started to plan fun outings for himself and Krissy. He made them a picnic and planned a sunset hike; he bought fishing rods and taught her how to fish; he even took her on a vacation to a place she had always wanted to explore. During these shared experiences, Krissy realized how long it had been since Sam had planned anything, never mind fun and exciting adventures. They both could sense the reemergence of the Real Sam.

ENJOY INTIMACY

Intimacy is a pillar of a healthy, balanced life, including sexual intimacy. Being vulnerable with another person is not easy, but it benefits your brain. Sharing life with the special people in your world facilitates the production of dopamine (pleasure) and serotonin (happiness) neurochemicals. Hugs and physical touch produce oxytocin (connection), making you feel good and helping you to bond with another person. People need physical touch. Following are five main types of intimacy that can help you create connection with your partner in new and exciting ways.

1. **Emotional intimacy** helps you connect with your partner on a deeper level, sharing your feelings, fears, challenges, and successes. It is a way that you can be seen and accepted as your authentic, true Self and be validated for daring to show up as such.
2. **Intellectual intimacy** involves the sharing of ideas. You can practice being a responsive listener who respects your partner's ideas. This can be facilitated by a routine with your partner, especially if you are in the midst of relationship repair from the damage of porn addiction. My husband and I hang out on our front porch almost every night sharing about our days. Sometimes we get into debates, like the other night when a one-hour discussion about coffee dilution ensued.

3. **Physical intimacy** includes affectionate touch, such as hugs, hand-holding, pats on the back, neck rubs, and so on. Studies have shown that hugs can produce high levels of oxytocin for enhanced feelings of connection.[1] Gentle touch will help you give and receive love.

4. **Experiential intimacy** can be the most fun type. You can dare to venture into new activities and hobbies together. My husband and I have built a hearty repertoire of things we like to do together—from golfing, museums, art shows, and rock concerts to attending conferences. Experience the world together for exciting connection.

5. **Spiritual intimacy**—the deeper connection fostered between oneself, their partner, and their divine inspiration—becomes a very important component for most of my clients. It can be a perpetual reminder of the bigger reasons they are committed to sexual health and integrity. Spiritual intimacy can include sharing philosophy, praying, and attending faith-based services or gatherings together.

Start practicing these forms of intimacy not only with your partner but with all the important people in your life. Hug your child, grab coffee with a coworker, share Scripture with your parent, tell your best friend your loftiest goal, debate which strength of coffee is most appealing with your son. Often, as your relationship goes on with someone, you find it lacks intimacy. You used to do fun things. Now you find yourself hanging out on the couch every night. Those aren't experiences. Do something new with your partner to bring you closer together. It doesn't have to be an earth-shaking experience. It can be something as simple as painting your living room, washing the car together, or picking apples. There is always room to try new things. Do many fun and interesting things with the people in your life to build intimacy all around you.

> ## Brain Hack Number 47
> ### *Try Something New*
>
> Do something new with your partner. Identify activities he or she likes to do, and you like to do, and then list shared experiences in each of the intimacy categories to put on your schedule. Remember, if it is not scheduled, it is not real.

MAKE YOUR PARTNER YOUR BEST FRIEND

Life is short and we all deserve to move through it with someone who knows us, loves us, and has our back. This notion is why I have long referred to my husband not only as my partner but as my best friend. Cliché, I know, but also true. A best friend is someone who loves you even with all your flaws, someone who won't change who you are but instead wants you to flourish by developing into the highest version of yourself, whatever that might look like for you. The depth of my relationship with my husband could only have been accomplished through successfully navigating many difficult life circumstances together. Our relationship has had its challenges, for sure, but through it all we keep coming back to support and encourage each other.

When we first started dating, my husband and I were enamored with each other, and I told him it was like I had found my best friend, a relationship I never could have imagined. He jokingly told me that people couldn't be best friends until they had known each other for one year. I now wholeheartedly agree with him. On our one-year dating anniversary, he took me out for a special dinner and the waiter presented us with a cake that read "Best Friends" in bold letters. The picture of us, looming over the cake, still hangs in our house all these years later. Getting to the place of being best friends, and not just partners, requires the compassion and empathy that come with increased emotional intelligence.

Conceptualizing each other as best friends isn't just endearing; it has helped us support each other along the way, especially when we didn't necessarily agree. It requires two things: staying emotionally committed to the journey together, and having empathy for each other's individual life experiences. For example, when my husband wanted to join the golf country club that I deemed too expensive, I supported him because, as best friends, I didn't want to stop him from making his own decision based on finances. I know it is his passion and I didn't want to hold him back from pursuing it. When I decided to learn to ride a motorcycle, which he deemed too dangerous, he supported me too.

RELATIONSHIPS: OUR GREATEST LEARNING OPPORTUNITIES

Our romantic relationships can be our best learning opportunities, if we let them. Within them we can discover who we really are and what we truly value. Fear of abandonment as a driving force can lead many relationships, especially those that include addiction, to fall into the category of codependency. Codependency often plays out with elements of enmeshment, resulting in the blurring of boundaries between partners, which is felt as lack of autonomy and diminished sense of self within the relationship. This often includes an inability to fully experience and understand your own unique thoughts, feelings, and needs. Codependency can manifest as one partner needing a great deal of support and the other "needing to be needed."

I related to this so much when I first discovered the concept. I had set my life up so that I had many people depending on me, and I ran myself ragged to keep up with the demands. Subconsciously it made me feel valued, but then I realized that if I was always taking care of my husband's and children's needs, above and beyond what I should, they never got the opportunity to do so themselves. In this way codependency robs some partners or children of the emotional-growth opportunities that can come from the challenges and strife in life.

As a person increasingly succumbs to addictive behaviors, their partner's increasing anxiety leads them to become enabling and controlling at the same time.[2] Subconsciously, their life feels out of control, and they grasp at trying to create stability. Poor boundaries permeate the relationship as the spouse focuses more heavily on the needs of their partner instead of their own needs. Effectively, they become the "giver," and inherently, the person with the addiction assumes the role of "taker."

Earlier we discussed the role that dopamine dependency plays in fostering narcissism and an egocentric view of pleasure. This mechanism is at play in codependency, and an underdeveloped concept of self is believed to be at the core of this dysfunctional relationship dynamic.[3] To improve the dynamic, it is imperative that you and your partner each develop a stronger sense of self. When you do this, you can have a healthy, *inter*dependent relationship dynamic that allows you each to flourish as top-tier individuals, and ultimately your relationship, to include security and shared happiness. When dysfunctional, codependent dynamics are improved through self-exploration, emotional growth, and intentional action, you can have the relationship you have always wanted.[4]

You might have defaulted into a codependent relationship dynamic, like I did, thinking it was perfectly natural and healthy because it was what was modeled for you. My parents had a very codependent, enmeshed relationship for all my life. I didn't become aware of it until I embarked upon my own personal development, and it blew my mind. I never realized how they would do everything together, neither choosing what really interested them but both defaulting to doing everything they *could* do together. I saw this play out in my own relationship. When I discovered this dynamic, I made an intentional, and at first uncomfortable, step to figure out what *I*, not *we*, like to do. It turned out that I like to box.

I realized codependence impacted both the hubs and me in that we would feel uncomfortable if we went to do something without the other person. He would feel "bad" golfing, and I never would go out with my girlfriends without inviting the men along too. With emotional growth, my husband and I have ventured into the world more confidently, knowing that we are free to do so in each other's eyes. We go our separate ways and happily unite at times to be together. With renewed commitment to ourselves and then each other, it has been incredibly freeing as individuals and empowering as a couple.

Remember, your best friend knows the Real You, flaws and all, and loves you. If you never show that version to your partner, you will never have the chance to have a strong, interdependent relationship. That is why it takes courage to open yourself up and be vulnerable.

PARTNERSHIP AND SEX-LIFE REWIRE PLAN

The vulnerability that you explore within the forms of intimacy discussed earlier in this chapter can help you to become more comfortable discussing your sexuality and sexual relationship with your partner. Communication is imperative to building a healthier sex life. With greater understanding of your individual identity and compassion for your partner's true Self, you can explore how to enjoy sex together in new ways.

I have developed a simple, three-part Sex Life Rewire Plan. If you follow these three steps, you can start rewiring your brain and overcome the effects of compulsive sexuality.

1. **Build dignity and integrity in your brain and life.** Once you are on your way toward healing your brain from porn use, tell your partner about your struggle. As scary as that sounds, it permanently breaks the shame cycle of porn and builds integrity and interdependency. It also releases your brain from neurorigidity so it can become more neuroplastic for lasting change and continued healing.

2. **Establish intimacy, empathy, and trust.** You must trust yourself so that your partner can also trust you. Building trust, developing intimacy, and being empathetic toward your partner's feelings help build emotional maturity. If you can't trust yourself because the Hijacker continues to have a slight grip on you, stay in a support group or work with your coach. The Hijacker is ingenious. Many people in recovery keep a coach or support group for life as a result. The insidious nature of porn addiction necessitates a long-term approach.

3. **Rewire your sexual arousal template through shared experiences.** Share sexual experiences with your partner by being present instead of being steeped in fantasy and driven toward intensity. You have been in a compulsive sexual pattern for a long time. It is time to experience a new, better sex life of sensuality and enjoyment. Develop a shared sexual arousal template to engage in sex that is pleasurable for both of you.

IF IT'S NOT SCHEDULED, IT'S NOT REAL

Sam planned sexual date nights once a week to reestablish a healthy sexual connection with his wife. He prepared romantic rendez-vous with dinner and candlelight that would help them be together sexually. It was difficult at first to have sex in such a planned way, especially for Sam, who had previously used sex for mood regulation. This scheduled sexual date night helped Sam see how much he used sex to regulate his mood, and stress reduction more specifically. He could now see how it was more challenging to turn sexuality on when he was not always in a hypersexual state. It was strange for him and required practice at first. He spent months learning to turn the hypersexuality off, or at least dial it down. Sexual date night helped him learn to be intimate and enjoy a healthy sexual experience.

As you are rebuilding a healthy sexual relationship with your partner, it can be extremely useful to schedule your sexual encounters.

Brain Hack Number 48
Schedule a Sex Date

Schedule a time with your partner for sexual encounters. This can become flexible eventually, but set it in stone for now.

Scheduling sex dates lets you know when you *are* having sex, which eases your mind as you recover from porn addiction. This way, your brain will know when it's getting its release, and this will keep your brain from going off the deep end. At the same time, both you and your partner know when you are *not* being sexual. This will also help you decrease the hypersexualization of your partner. Be sure to share responsibility for who initiates. If you don't do this, one person may run the risk of feeling rejected, and the other may feel forced into rejecting sexual advances.

It is also essential to make room for nonsexual experiences. Plan one nonsexual date night each week as well. This will help to decrease hypersexuality associated with your partner and build other intimacies. Try to do something mutually agreed upon and pleasurable for both you and your partner. Weave intimacy throughout life; take hypersexuality out.

Brain Hack Number 49
Schedule a Nonsexual Date Night

Schedule a time with your partner for a nonsexual date night. Do something fun that you both will enjoy. Bring a zest for life back into your relationship.

PARTNER RECOVERY

Reestablishing trust and intimacy with your partner may also involve understanding what they have been through and the challenges they have faced due to your addiction and associated behaviors. It can devastate your partner when they find out you have a porn problem. They may have started to question their reality after months or years of being deceived, lied to, and manipulated.

My client Jim would watch porn in his home office every night after his wife, Joan, went to bed. Joan would lie awake in bed feeling suspicious because there had been many times she had quietly approached Jim's office to get him to come to bed, and he would close out his browser and jump up when she entered. She had asked Jim many times if he watched porn. He constantly reassured her that he didn't. When she pressed the conversation, he would be upset with her for not believing him and insinuate that she had trust issues. One night she walked in on him masturbating, upon which she checked his search history to find years' worth of nightly porn use in it. That equated to a decade of being convinced what she believed to be true was not.

Partner betrayal trauma has been shown to be similar in the brain to post-traumatic stress disorder (PTSD).[5] The day your partner discovers they didn't know the Real You can be earth-shattering. So extend compassion toward her or him during this difficult time. Your partner must resolve the trauma surrounding your dishonesty, sexual acting out, and lack of integrity. And then you can work toward rebuilding those aspects *with* your partner. But first, they will need to become emotionally healthier. I encourage impacted partners to reframe "discovery day" not only as the day they learned that they have been lied to and manipulated about your hypersexual behaviors but also as a day of rebirth. It is the first day of the rest of their lives, if you will. It can also be the start of a new and improved relationship for both of you.

Recovery for your partner is congruent with yours, but it's entirely different. Most partners need healing; if they engage in it, your health will improve too. Partners often struggle with childhood trauma and dysfunction, attachment issues, unhealthy coping mechanisms, and abandonment of the authentic version of themselves as well.

Sonja grew up with an overbearing, alcoholic father. She never felt completely safe around him. This led her to engage in a significant amount of people-pleasing behaviors as she fawned to survive. When she married Mark, she finally had the opportunity to feel safe, or so she thought. But not long into their marriage she sensed something off about Mark's behaviors. She had walked in on him masturbating in the shower in compromising positions too many times. The first time she caught him, he assured her that he was just trying that act for the first time. By the third time, his alibi was wearing thin. The distrust and hypervigilance she had developed for survival in her youth grew.

Your partner's healing journey—where they develop their strength and communication skills while getting on purpose in their own life—will also benefit you. The dynamic is different depending on the relationship, but most relationships flourish when each partner is allowed and encouraged to develop and grow in a parallel manner of interdependency. It is truly beautiful when people heal beside one another, becoming strong not only in themselves but also for each other.

This process will likely necessitate your partner's forgiveness of your dishonesty, lies, manipulation, and even infidelity. Studies show that a partner's secretive porn use registers as infidelity for many spouses.[6] Take note of that. Forgiveness is an act and also a process. Like your recovery, your partner's forgiveness will be exercised and strengthened over time. Learning to have patience while offering encouragement can help your relationship heal as fast as possible. At the same time, your partner may say and do things out of fear, anger, and hurt. Forgiveness must go both ways. When you forgive your partner for their unbecoming behavior, it enhances their ability to forgive you. Give to receive.

NO PARTNER, NO PROBLEM

You may not have a partner but would like to have one. Many people turn to porn because the risk of rejection in dating is high. If you are in a relationship with your screen and hand, you don't have room for a partner. Remember, if you are stuck in the initial lust phase of courtship, attracting a partner interested in a more mature, romantic-love type of relationship will be challenging. If your brain is consistently exposed to porn, you will have difficulties attracting a healthy mate because of your brain performance pattern and subsequent emotionally dysregulated internal states.

Dating can be terrifying. When you practice intimacy without attachment to outcomes, it becomes easier. Try to engage yourself in groups of like-minded friends and acquaintances to meet new people. Don't rely on dating apps. Don't hit the Easy button here. Instead, make plans to consistently go out into your community to places, events, and activities that revolve around your authentic identity's purpose—the one you have been creating and establishing along our journey together. If you like to play chess, join a chess club. If you are more of a volleyball person, join recreational volleyball. Put some effort into discovering what's happening in your town or city. I think you will be amazed by the sheer quantity and quality of different community events and groups.

My client Bob trepidatiously joined a biking club at my behest. He didn't think it would do anything positive for his life. He was pleasantly surprised when he met a woman on a bike trail one day and struck up a conversation with her that bloomed into a beautiful relationship. Let your new relationships grow organically. Go old school. With your newly established healthy brain energy, learn to sense the energy of people around you. Learn to connect with others in a purposeful, healthy way.

If you don't find a date on your first visit to your new organization, club, or activity, don't fret; belonging to a group can be very powerful for your brain. Loneliness and social isolation can lead to cognitive decline, whereas social belonging has a protective effect by improving cognition and reducing stress.[7] This way, you will learn to sense a healthy attraction, not just hypersexuality. Then, dare to approach and engage with people who strike your fancy. Do it for the connection, not the sex.

LIKE ATTRACTS LIKE; STAY PRESENT WHEN YOU CREATE A GLORIOUS LIFE.

Move slowly in your new relationship, which is the opposite of how sexuality is generally portrayed in pornography. Start with a coffee date, move on to dinner, and eventually, physical intimacy. In this way you can find an emotionally healthy partner to match your new place in life. Like attracts like. Don't turn to masturbation as a stress reducer or a means of fantasy exploration anymore. It will only take you back to porn and make it challenging to create and maintain the true intimacy you are looking for. Fight the urges. Stay present while you create a glorious life.

If you are not looking for a partner or a relationship at the moment, that is fine too. But be aware of the challenges just described. Sexual well-being is considered one of the most important aspects of one's overall quality of life.[8] Also, it is shown to be moderated by brain function related to dopamine, a system you have been overusing for some time. As you reinvent your overall identity, it is essential to consider what healthy sexuality looks like for you. Remember, sex is not shameful; porn is. Healthy sex helps you thrive.

Brain Hack Number 50
Join a Social Group

Join a purposeful, like-minded group for engagement with others. As your brain heals and you objectify less, it will be easier to establish an intimate relationship with a potential partner. Follow a natural progression with your potential partner: friends, date once, date multiple times, intimacy, kissing, heavy petting (yes, I just said "heavy petting"), and finally, sex.

HEALTHY LUST AND FANTASY INTEGRATION GUIDE

You must build healthy sexuality and avoid addictive sexual practices. To reduce hypersexuality, you cannot keep lust for other people in the mix. But you *can* lust after your partner. Make it part of your foreplay. Lusting for your partner healthily can keep your sex life exciting and fiery. But first, a note of caution. These notions might be challenging to integrate into a healthy sex life if you have struggled with addictive sexuality for a long time. Use the following guide to rewire your brain toward the optimal mode.

Healthy Lust

Train your brain to lust after your partner and your partner only. Think sensual thoughts toward sensual touch. Choose selfless, shared intimacy over selfish, maximal pleasure.

Follow these guidelines to incorporate healthy lust into your relationship. By adhering to these guiding principles, you will succeed in building neural pathways for healthy sexuality and *not* using your partner to initiate and perpetuate addictive sexuality.

Schedule sexual times and allow yourself to get excited about being with your partner sexually.

If you find yourself lusting after others, redirect your thoughts to your partner and your life.

As lovers, be sexually playful with each other without sexualizing all activities all day long. Hypersexualizing involves the objectification of your partner. Being sexually playful builds connection.

Healthy Fantasy

Building fantasy into your healthy sexual relationship with another human partner can fulfill some of your heightened sexual desires. Follow these principles to keep fantasy healthy and not addictive.

Incorporate fantasy with your partner in a mutually agreeable way. You and your partner should agree upon the inclusion and eroticism of the type of fantasy to be experienced together.

Be sure the fantasy does not objectify your partner. It should be pleasurable for both of you. It should not be used solely for your enjoyment.

Stay away from porn fantasies. Do not include any triggering fantasy you have consumed via pornography. The neural pathways in your brain have been traversed repeatedly by the scenes you have watched. If you act these scenes out with your partner, you will likely have a fantasy in your mind, either in the moment or later on, that does not directly connect you to your partner in the real world. Instead, stay present in an erotic experience both of you can enjoy.

If you want to keep healthy masturbation in the mix with your partner, make it part of the garden. Break the pattern of secretive masturbation to extinguish the shame surrounding it. This way, you will enjoy masturbation more than ever before.

BUILDING SEXUAL INTEGRITY

The truth will set you free. You likely hear that all the time, but it's important and valid. And it's especially true when overcoming porn or sex addiction. Secrets hurt. Secrets hold you back. You can't let the Hijacker lie to you again. He knows if you are keeping secrets. He wants you to keep them because it is how he controls your mind. Secrets create shame and progressively lock your brain into neurorigidity. So many people experience a relapse into sex addiction for this reason. Tell someone if you hear a voice telling you to keep a secret. You might even want to take a polygraph test to prove that you are honest with yourself. Many people recovering from sex addiction do this for their own sake. It will keep you on your toes. It can maintain honesty with yourself and your partner. I've seen it work extraordinarily well for some.

Building sexual integrity includes feeling relaxed and confident about your sexual self. It is neither secretive nor shameful. Permanently shed light on the dark so you can remain integrated. This is why you *must* avoid any behavior that creates feelings of shame. Sexual integrity involves pleasure *and* connection, not one or the other. You must learn how to talk about sex positively and healthily. It involves the following key components:

- Pleasure with connection
- Talking about sex and both partners' sexual desires
- Accepting your body without shame
- Exploring your body, your partner's body, and sexuality in a healthy way
- Cautiously integrating masturbation and fantasy (if you can or want to)
- Integrating love and a healthy lust

> ### Brain Hack Number 51
> *List Your Secrets*
>
> List any secrets you have had before, thank them for protecting you in the past, and say goodbye with gratitude that you don't need them anymore. Remember that secrets are a manipulative mechanism of the Hijacker to keep you bound to him for life. Set yourself free by not keeping secrets.

"CUPID'S POISONED ARROW": REWIRE YOUR RELATIONSHIP

Cupid was said to have had two arrows: one put you under the spell of love; the other made you a slave to sex and pleasure.[9] To stay successful in your journey of brain rewiring, you must create healthy relationship dynamics and healthy sexuality. That is the only way to avoid the second, poisoned arrow.

There are some incredible stories I could tell about the convoluted and twisted paths of people's relationships following the discovery of their porn addiction. For some, out of shame, they let their partners dictate their actions. For Jeff, going out was triggering for him as he continued to look at other women's bodies in the presence of his wife, but staying home forever, as his wife wanted him to do, was not how he would solve that problem. Instead, I encouraged him to go out and practice diverting his gaze or connecting in a healthy way with others instead of objectifying them. Another client, Kaleb, chose to wear a chastity belt to keep from touching himself. Again, self-soothing through masturbation is a genuine concern, but locking oneself away is not the long-term strategy for that issue.

The real solution involves addressing and resolving the complex ideas presented in this book. It is critical to establishing healthy relationships and sexuality. It's about learning to use sex for intimacy, bonding, and connection, not for mood regulation. Sex is fundamentally relational; it should be shared between two people in an interdependent relationship, not one based on codependency or disengagement.

Now, let's learn how to make your brain rewire permanent.

PART 4

HARDWIRE:

MAKING YOUR BRAIN
REWIRE STICK

CHAPTER 13

YOUR FUTURE: HARDWIRING YOUR BRAIN FOR LASTING SUCCESS

*If we are facing in the right direction, all
we have to do is keep on walking.*
JOSEPH GOLDSTEIN

A TRANSFORMATIONAL JOURNEY

It's all about lifestyle. Sam needed to change his lifestyle to stay out of porn. He changed it to include less stress overall and more varied, healthy stress management. With increased intimacy, more intention, and satisfying, healthy sexuality, Sam had a recipe for success in the long term.

This is why I characterize porn recovery as a transformational journey. If you grew up with porn use as your main coping mechanism for life's challenges, it is imperative to restyle your life to remove porn and add a toolbox of healthy coping mechanisms.

Sam created a daily and weekly schedule without porn that served his true Self and helped him live the life he had always wanted. It was simultaneously easy and difficult. And this is what it looked like: Sam established and practiced a morning routine that he loved. He meditated, journaled, read, stretched, and set intentions to prepare himself to thrive each day without fail. It became an essential habit. He did his most important work in the morning when he was fresh, took brain breaks throughout the day to refresh his mind, socialized with colleagues at lunch, exercised three days a week after work, enjoyed dinner with his family most evenings, watched his favorite shows and movies to wind down, and read before bed. Poker with the guys on Wednesday nights was a lifesaver. It perfectly broke up the week to keep Sam going. He made weekend plans to bike and hike with his kids, have lunch with friends, and enjoy a date night with Krissy, and he engaged in his spiritual rest practice on Sundays. It became a full life that had no room for porn.

Now that Sam had relinquished his porn habit, healed his brain, and created his authentic, healthy lifestyle, he was more purposefully engaged in his life than ever. With enhanced focus and motivation, things skyrocketed for Sam at work. He always thought he was being held back by something in his life. He *never* suspected it was porn. But now that he had quit it, he became top of the class in his organization and received compensation and accolades for his achievements. Not only did he excel at work, but he enjoyed it much more too. He was blown away and so grateful for this aspect of his journey. Where he had struggled so much to perform well at work before, now it had become so easy.

With newfound self-confidence and a lot less social anxiety since quitting porn, Sam even made new friends. He was less intimidated and began to go on "man dates," as I call them, with colleagues and acquaintances. Friendships blossomed, and Sam enjoyed more engagement and camaraderie than ever before.

Sam's sex life was better than ever too. Through open and honest communication and relearning how to be with Krissy, he began to enjoy intimacy and the pleasures of sex in new and profound ways. You can have that too.

Although Sam's kids did not know about his struggles with porn, their relationship had been strained and fraught with tension. This got better in many ways as well. Sam was softer and kinder with them. In return, they came to him more often for advice, support, and love. He returned those gestures with love, which accumulated exponentially over time.

Although the last thing Sam wanted to do was to stay in porn-recovery coaching, he realized it was a critical piece of his successful hardwire program. The Hijacker tried to take him back to porn a few times during his recovery. Without a consistently safe, closed community led by a professional, he was at risk of relapse.

Only through consistent hardwiring of actions, thoughts, and feelings can you cement the changes you have begun to create within your brain. First, you set the intention, then take an action step, and in doing so, you expect it to work out for you. Then, when it does, allow yourself to receive the rewards while remaining in an awe-inspired state of gratitude. In this manner, big things will begin to take shape for you too.

It is not rocket science but neuroscience, and it works. Create the exact life that you have dreamed of for yourself. Become and stay the true Self you know you can be. At last, you can be the Real

You. This is how you will create a life you *love*, and when you do, it will be one you won't want to escape from through porn or sexual fantasy. Life will be too precious.

NEUROPLASTICITY REVISITED

Neuroplasticity is such a wonderful thing. But it always holds a cautionary tale. When discussing your hardwire process, it is crucial to remember how it operates. Depending on how you treat it, neuroplasticity can be your best friend or worst enemy. If you create a lifestyle that uses neuroplasticity to continually wire your brain in a healthy mode, you will be all set. Your brain will be your lifelong best friend. It can help you to stay committed to your goals and achieve contentedness in your work, relationships, and life.

NEUROPLASTICITY IS SUCH A WONDERFUL THING. BUT IT ALWAYS HOLDS A CAUTIONARY TALE.

If you begin to break down the foundation of your healthy lifestyle, neuroplasticity can yet again become your worst enemy. Scientists have proclaimed that addiction is a "pathological, yet powerful, form of learning and memory."[1] Not only that, but Delta FosB, a powerful protein in the brain, is known to act like a "molecular switch" that can activate an old addictive process in the brain more readily.[2] This means that if you begin to slide out of the outer circle of sustained recovery toward the danger zone of the inner circle of hypersexuality, you may default to the Easy button of porn, masturbation, and your previous behaviors. Thus, it is crucial to maintain the healthy lifestyle that enables you to stay on the path of intentional living. To do this, it might be easier to gamify your thoughts and behaviors in a way that continually reward you toward the life of your dreams.

Brain Hack Number 52
Gamify Daily Progress

Gamify, with points, your recovery progress each day by accounting for actions that you took that day to move yourself toward, or away from, your goals. Recognize that all positive actions reinforce neuroplasticity for solid recovery progress, while any self-sabotaging instances threaten to move you backward or obliterate your progress altogether. If you identify any triggering events or yellow-circle behaviors, be sure to revisit your pivot plan in chapter 7 to keep neuroplasticity working in your favor.

FIVE-STEP HARDWIRE PLAN: *SPARG* TO SUCCEED

The steps you need to take to hardwire your new, porn-free lifestyle fall into a few basic categories. SPARG can be your easy-to-use acronym to remember the five steps to hardwire your brain after all your hard work. Here are the steps, followed by an explanation of each one:

1. Self-regulation through stress awareness and management
2. Personality integration for optimal performance
3. Authentic interactions and communication
4. Relationship management with vulnerability
5. Goal pursuit for healthy feelings

1. Self-Regulation Using the Stress Scales

Perhaps nothing challenges the enactment of your hardwire lifestyle more regularly than stress. Stress is by far the number one risk factor for relapse. Take that in for a moment.

Self-regulation becomes increasingly important during times of stress because that is when it is the most challenging. Having a plan helps. When stress starts, I make a plan to punch the General (my boxing bag), work out, and get together and laugh with friends. Your stress-management plan will require your newly developed pillars of emotional intelligence—namely, self-awareness and self-regulation. Ultimately, these will help your social awareness and relationship management.

So, what is the best way to keep your stress levels in check? Here are two critical pointers that have worked well for my clients in preventing relapse.

1. Stay aware of your stress levels because they constantly fluctuate.
2. Manage stress in healthy ways according to the level you are experiencing at any given moment.

Staying aware of your stress levels and managing them is the secret to porn recovery. In fact, it is essential to your success. To do that, you must check in with yourself every day on any stressors that have been added to your life.

But stress is sneaky. So many of us are addicted to stress itself. With early stressful life experiences and continual adversity in daily life, neurobiological alterations often occur that activate a nonstop stress response. Continual stress activation can cause strained brain, low self-awareness, and the risk of addiction.

I know I fell into this category in the past. It can be very difficult to realize how stressed out you are until you are already at your limit. We will work on a way to help you identify your stress level shortly. But for now, it is important to know that stress can affect your recovery efforts and cause relapse. Addressing stress requires added management and relief.

Balance Your Stress Scales

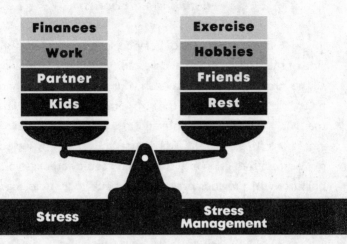

I envision healthy stress management as a set of scales. On one side, the scale is filled with stress in many shapes and forms, such as work, bills, partners, kids, parents, obligations, and the list goes on and on. On the other side, the scale should be lined with healthy stress management. It might include cooking, bike rides, action movies, workouts, or meeting friends for dinner. Learn to identify how much stress you are enduring on any given day and be sure to offset it at matching levels, keeping your scales balanced.

If the scales tip to the left due to more stress, it is time to double down and add more stress management to the other side to balance the scales as quickly as possible. If you are busier because of a big work project, it can be hard to relax. If you are sick, it is more challenging to exercise. In these times, it is even more crucial to find a way to include stress management. Healthy stress management will keep you away from the screen.

Brain Hack Number 53
Drawing Your Scales

In your journal, draw a set of balance scales with plates on each side of the fulcrum in the middle. On the left scale, draw or list all the stressors that you have on your plate that day. Then, on the right scale, identify the stress-management activities that you will engage in to offset stress when it piles on. With increasing stress, you should balance your scales by including more stress-reduction exercises. Using self-awareness you have built from the previous brain hacks, check your stress scales daily. Then do the activities on the right scale for increased self-regulation in a healthy manner. Doing so will make you more effective in managing your life and relationships.

2. Personality Integration for Optimal Performance

Maintaining your goals and purpose keeps your personality integrated as you move into the future as the Real You, your true Self. This way, you can leave not only pornography behind but maybe even all your self-sabotaging habits. Straying from your plan can create a crack in the foundation that develops into a chasm over time, leading to the disintegration of your personality.

There are two important factors in the integration of personality: coherence and congruence.[3] Coherence occurs when your objectives—smaller goals that lead to the larger goal—are related to each other and toward the higher-level goal you set for yourself. Each objective is a goal in and of itself, and all objectives converge in pursuit of your ultimate achievements. For example, back when I was in school, I worked toward a PhD, training in two areas, while also reading and engaging in coaching programs outside of formal education. Those individual objectives and goals have melded together to help me create the programs and coaching practice that I offer today.

People with coherent organization use wisdom and creativity to strive toward a life of happiness and are less likely to create personal strivings that lead only toward pleasure. After years of being in the dopamine-induced, pleasure-seeking behavior of porn addiction, your personality could likely benefit from improved coherence.

Congruence emerges in personal striving when the goals are self-determined, intrinsically motivated, and purposeful within a balanced, healthy lifestyle. The stories we tell ourselves about ourselves can influence our short-term objectives and our long-term goals. For me, I told myself the story that being smart and getting more degrees was important. When I stopped going to school, it was because I realized I was telling myself that story for the approval of other people. I was tired and wanted a break to enjoy my beautiful family.

The congruent coherence of your personality can help you evolve into your true Self and has been shown to be important in how you show up in your life and relationships each day. Essentially, the more integrated your personality is, the more purposeful and self-actualized your life can be.

There are three levels of personality integration. The top-tier is fully integrated, living peacefully and purposefully. Thriving. In between is the lifestyle of striving—always moving toward your goal but with some ups and downs. At the lowest level is suffering in addiction using self-soothing and self-stimulating to offset the discomfort of limited emotional regulation skills. Surviving.

As you set goals for your life and integrate your personality, you will strive for more. Even if you don't make it all the way up the mountain of recovery, you will be happier and healthier by continuing to strive toward it. Stay present and enjoy the journey.

THREE LEVELS OF PERSONALITY INTEGRATION
TOWARD YOUR AUTHENTIC IDENTITY

Level 1: Personality Integration:
Peace, Purpose, Well-Being

- Superconscious lifestyle: living with integrity and purpose toward self-actualization
- Optimal brain pattern for neurological regulation
- 100 percent authentic identity, true Self
- Healthy lifestyle, including work, hobbies, and relationships
- Outer-circle behaviors: healthy sexuality with a romantic partner
- Long-term emotional regulation skills through stress reduction and management
- Thriving

Level 2: Mid-Level (Dis)Integration: Fault Line

- Conscious and subconscious lifestyle: living with inconsistent integrity and happiness
- Strained brain (neurological dysregulation)
- 50 percent true Self and 50 percent Dr. Jekyll and Mr. Hyde
- Back-and-forth between joy and anxiety that leads to pleasure-seeking; may lose sight of your purpose and begin to act out of fear
- Middle-circle behaviors: some hypersexual behaviors
- Inconsistent use of healthy emotional regulation strategies, which leads to increased stress
- Striving

Level 3: Disintegrated Personality: Anxiety, Self- Soothing and Self-Stimulating, Addiction

- Unconscious lifestyle: living dictated by fear and discomfort
- Drained brain (neurological dysregulation)
- 100 percent Dr. Jekyll and Mr. Hyde
- Inner-circle behaviors: hypersexuality consistently
- Self-sabotaging and self-soothing behaviors take hold
- Surviving

Brain Hack Number 54
Permanent Personality Integration

Write a description of the incoherent, incongruent version of your personality. You've been him or her; you know what it is like. This version of you might include anxiety, depression, anger, and constant pleasure-seeking. Draw a picture of him with descriptors of what he thinks and feels. Get a clear picture of his energy field and how he is affecting others. Now conceptualize the most integrated version of yourself. Draw her with thought and feeling descriptors. What are her personal strivings? What goals does she have? How do the goals converge toward self-actualization? What daily action steps does it take to stay in this version?

Discover your fault line. How will you know you are disintegrating before you get there?

3. Authentic Interactions and Communication

Communicating your feelings and needs can be incredibly difficult. Interacting with an emotionally immature or less mature person makes this excruciating. Learning to approach and engage in interactions in a healthy way will keep you integrated. Say what you want to say when you need to do so. Say it with kindness, compassion, and grace. And with discretion, of course. Strive to communicate your thoughts and feelings openly while not oversharing or making yourself uncomfortable. I have been practicing a strategy that I call "transparency with discernment" for years. I try to be as much of my true Self as possible when interacting with someone, while considering their level of emotional maturity, the depth of my relationship with them, and whether they can be trusted with my deeper feelings. Living authentically isn't always easy, but it is always worth it.

Brain Hack Number 55
Engaging Interactions

Listen more, ask questions, and focus on others—not always on yourself. Share your ideas and concerns. Know your values. Know what you need. Don't be afraid to ask for what you truly desire. Create more openness in your relationships. Practice transparency with discernment. Be real, be present.

4. Relationship Management with Vulnerability

Early on you identified the defense mechanisms you have defaulted to for much of your life. Now it is time to move forward without them. So, what will you do instead? Managing your relationship with more vulnerability includes constantly reevaluating your own characteristics and authentic needs, especially those that might differ from those of your partner, so you can handle relationship situations in a new, healthier, more authentic manner. This can help maintain top-tier levels of interdependency, secure attachment, and best-friend status. Communication, respect for each other's varied needs, and collaboration can help you and your relationships thrive.

5. Goal Pursuit for Healthy Feelings

A self-actualized life should feel good. You have spent so much time up until now avoiding feelings or feeling bad. Moving forward, I want you to feel great and know that you do. To do that, it is important to set healthy goals for your benefit. Surround yourself with people who make you feel valued and loved. You want to make enough money to feel secure and obtain what I call "financial peace"—never having to worry about money. Remember, financial stress is a significant trigger for porn use.

Like Sam, you are going to set goals for the future that will help you keep your personality integrated. You have been on a journey. It is time to come home to the true Self in the life that stabilizes your well-being. A permanent staycation, if you will. This involves creating a physical environment in your home that you enjoy—one that makes you feel safe and secure—and surrounding yourself with people who bring your mood up, not down. You want to spend your time and energy in positive, brain-boosting, and brain-neutral ways. For example, my home, with its porches for sunrises and sunsets, helps me to start and end the day peacefully. Sitting on them each day adds significant peace to my life. I deliberately sought a home with these views. I set the goal, took the action steps, and made it happen so that every morning and evening I can experience joy. You can do that too.

Like I told you in the introduction, the neuroscience of goal striving requires a strong will and a deliberate way. It is a "detour from the path of least resistance" that necessitates intentional intervention.[4] I find it important to set intentional goals in nine main areas of life:

1. intellectual,
2. emotional,
3. physical,
4. spiritual,
5. familial (romantic partnership and parenting),
6. social,
7. financial,
8. career, and
9. hobbies/relaxation.

Brain Hack Number 56
Identify Goals to Get You on Purpose

In your journal, list your goals in the nine main areas of life that I just listed.

Next, pick your three most important goals and then prioritize them, numbering them 1, 2, and 3. It's most healthy to focus on one at a time.

After you do this activity, you should have some sense of the top three goals you'd like to achieve or at least make serious progress toward in the future. This doesn't mean you can't begin to address the other areas, but it does mean that you will focus on the main three and assess change toward achieving them. Schedule time in your flexibly scheduled life.

HARDWIRING INTEGRITY

Feelings of shame and inadequacy drive people toward the screen. Now that you have put down the shame of the past fueled by trauma and continual porn use, you can create a new life that will establish integrity. But first, you must know what that life involves for you.

It comes down to this: What do you need in this one precious life of yours to be happy? *You.* Not your brother, grandmother, partner, or best friend. *You.* Figure it out, and then have the courage to create it for yourself, while communicating and staying connected with the people who are most important to you. You deserve this much from your life.

Keep your word. Be radically honest. Stay in integrity with yourself, even if it challenges you to grow. This means if you tell someone you will do something, do it. This way, you can look yourself in the eye and know in your heart that you are on point. Never intentionally do anything to be harmful to another person. You can hold your head high and your shoulders back and take the world on with this newfound strength that gives you peace.

KEEP YOUR WORD. BE RADICALLY HONEST. STAY IN INTEGRITY.

Integrity is not always the easiest skill to pull off. However, it is easy to know when you need to exercise it. When you get a pang in your chest or gut that tells you that you are on the precipice of doing or saying something that will make you feel guilty or shameful, that is the time to step forward with courage in the face of fear and use your strength like the hero you have become. If you want to lie, don't. Tell the truth even if the other person doesn't like it. For example, if you feel a strong need to try something new, like riding a motorcycle, and your partner doesn't want you to, kindly tell her why it is important to you and continue to have conversations about it. Don't give up on the dreams of your true Self.

Living intentionally can ruffle some feathers. My client Jim wanted a tattoo, but his wife told him she didn't want him to get it. So he didn't. After years of resenting her for limiting him, he went and got one anyway. It created a rift in their relationship that remained for a long time. This distress could have been avoided through greater acceptance of each other's authentic desires and healthier communication. My husband and I had similar dynamics for quite a while too, until we did this type of self-exploration. Now we support each other's goals and dreams even if it is difficult for us to understand the other's internal motivations. We communicate to understand each other's passions so we *can* provide the support that is necessary. This has led us each to be happier in our own lives and is creating a healthier shared life experience.

When you stay in integrity, other people will respect you for acting confidently in what you want to accomplish in your life. In this way, you can live a life free of regrets. It will pay off in dividends.

CONCLUSION

That place of true healing is a fierce place. It's a
giant place. It's a place of monstrous beauty and
endless dark and glimmering light. And you have
to work really, really, really hard to get there, but
you can do it.

CHERYL STRAYED

WHAT A RELIEF

Sam's Mercedes-Maybach convertible wasn't the goal he was working to achieve. Still, it was a benefit of the transformation he created within himself. When he confidently walked back into my office as a new man, with beautiful Krissy on his arm, love and peace in his heart, and an optimized brain in his head, it was because—for the first time in his life—he was walking in as the Real Sam. He was on purpose in his work, and it was paying off. He was vulnerable, authentic, and intentional in his relationship, and so it flourished. He anchored love for himself in his beloved hobbies, feeding his soul. Life was good.

Although he stumbled initially, Sam unwired his unhealthy

brain pattern and the subsequent habits that drove him back into the screen for decades. He befriended neuroplasticity and harnessed it to work with and for him, instead of against him. In doing so, he rewired his brain to perform optimally. Day by day, as he engaged in new actions, challenged his old, distorted thought system, and truly felt his feelings instead of ignoring them, Sam transitioned into a new, calmer, more focused version of himself. At first, his self-awareness was low, and he couldn't tell if he was changing, but then he hit a point in his recovery when he *knew* it was working and that he *would* succeed. What a relief. At this point in his porn-brain rewire, he set goals for his future to hardwire his brain for lasting success. With his personality integrated at the healthiest levels and warning alarms set to alert him at the first signs of disintegration, Sam was poised for long-term happiness without the need for porn.

When I asked Sam what he felt to be the greatest benefit of leaving porn behind, he paused. He thought about the question for a while. Then, when he finally began to answer, he had difficulty putting it into words. The idea he communicated was this: "I almost lost everything I cared about because I stopped caring about everything. I didn't realize how much porn had changed my view of almost everything in my life." He could see the distortion clearly once his brain had healed, and he proclaimed to never let that happen again. He realized he had been caught up in the constant pleasure-seeking lifestyle that can never truly make a person happy. It made him less happy every step of the way.

He continued, "I almost let porn take away my professional work because I stopped loving it. Porn almost destroyed my marriage, which I cherish. Porn allowed me to persecute my precious wife in ways I never thought possible. I was angry and unpleasant most of the time. I lied to her, manipulated her, lusted after women in front of her, and I was even pulled toward cheating. My kids suffered from my mood swings and constant snapping at them.

Through my brain training, I could see my brain pattern and how messed up it was. It was impaired and influenced my decisions and actions. I became someone I couldn't recognize without even seeing it. Unbelievable. I have seen my brain heal and feel it in my mind, body, and spirit. I am living a new life. I never knew life could be so good, and I finally feel I deserve it. Thankfully, I have the rest of my life to live as the man I have always wanted to be."

—

After wearing the two-faced mask of Dr. Jekyll and Mr. Hyde for so long, Sam was finally free. He no longer needed to "keep up with the Joneses" or "put on airs." Instead, he could be just Sam, the Real Sam, everywhere he went. In doing so, he conserved his brain's energy by staying out of the pendulum effect. His brain never swung incredibly fast or slow. His brain was optimized, and his life was amazing. He could take deep breaths, mask-free.

Freedom to be and love yourself is the greatest gift on the other side of your porn-brain rewire. When that is accomplished, others are free to love and accept you as you are, the Real You. And they will. The wounds of the innocent child within you will heal. The Hijacker will disappear as you grow into the deserving adult you have strived to become.

Without the Easy button to turn to, you will be inspired to look inward and feel what you want and need at any given moment. You will have the brain power to exercise executive control to move toward your dreams, step-by-step, without losing your footing. You will create the big picture of the life you want and have the passion, motivation, and drive to wake up each day and live it. And when you do, the narcissistic bubble made by the dopamine-driven cycle of porn use will pop. In its place, you will find that when you give, you are better able to receive. The contribution that you, and only the Real You, can impart to this world is amazing, special, and important. It is why you are here, to make your lasting mark. Now you are equipped and psyched to do it. You are no longer surviving; you are thriving.

You may stumble from time to time. You may experience some bumps in the road. Transformation is not always linear. It will have its ups and downs. But you will be prepared. Within these pages, you have accessed the strategies you need. If it is difficult to implement the techniques by yourself; you may want to seek professional assistance such as brain-health coaching, which has been shown to be highly effective for people of all ages.[1] With the knowledge of the neurological underpinnings of porn addiction, personalized guidance can move you forward faster. Remember, those who quit an undesirable behavior succeeded significantly more with support. If you are struggling, don't give up; get help.

When you pass through a valley on your way to another transitional peak, remember this: the valley reminds you that change is necessary to keep moving forward. In my journey, I have found that it is darkest before dawn. I have learned *never* to give up because it is when I feel like giving up that I reach another summit. Relief is what you will find at the top of that mountain. Relief and peace await you.

AFTERWORD

As I told you in the introduction, I put my heart, mind, and soul into this book with the hope that it will help you succeed. And as you use this book as your guide to reach your full potential, it is time for you to invest that same devotion into your journey. With a healthier brain in your head and intentionality of your thoughts and actions, you can create the lifestyle you always wanted and that you deserve. You can move through the world in new and exciting ways. By reading this book and engaging with it, you have transcended your mind over explicit matter. Once risen, it cannot sink again. It's like a secret. Once you know it, you can never unknow it. Well, now you know. Knowledge is power. You will never be the same.

ACKNOWLEDGMENTS

I would like to acknowledge all the wonderful people who have supported me on the journey of pursuing porn addiction recovery, not always an easy subject, as a focal point of my career, and ultimately, in the writing of this book. Receding the tsunami of porn addiction for my children and their generation has always been a strong motivational factor for me. Aoife, Declan, Fiona, Seamus, and Saoirse, thank you for inspiring me and for championing my cause with spirit and vigor. You are precious to me, and I am so fortunate to have you all in my life.

To my family, I love you.

Jonathan Merritt, my agent, believed in this book before he even knew it was written. Your commitment to positive change and dedication to bringing this book to life will never be forgotten. I will be forever grateful. Thank you.

My editorial team at W Publishing was incredible with thoughtful and intentional feedback to help me enhance the impact of this book. I appreciate your hard work and care in the process.

To my besties, your love and support mean everything to me. I never imagined I would have a neo-family like you all.

Cosmas, my husband and best friend of many years, thank you for always pushing me to achieve my goals, even when doing so challenged you to step out of your comfort zone. Together, we can make lemonade out of lemons.

To everyone at the Christopher Ferebee Agency and W Publishing, I cannot thank you enough for believing in this book and helping me usher it into the hands of people who need it.

Thank you to my team at Dr. Trish Leigh & Co. You are all amazing, and the synergy we create to help people around the world is magnificent. Together we really can change the world one brain at a time.

NOTES

Introduction

1. Ricardo Irizarry et al., "How the Rise of Problematic Pornography Consumption and the COVID-19 Pandemic Has Led to a Decrease in Physical Sexual Interactions and Relationships and an Increase in Addictive Behaviors and Cluster B Personality Traits: A Meta-Analysis," *Cureus* 15, no. 6 (June 2023): e40539, https://doi.org/10.7759/cureus.40539.
2. Stefan G. Hofmann et al., "The Efficacy of Cognitive Behavioral Therapy: A Review of Meta-Analyses," *Cognitive Therapy and Research* 36, no. 5 (2012): 427–440, https://doi.org /10.1007/s10608-012-9476-1; Shian-Ling Keng, Moria J. Smoski, and Clive J. Robins, "Effects of Mindfulness on Psychological Health: A Review of Empirical Studies," *Clinical Psychology Review* 31, no. 6 (2011): 1041–56, https://doi.org/10.1016/j.cpr.2011.04.006; Donald Posson, "Automated Neurofeedback as a Primary Addictions Intervention," program at the Global Conference on Addiction Medicine, Behavioral Health and Psychiatry, Baltimore, MD, October 2024, https://addiction-behavioral-conferences.magnusgroup.org /program/scientific-program/2024/automated-neurofeedback-as-a-primary-addictions -intervention; Tom Hendriks et al., "The Efficacy of Multi-Component Positive Psychology Interventions: A Systematic Review and Meta-Analysis of Randomized Controlled Trials," *Journal of Happiness Studies* 21 (2020): 357–90, https://doi.org/10.1007/s10902-019-00082-1.
3. Martin Oscarsson et al., "A Large-Scale Experiment on New Year's Resolutions: Approach-Oriented Goals Are More Successful Than Avoidance-Oriented Goals," *PLoS One* 15, no. 12 (2020): e0234097, https://pubmed.ncbi.nlm.nih.gov/33296385/.
4. Nicholas Guenzel and Dennis McChargue, "Addiction Relapse Prevention," StatPearls, last updated July 21, 2023, https://www.ncbi.nlm.nih.gov/books/NBK551500/.
5. Elliot Berkman, "The Neuroscience of Goals and Behavior Change," *Consulting Psychology Journal: Practice and Research* 70, no. 1 (2018): 28–44, https://doi.org/10.1037/cpb0000094.

Chapter 1: Compulsive Porn Use and Hypersexuality

1. Igor Marchetti, "The Structure of Compulsive Sexual Behavior: A Network Analysis Study," *Archives of Sexual Behavior* 52, no. 3 (2023): 1271–84, https://doi.org/10.1007 /s10508-023-02549-y.
2. Timothy W. Fong, "Understanding and Managing Compulsive Sexual Behaviors," *Psychiatry* 3, no. 11 (2006): 51–8, https://pmc.ncbi.nlm.nih.gov/articles/PMC2945841/; Michal Privara and Petr Bob, "Pornography Consumption and Cognitive-Affective Distress," *Journal of Nervous and Mental Disease* 211, no. 8 (2023): 641–46, https://doi.org/10.1097 /NMD.0000000000001669; Tim Jacobs et al., "Associations Between Online Pornography

255

Consumption and Sexual Dysfunction in Young Men: Multivariate Analysis Based on an International Web-Based Survey," *JMIR Public Health and Surveillance* 7, no. 10 (2021): e32542, https://doi.org/10.2196/32542.

3. Simone Kühn and Jürgen Gallinat, "Brain Structure and Functional Connectivity Associated with Pornography Consumption: The Brain on Porn," *JAMA Psychiatry* 71, no. 7 (2014): 827–34, https://doi.org/10.1001/jamapsychiatry.2014.93.

4. Mehdi D. Molla, Mahmoud Shirazi, and Zahra Nikmanesh, "The Role of Difficulties in Emotion Regulation and Thought Control Strategies on Pornography Use," *Practice in Clinical Psychology* 6, no. 2 (2018): 119–28, https://doi.org/10.29252/nirp.jpcp.6.2.119.

5. Debby Herbenick et al., "Diverse Sexual Behaviors and Pornography Use: Findings from a Nationally Representative Probability Survey of Americans Aged 18 to 60 Years," *Journal of Sexual Medicine* 17, no. 4 (2020): 623–33, https://doi.org/10.1016/j.jsxm.2020.01.013; https://www.commonsensemedia.org/press-releases/new-report-reveals-truths-about-how-teens-engage-with-pornography.

6. Paul J. Wright, Debby Herbenick, and Bryant Paul, "Adolescent Condom Use, Parent-Adolescent Sexual Health Communication, and Pornography: Findings from a U.S. Probability Sample," *Health Communication* 35, no. 13 (2020): 1576–82, https://doi.org/10.1080/10410236.2019.1652392.

7. Rubén de Alarcón et al., "Online Porn Addiction: What We Know and What We Don't—A Systematic Review," *Journal of Clinical Medicine* 8, no. 1 (2019): 91, https://doi.org/10.3390/jcm8010091.

8. Rafael Ballester-Arnal et al., "Pornography Consumption in People of Different Age Groups: An Analysis Based on Gender, Contents, and Consequences," *Sexuality Research and Social Policy* 20 (2023): 766–79, https://doi.org/10.1007/s13178-022-00720-z.

9. Colin Hesse and Kory Floyd, "Affection Substitution: The Effect of Pornography Consumption on Close Relationships," *Journal of Social and Personal Relationships* 36, no. 11–12 (2019): 3887–3907, https://doi.org/10.1177/0265407519841719.

10. Cameron Wong, Yo-Der Song, and Aniket Mahanti, "YouTube of Porn: Longitudinal Measurement, Analysis, and Characterization of a Large Porn Streaming Service," *Social Network Analysis and Mining* 10, no. 62 (2020), https://doi.org/10.1007/s13278-020-00661-8.

11. Josh McDowell, *The Porn Phenomenon: The Impact of Pornography in the Digital Age* (Barna Group, 2016), 24.

12. McDowell, *The Porn Phenomenon*, 24.

13. Brian Y. Park et al., "Is Internet Pornography Causing Sexual Dysfunctions? A Review with Clinical Reports," *Behavioral Sciences* 6, no. 3 (2016): 17, https://doi.org/10.3390/bs6030017.

14. Park et al., "Is Internet Pornography Causing Sexual Dysfunctions?"

15. Martin P. Kafka, "Hypersexual Disorder: A Proposed Diagnosis for DSM-V," *Archives of Sexual Behavior* 39, no. 2 (2010): 377–400, https://doi.org/10.1007/s10508-009-9574-7.

16. Kafka, "Hypersexual Disorder."

17. Kafka, "Hypersexual Disorder"; Patrick Carnes, *Out of the Shadows: Understanding Sexual Addiction*, 3rd ed. (Center City, MN: Hazelden Publishing, 2001).

18. Ana J. Bridges et al., "Pornography Use and Sexual Objectification of Others," *Violence Against Women* 30, no. 1 (2024): 228–48, https://doi.org/10.1177/10778012231207041.

19. Nicky Stanley et al., "Pornography, Sexual Coercion and Abuse and Sexting in Young People's Intimate Relationships: A European Study," *Journal of Interpersonal Violence* 33, no. 19 (2018): 2919–44, https://doi.org/10.1177/0886260516633204.

20. Jodie L. Baer, Taylor Kohut, and William A. Fisher, "Is Pornography Use Associated with Anti-Woman Sexual Aggression? Re-examining the Confluence Model with Third Variable Considerations," *Canadian Journal of Human Sexuality* 24, no. 2 (2015): 160–73, https://utppublishing.com/doi/10.3138/cjhs.242-A6.

21. Privara and Bob, "Pornography Consumption and Cognitive-Affective Distress."

22. Julie M. Albright, "Sex in America Online: An Exploration of Sex, Marital Status, and Sexual

Identity in Internet Sex Seeking and Its Impacts," *The Journal of Sex Research* 45, no. 2 (2008): 175–86, https://doi.org/10.1080/00224490801987481.

23. Carson R. Dover and Brian J. Willoughby, "Sexual Behaviors as a Mediator Between Pornography Use and Heterosexual Relationship Outcomes," *Archives of Sexual Behavior* 53, no. 2 (2024): 689–701, https://doi.org/10.1007/s10508-023-02698-0; Cicely Marston and R. Lewis, "Anal Heterosex Among Young People and Implications for Health Promotion: A Qualitative Study in the UK," *BMJ Open* 4, no. 8 (2014): e004996, https://doi.org/10.1136/bmjopen-2014-004996.

24. Goran Koletić, "Longitudinal Associations Between the Use of Sexually Explicit Material and Adolescents' Attitudes and Behaviors: A Narrative Review of Studies," *Journal of Adolescence* 57, no. 1 (2017): 119–33, https://doi.org/10.1016/j.adolescence.2017.04.006.

25. Albright, "Sex in America Online."

26. Samuel L. Perry, "Pornography Use and Marital Separation: Evidence from Two-Wave Panel Data," *Archives of Sexual Behavior* 47, no. 6 (2018):1869–1880, https://doi.org/10.1007/s10508-017-1080-8.

27. Perry, "Pornography Use and Marital Separation."

28. Perry, "Pornography Use and Marital Separation."

29. Christina L. Scott and Angelberto Cortez Jr., "No Longer His and Hers, but Ours: Examining Sexual Arousal in Response to Erotic Stories Designed for Both Sexes," *Journal of Sex and Marital Therapy* 37, no. 3 (2011): 165–75, https://doi.org/10.1080/0092623X.2011.560529.

30. W. S. Chung et al., "Gender Difference in Brain Activation to Audio-Visual Sexual Stimulation; Do Women and Men Experience the Same Level of Arousal in Response to the Same Video Clip?" *International Journal of Impotence Research* 25 (2013): 138–42, https://doi.org/10.1038/ijir.2012.47.

31. Arjun Kharpal, "Kinky! The Saucy Business Sparked by '50 Shades,'" CNBC, February 13, 2015, https://www.cnbc.com/2015/02/13/oy-sales-set-for-50-shades-of-grey-boost.html.

32. "A Sex Expert Reveals the Real Reason Women Read Erotic Fiction," *Australian Women's Weekly*, September 27, 2022, https://www.womensweekly.com.au/health/why-women-read-erotic-fiction-17262/.

33. Christopher Ingraham, "Sex Toy Injuries Surged after 'Fifty Shades of Grey' Was Published," *Washington Post*, February 10, 2015, https://www.washingtonpost.com/news/wonk/wp/2015/02/10/sex-toy-injuries-surged-after-fifty-shades-of-grey-was-published/.

34. Amber Martin, "*Fifty Shades* of Sex Shop: Sexual Fantasy for Sale," *Sexualities* 16, no. 8 (2013): 980–84, https://doi.org/10.1177/1363460713508901.

35. Megan K. Maas and Shannamar Dewey, "Internet Pornography Use Among Collegiate Women: Gender Attitudes, Body Monitoring, and Sexual Behavior," *Sage Open* 8, no. 2 (2018), https://doi.org/10.1177/2158244018786640.

36. Sophie Gilbert, "What the Sexual Violence of *Game of Thrones* Begot," *Atlantic*, May 4, 2021, https://www.theatlantic.com/culture/archive/2021/05/game-of-thrones-the-handmaids-tale-them-tv-sexual-violence/618782/.

37. Eliana Dockterman, "*Game of Thrones*' Woman Problem Is About More Than Sexual Assault," *Time*, June 11, 2015, https://time.com/3917236/game-of-thrones-woman-problem-feminism/.

38. L. Monique Ward, "Media and Sexualization: State of Empirical Research, 1995–2015," *The Journal of Sex Research* 53, no. 4–5 (2016): 560–77, https://doi.org/10.1080/00224499.2016.1142496.

39. Vanessa R. Schick et al., "Genital Appearance Dissatisfaction: Implications for Women's Genital Image Self-Consciousness, Sexual Esteem, Sexual Satisfaction, and Sexual Risk," *Psychology of Women Quarterly* 34, no. 3 (2010): 394–404, https://doi.org/10.1111/j.1471-6402.2010.01584.x.

40. Hesse and Floyd, "Affection Substitution: The Effect of Pornography Consumption."

41. Albright, "Sex in America Online."

42. Thomas V. Hicks and Harold Leitenberg, "Sexual Fantasies about One's Partner Versus

Someone Else: Gender Differences in Incidence and Frequency," *The Journal of Sex Research* 38, no. 1 (2001): 43–50, https://doi.org/10.1080/00224490109552069.

43. Jennifer Jacquet, *The Playbook: How to Deny Science, Sell Lies, and Make a Killing in the Corporate World* (New York: Pantheon, 2022).

44. Jacquet, *The Playbook*.

45. Tate Ryan-Mosley, "How Generative AI Is Boosting the Spread of Disinformation and Propaganda," MIT Technology Review, October 4, 2023, https://www.technologyreview .com/2023/10/04/1080801/generative-ai-boosting-disinformation-and-propaganda-freedom -house/.

46. "Tactics of Disinformation," Cybersecurity and Infrastructure Security Agency (CISA), n.d., https://www.cisa.gov/sites/default/files/publications/tactics-of-disinformation_508.pdf.

47. Donald J. Hilton Jr., "Pornography Addiction—A Supranormal Stimulus Considered in the Context of Neuroplasticity," *Socioaffective Neuroscience & Psychology* 3, no. 1 (2013), https://doi.org/10.3402/snp.v3i0.20767; Deirdre Barrett, *Supernormal Stimuli: How Primal Urges Overran Their Evolutionary Purpose* (W. W. Norton, 2010).

Chapter 2: Your Porn Brain

1. Anil Gulati, "Understanding Neurogenesis in the Adult Human Brain," *Indian Journal of Pharmacology* 47, no. 6 (2015): 583–4, https://doi.org/10.4103/0253-7613.169598; Sandra Ackerman, foreword to *Discovering the Brain* (National Academies Press, 1992), iii–iv, https://www.ncbi.nlm.nih.gov/books/NBK234155/.

2. Soyoung Q. Park et al., "A Neural Link Between Generosity and Happiness," *Nature Communications* 8, no. 15964 (2017), https://doi.org/10.1038/ncomms15964; Dariush Dfarhud, Maryam Malmil, and Mohammad Kahnahmadi, "Happiness & Health: The Biological Factors—Systematic Review Article," *Iranian Journal of Public Health* 43, no. 11 (2014): 1468–77, https://pmc.ncbi.nlm.nih.gov/articles/PMC4449495/.

3. Daniel Z. Lieberman and Michael E. Long, *The Molecule of More: How a Single Chemical in Your Brain Drives Love, Sex, and Creativity—and Will Determine the Fate of the Human Race* (Dallas, TX: BenBella Books, 2019).

4. Jon E. Grant et al., "Introduction to Behavioral Addictions," *American Journal of Drug and Alcohol Abuse* 36, no. 5 (2010): 233–41, https://doi.org/10.3109/00952990.2010.491884.

5. Todd F. Heatherton, "Neuroscience of Self and Self-Regulation," *Annual Review of Psychology* 62 (2011): 363–90, https://doi.org/10.1146/annurev.psych.121208.131616.

6. Marta Kopańska et al., "Quantitative Electroencephalography (QEEG) as an Innovative Diagnostic Tool in Mental Disorders," *International Journal of Environmental Research and Public Health* 19, no. 4 (2022): 2465, https://doi.org/10.3390/ijerph19042465.

7. William H. Walker II et al., "Circadian Rhythm Disruption and Mental Health," *Translational Psychiatry* 10, no. 28 (2020), https://doi.org/10.1038/s41398-020-0694-0.

8. Alessandro Musetti et al., "The Interplay Between Problematic Online Pornography Use, Psychological Stress, Emotion Dysregulation and Insomnia Symptoms During the COVID-19 Pandemic: A Mediation Analysis," *Nature and Science of Sleep* (2022): 83–92, https:// doi.org/10.2147/NSS.S348242; Aishwariya Jha and Debanjan Banerjee, "Neurobiology of Sex and Pornography Addictions: A Primer," *Journal of Psychosexual Health* 4, no. 4 (2022): 227–36, https://doi.org/10.1177/26318318221116042.

9. Pierre Trifilieff and Diana Martinez, "Imaging Addiction: D2 Receptors and Dopamine Signaling in the Striatum as Biomarkers for Impulsivity," *Neuropharmacology* 76, part B (2014): 498–509, https://doi.org/10.1016/j.neuropharm.2013.06.031.

10. Brian Y. Park et al., "Is Internet Pornography Causing Sexual Dysfunctions? A Review with Clinical Reports," *Behavioral Sciences* 6, no. 3 (2016): 17, https://doi.org/10.3390/bs6030017.

11. D. O. Hebb, *The Organization of Behavior: A Neuropsychological Theory* (New York: Psychology Press, 2002), https://doi.org/10.4324/9781410612403.

12. Gaëtan Vignoud, Laurent Venance, and Jonathan D. Touboul, "Anti-Hebbian Plasticity

Drives Sequence Learning in Striatum," *Communications Biology* 7, no. 555 (2024), https://doi.org/10.1038/s42003-024-06203-8.

13. Norman Doidge, *The Brain's Way of Healing: Remarkable Discoveries and Recoveries from the Frontiers of Neuroplasticity* (New York: Penguin Life, 2015).

14. In-Seon Lee et al., "Operant and Classical Learning Principles Underlying Mind-Body Interaction in Pain Modulation: A Pilot fMRI Study," *Scientific Reports* 11, no. 1663 (2021), https://doi.org/10.1038/s41598-021-81134-6; Riya R. Kanherkar et al., "Epigenetic Mechanisms of Integrative Medicine," *Evidence-Based Complementary and Alternative Medicine* (2017): 4365429, https://doi.org/10.1155/2017/4365429.

15. *Merriam-Webster*, s.v. "epi-," accessed August 16, 2024, https://www.merriam-webster.com /dictionary/epi-.

16. Tim Denison and Martha J. Morrell, "Neuromodulation in 2035: The Neurology Future Forecasting Series," *Neurology* 98, no. 2 (2022): 65–72, https://doi.org/10.1212 /WNL.0000000000013061.

17. Meghan E. Martz et al., "Neuromodulation of Brain Activation Associated with Addiction: A Review of Real-Time fMRI Neurofeedback Studies," *NeuroImage: Clinical* 27 (2020): 102350, https://doi.org/10.1016/j.nicl.2020.102350; Eugene G. Peniston and Paul J. Kulkosky, "Neurofeedback in the Treatment of Addictive Disorders," in *Introduction to Quantitative EEG and Neurofeedback*, ed. James R. Evans and Andrew Abarbanel (Academic Press,1999), 157–79, https://doi.org/10.1016/B978-012243790-8/50008-0; Chao Chen et al., "Efficacy Evaluation of Neurofeedback-Based Anxiety Relief," *Frontiers in Neuroscience* 15 (2021): 758068, https://doi.org/10.3389/fnins.2021.758068; J. Fernández-Alvarez et al., "Efficacy of Bio- and Neurofeedback for Depression: A Meta-Analysis," *Psychological Medicine* 52, no. 2 (2022): 201–16, https://doi.org/10.1017/S0033291721004396.

18. Kenji Satake, "Advances in Earthquake and Tsunami Sciences and Disaster Risk Reduction Since the 2004 Indian Ocean Tsunami," *Geoscience Letters* 1, no. 15 (2014), https://doi.org /10.1186/s4056-014-0015-7.

19. Ricardo Irizarry et al., "How the Rise of Problematic Pornography Consumption and the COVID-19 Pandemic Has Led to a Decrease in Physical Sexual Interactions and Relationships and an Increase in Addictive Behaviors and Cluster B Personality Traits: A Meta-Analysis," *Cureus* 15, no. 6 (2023): e4053, https://doi.org/10.7759/cureus.40539.

20. K. Michael Cummings and Robert N. Proctor, "The Changing Public Image of Smoking in the United States: 1964–2014," *Cancer Epidemiology, Biomarkers & Prevention* 23, no. 1 (2014): 32–6, https://doi.org/10.1158/1055-9965.EPI-13-0798.

Chapter 3: What Is Healthy Sex Anyway?

1. Derek Kreager and Jeremy Staff, "The Sexual Double Standard and Adolescent Peer Acceptance," *Social Psychology Quarterly* 72, no. 2 (2009): 143–64, https://doi.org /10.1177/019027250907200205; Sarah Ashton, Karalyn McDonald, and Maggie Kirkland, "Women's Experiences of Pornography: A Systematic Review of Research Using Qualitative Methods," *Journal of Sex Research* 55, no. 3 (2018): 334–47, https://doi.org/10.1080 /00224499.2017.1364337.

2. Niki Fritz et al., "A Descriptive Analysis of the Types, Targets, and Relative Frequency of Aggression in Mainstream Pornography," *Archives of Sexual Behavior* 49, no. 8 (2020): 3041–53, https://doi.org/10.1007/s10508-020-01773-0; Gemma Mestre-Bach, Alejandro Villena-Moya, Carlos Chiclana-Actis, "Pornography Use and Violence: A Systematic Review of the Last 20 Years," *Trauma, Violence, & Abuse* 25, no. 2 (2024): 1088–1112, https://doi.org /10.1177/15248380231173619.

3. Alexandra Katehakis, *Erotic Intelligence: Igniting Hot, Healthy Sex While in Recovery from Sex Addiction* (New York: Simon and Schuster, 2010).

4. Dan P. McAdams and Kate McLean, "Narrative Identity," *Current Directions in Psychological Science* 22, no. 3 (2013): 233–38, https://doi.org/10.1177/0963721413475622; Gerald Adams

and Sheila Marshall, "A Developmental Social Psychology of Identity: Understanding the Person-in-Context," *Journal of Adolescence* 19, no. 5 (1996): 429–42, https://doi.org/10.1006/jado.1996.0041.

5. Erica M. Webster, "The Impact of Adverse Childhood Experiences on Health and Development in Young Children," *Global Pediatric Health* (February 2022), https://doi.org/10.1177/2333794X221078708.

6. Michael H. Miner, Janna Dickenson, and Eli Coleman, "Effects of Emotions on Sexual Behavior in Men with and without Hypersexuality," *Sex Addict Compulsivity* 26, no. 1–2 (2019): 24–41, https://www.tandfonline.com/doi/full/10.1080/10720162.2018.1564408.

7. Amber Craig et al., "The Impact of Sexual Arousal and Emotion Regulation on Men's Sexual Aggression Proclivity," *Journal of Interpersonal Violence* 37, nos. 1–2 (2022), https://journals.sagepub.com/doi/10.1177/0886260520915544.

8. Jack Bauer, "Nature, Nurture, and 'Ndividuality: Why Personal Growth Is Possible," in *The Transformative Self: Personal Growth, Narrative Identity, and the Good Life* (New York: Oxford Academic, 2021), 329–50, https://doi.org/10.1093/oso/9780199970742.003.0011.

9. Noël Clark, *The Etiology and Phenomenology of Sexual Shame: A Grounded Theory Study* (Seattle: Seattle Pacific University, 2017).

10. "Jim Carrey Declares He Has No Identity in Latest Surreal Interview," *Telegraph*, October 6, 2017, https://www.telegraph.co.uk/films/2017/10/06/jim-carrey-declares-has-no-identity-latest-surreal-interview/.

11. Margareta Sjöblom et al., "Health Throughout the Lifespan: The Phenomenon of the Inner Child Reflected in Events During Childhood Experienced by Older Persons," *International Journal of Qualitative Studies on Health and Well-Being* 11, no. 1 (2016): 31486, https://doi.org/10.3402/qhw.v11.31486.

12. Daniel Goleman, *Emotional Intelligence: Why It Can Matter More Than IQ*, 10th ed. (New York: Bantam Books, 2007).

13. Vinicius Jobim Fischer et al., "The Relationship Between Emotion Regulation and Sexual Function and Satisfaction: A Scoping Review," *Sexual Medicine Reviews* 10, no. 2 (2022): 195–208, https://doi.org/10.1016/j.sxmr.2021.11.004.

14. Fischer et al., "The Relationship Between Emotion Regulation and Sexual Function and Satisfaction."

15. Justin Dubé et al., "Emotion Regulation in Couples Affected by Female Sexual Interest/Arousal Disorder," Archives of Sexual Behavior 48, no. 8 (2019): 2491–2506, https://doi.org/10.1007/s10508-019-01465-4.

16. Theodore W. Frick, "The Theory of Totally Integrated Education (TIE)," in *Learning, Design, and Technology*, ed. J. Michael Spector, Barbara Lockee, and Marcus Childress (Springer, 2020), https://doi.org/10.1007/978-3-319-17727-4_69-3.

Chapter 4: The Hijacker: The Impact of Trauma, Abuse, and Neglect on the Brain

1. Brené Brown, *Rising Strong: The Reckoning. The Rumble. The Revolution* (London: Vermilion, 2015).

2. Haci-Halil Uslucan and Urs Fuhrer, "Intergenerational Transmission of Violence," in *Cultural Transmission: Psychological, Developmental, Social, and Methodological Aspects*, ed. Ute Schönpflug (New York: Cambridge University Press, 2008): 391–418.

3. David S. Black et al., "A Further Look at the Intergenerational Transmission of Violence: Witnessing Interparental Violence in Emerging Adulthood," *Journal of Interpersonal Violence* 25, no. 6 (2010): 1022–42, https://doi.org/10.1177/0886260509340539; Uslucan and Fuhrer, "Intergenerational Transmission of Violence."

4. M. Glasser et al., "Cycle of Child Sexual Abuse: Links Between Being a Victim and Becoming a Perpetrator," *British Journal of Psychiatry* 179, no. 6 (2001): 482–94, https://doi.org/10.1192/bjp.179.6.482.

5. E. H. Erikson, *Childhood and Society*, 2nd ed. (New York: W.W. Norton, 1963).
6. Gabriel A. Orenstein and Lindsey Lewis, "Erikson's Stages of Psychosocial Development," StatPearls, updated November 7, 2022, https://www.ncbi.nlm.nih.gov/books/NBK556096/.
7. Cardoso J, Ramos C, Brito J, et al. Predictors of Pornography Use: Difficulties in Emotion Regulation and Loneliness. J Sex Med 2022;19:620–628.
8. Yael Dvir et al., "Childhood Maltreatment, Emotional Dysregulation, and Psychiatric Comorbidities," *Harvard Review of Psychiatry* 22, no. 3 (2014): 149–61, https://doi.org/10.1097/HRP.0000000000000014.
9. Gal Richter-Levin and Carmen Sandi, "Labels Matter: Is It Stress or Is It Trauma?" *Translational Psychiatry* 11 (2021): 385, https://doi.org/10.1038/s41398-021-01514-4.
10. Shulamith Straussner and Alexandrea Calnan, "Trauma Through the Life Cycle: A Review of Current Literature," *Clinical Social Work Journal* 42 (2014): 323–35, https://doi.org/10.1007/s10615-014-0496-z.
11. Bessel van der Kolk, *The Body Keeps the Score: Brain, Mind, and Body in the Healing of Trauma* (New York: Viking, 2014).
12. Zukiswa Zingela et al., "The Psychological and Subjective Experience of Catatonia: A Qualitative Study," *BMC Psychology* 10, no. 1 (2022): 173, https://doi.org/10.1186/s40359-022-00885-7.
13. Michal Privara and Petr Bob, "Pornography Consumption and Cognitive-Affective Distress," *Journal of Nervous and Mental Disease* 211, no. 8 (2023): 641–46, https://doi.org/10.1097/NMD.0000000000001669.
14. Will Smith and Mark Manson, *Will* (Penguin Press, 2021).
15. Jill Bolte Taylor, *My Stroke of Insight: A Brain Scientist's Personal Journey* (New York: New American Library, 2009).
16. Jennifer R. Piazza et al., "Affective Reactivity to Daily Stressors and Long-Term Risk of Reporting a Chronic Physical Health Condition," *Annals of Behavioral Medicine* 45, no. 1 (2013): 110–20, https://doi.org/10.1007/s12160-012-9423-0.
17. Ryan Bailey and Jose Pico, "Defense Mechanisms," StatPearls, updated May 22, 2023, https://www.ncbi.nlm.nih.gov/books/NBK559106.
18. Margareta Sjöblom et al., "Health Throughout the Lifespan: The Phenomenon of the Inner Child Reflected in Events During Childhood Experienced by Older Persons," *International Journal of Qualitative Studies of Health and Well-Being* 11, no. 1 (2016): 31486, https://doi.org/10.3402/qhw.v11.31486.

Chapter 5: Reparenting Your Authentic, True Self

1. "Warriors," by Imagine Dragons, produced by KIDinaKORNER and Interscope, single released September 18, 2014.
2. C. R. Kneisl, "Healing the Wounded, Neglected Inner Child of the Past," *Nursing Clinics of North America* 26, no. 3 (1991): 745–55, https://doi.org/10.1016/S0029–6465(22)00285–7.
3. Michael H. Bernstein et al., *The Nocebo Effect: When Words Make You Sick* (Mayo Clinic Press, 2024).
4. Adriaan Louw et al., "Sham Surgery in Ortopedicas: A Systematic Review of the Literature," *Pain Medicine* 18, no. 4, (2017): 736–50, https://doi.org/10.1093/pm/pnw164.
5. Swapna Munnangi et al., "Placebo Effect," StatPearls, updated November 13, 2023, https://www.ncbi.nlm.nih.gov/books/NBK513296/.
6. Karin Meissner et al., "The Placebo Effect: Advances from Different Methodological Approaches," *Journal of Neuroscience* 31, no. 45 (2011):16117–24, https://doi.org/10.1523/JNEUROSCI.4099-11.2011.

Chapter 6: Understanding the Porn Habit

1. Patrick Carnes and Ken Rosenberg, "Sexual Compulsivity and Addiction," Seminar 3, New York Hilton Mercury Ballroom, American Psychiatric Association, May 3, 2014,

NOTES

https://static1.squarespace.com/static/61de459c71bceb590bd88e2f/t
/6204aedcd27df278768d8186/1644474093208/03SMKnit.pdf.

2. Tim Jacobs et al., "Associations Between Online Pornography Consumption and Sexual Dysfunction in Young Men: Multivariate Analysis Based on an International Web-Based Survey," *JMIR Public Health and Surveillance* 7, no. 10 (2021): e32542, https://doi.org/10.2196/32542.

3. Nicolas Sommet and Jacques Berent, "Porn Use and Men's and Women's Sexual Performance: Evidence from a Large Longitudinal Sample," *Psychological Medicine* 53, no. 7 (2023): 3105–3114, https://doi.org/10.1017/S003329172100516X.

4. Max Oginsky et al., "Eating 'Junk-Food' Produces Rapid and Long-Lasting Increases in NAc CP-AMPA Receptors: Implications for Enhanced Cue-Induced Motivation and Food Addiction," *Neuropsychopharmacology*.41, no. 13 (2016): 2977–86, https://doi.org/10.1038/npp.2016.111; S. Kühn et al., "The Neural Basis of Video Gaming," *Translational Psychiatry* 1 (2011): e53, https://doi.org/10.1038/tp.2011.53; Sergey Yu Tereshchenko, "Neurobiological Risk Factors for Problematic Social Media Use as a Specific Form of Internet Addiction: A Narrative Review," *World Journal of Psychiatry* 13, no. 5 (2023): 160–73, https://doi.org/10.5498/wjp.v13.i5.160; Núria Aragay et al., "Differences in Screen Addiction in the Past 15 Years," *International Journal of Environmental Research and Public Health* 21, no. 1 (2024): 1, https:///doi.org/10.3390/ijerph21010001; George Koob and Nora Volkow, "Neurocircuitry of Addiction," *Neuropsychopharmacology* 35 (2010): 217–38, https://doi.org/10.1038/npp.2009.110.

5. Igor Marchetti, "The Structure of Compulsive Sexual Behavior: A Network Analysis Study," *Archives of Sexual Behavior* 52, no. 3 (2023): 1271–1284, https://doi.org/10.1007/s10508-023-02549-y.

6. Shane W. Kraus et al., "Compulsive Sexual Behaviour Disorder in the ICD-11," *World Psychiatry* 17, no. 1 (2018):109–10, https://doi.org/10.1002/wps.20499.

7. Niko Tinbergen, *The Herring Gull's World; A Study of the Social Behaviour of Birds* (London: Collins, 1953).

8. Donald L. Hilton Jr., "Pornography Addiction—A Supranormal Stimulus Considered in the Context of Neuroplasticity," *Socioaffective Neuroscience and Psychology* 3, no. 1 (2013): 20767, https://doi.org/10.3402/snp.v3i0.20767.

9. J. C. Froehlich, "Opioid Peptides," *Alcohol Health and Research World* 21, no. 2 (1997): 132–6, https://pmc.ncbi.nlm.nih.gov/articles/PMC6826828/.

10. Kyle Pitchers et al., "Endogenous Opioid-Induced Neuroplasticity of Dopaminergic Neurons in the Ventral Tegmental Area Influences Natural and Opiate Reward," *Journal of Neuroscience* 34, no. 26 (2014): 8825–36, https://doi.org/10.1523/JNEUROSCI.0133-14.2014.

11. Adam G. Jones and Nicholas L. Ratterman, "Mate Choice and Sexual Selection: What Have We Learned Since Darwin?" in *In the Light of Evolution: Volume III: Two Centuries of Darwin*, ed. John C. Avise and Francisco J. Ayala (Washington, DC: National Academies Press, 2009), 169–90, https://www.ncbi.nlm.nih.gov/books/NBK219729.

12. David M. Buss, "Sex Differences in Human Mate Preferences: Evolutionary Hypotheses Tested in 37 Cultures," *Behavioral and Brain Sciences* 12, no. 1 (1989): 1–49, https://doi.org/10.1017/S0140525X00023992.

13. J. R. Wilson et al., "Modification in the Sexual Behavior of Male Rats Produced by Changing the Stimulus Female," *Journal of Comparative and Physiological Psychology* 56, no. 3 (1963): 636–44, https://doi.org/10.1037/h0042469.

14. Wilson et al., "Modification in the Sexual Behavior of Male Rats"; Dennis F. Fiorino, Ariane Coury, and Anthony G. Phillips, "Dynamic Changes in Nucleus Accumbens Dopamine Efflux during the Coolidge Effect in Male Rats," *Journal of Neuroscience* 17, no. 12 (1997): 4849–55, https://doi.org/10.1523/JNEUROSCI.17-12-04849.1997.

15. Sarah Blumenthal and Larry Young, "The Neurobiology of Love and Pair Bonding from Human and Animal Perspectives," *Biology* 12, no. 6 (2023): 844, https://doi.org/10.3390/biology12060844.

16. Offspring: Human Fertility Behavior in Biodemographic Perspective, National Research Council (US) Panel for the Workshop on the Biodemography of Fertility and Family Behavior, ed. Kenneth Wachter and Rodolfo Bulatao (Washington, DC: National Academies Press, 2003), https://doi.org/10.17226/10654.

17. Dan Sullivan and Benjamin Hardy, *Who Not How: The Formula to Achieve Bigger Goals Through Accelerating Teamwork* (Carlsbad, CA: Hay House Business, 2020), 24.

18. Abraham Maslow, *Toward a Psychology of Being* (1962), https://doi.org/10.1037/10793-000.

19. Georgios Paslakis, Carlos Chiclana-Actis, and Gemma Mestre-Bach, "Associations Between Pornography Exposure, Body Image and Sexual Body Image: A Systematic Review," *Journal of Health Psychology* 27, no. 3 (2022): 743–60, https://doi.org/10.1177/1359105320967085.

20. Germano Vera Cruz et al., "Finding Intimacy Online: A Machine Learning Analysis of Predictors of Success," *Cyberpsychology, Behavior, and Social Networking* 26, no. 8 (2023), https://doi.org/10.1089/cyber.2022.0367.

21. Ángel Castro and Juan Ramón Barrada, "Dating Apps and Their Sociodemographic and Psychosocial Correlates: A Systematic Review," *International Journal of Environmental Research and Public Health* 17, no. 18 (2020): 6500, https://doi.org/10.3390/ijerph17186500; Jessica Strubel and Trent Petrie, "Love Me Tinder: Body Image and Psychosocial Functioning Among Men and Women," *Body Image* 21 (2017): 34–8, https://doi.org/10.1016/j.bodyim.2017.02.006.

22. Elisha Fieldstadt, "Billie Eilish Reveals She Watched Porn at Young Age, Calls It 'a Disgrace,'" NBC News, December 15, 2021, https://www.nbcnews.com/news/us-news/billie-eilish -reveals-watched-porn-young-age-calls-disgrace-rcna8863.

Chapter 7: How to Stop Watching Porn

1. Crystal Hollenbeck and Barbara Steffens, "Betrayal Trauma Anger: Clinical Implications for Therapeutic Treatment Based on the Sexually Betrayed Partner's Experience Related to Anger after Intimate Betrayal," *Journal of Sex & Marital Therapy* 50, no. 4 (2024): 456–67, https://doi.org/10.1080/0092623X.2024.2306940.

2. Dahlia W. Zaidel, "Art and Brain: Insights from Neuropsychology, Biology and Evolution," *Journal of Anatomy* 216, no. 2 (2010): 177–83, https://doi.org/10.1111/j.1469-7580.2009.01099.x; Hyunju Jo, Chorong Song, and Yoshifumi Miyazaki, "Physiological Benefits of Viewing Nature: A Systematic Review of Indoor Experiments," *International Journal of Environmental Research and Public Health* 16, no. 23 (2019): 4739, https://doi.org/10.3390/ijerph16234739.

3. Anna Lembke, *Dopamine Nation: Finding Balance in the Age of Indulgence* (Dutton, 2021).

Chapter 8: Overcoming Obstacles in Your Path

1. George Lucas, dir., *Star Wars: Episode I—The Phantom Menace*, Lucasfilm Ltd., released by Twentieth Century Fox Film Corporation, 2013.

2. *Three Circles: Defining Sobriety in Sex Addiction Anonymous* (Minneapolis, MN: SAA Literature, 1991).

Chapter 9: Drafting Your Offensive Plan

1. Sucharit Katyal and Philippe Goldin, "Alpha and Theta Oscillations Are Inversely Related to Progressive Levels of Meditation Depth," *Neuroscience of Consciousness* 2021, no. 1 (2021): niab042, https://doi.org/10.1093/nc/niab042.

2. Rebecca Divarco et al., "Stimulated Brains and Meditative Minds: A Systematic Review on Combining Low intensity Transcranial Electrical Stimulation and Meditation in Humans," *International Journal of Clinical and Health Psychology* 23, no. 3 (2023): 100369, https://doi.org/10.1016/j.ijchp.2023.100369; Luke Sniewski et al., "Meditation as an Intervention for Men with Self-Perceived Problematic Pornography Use: A Series of Single Case Studies," *Current Psychology* 41 (2022): 5151–162, https://doi.org/10.1007/s12144-020-01035-1; William Van Gordon, Edo Shonin, and Mark D. Griffiths, "Meditation Awareness Training for the Treatment of Sex Addiction: A Case Study," *Journal of Behavioral Addictions* 5, no. 2 (2016): 363–72. https://doi.org/10.1556/2006.5.2016.034.

3. Wayne W. Dyer, *Getting in the Gap: Making Conscious Contact with God Through Meditation* (Carlsbad, CA: Hay House Inc., 2014).

4. Gareth Edwards, dir., *Rogue One: A Star Wars Story* (Burbank, CA: Buena Vista Home Entertainment, 2016).

5. Primavera Spagnolo and David Goldman, "Neuromodulation Interventions for Addictive Disorders: Challenges, Promise, and Roadmap for Future Research," *Brain* 140, no. 5 (2017): 1183–1203, https://doi.org/10.1093/brain/aww284.

6. Daisuke Ishikawa et al., "Operant Conditioning of Synaptic and Spiking Activity Patterns in Single Hippocampal Neurons," *JNeurosci* 34, no. 14 (2014): 5044–53, https://doi.org /10.1523/JNEUROSCI.5298–13.2014.

7. Meghan E. Martz et al., "Neuromodulation of Brain Activation Associated with Addiction: A Review of Real-Time fMRI Neurofeedback Studies," *NeuroImage: Clinical* 27 (2020): 102350, https://doi.org/10.1016/j.nicl.2020.102350.

8. Daniela J. Pereira et al., "Neurofeedback-Dependent Influence of the Ventral Striatum Using a Working Memory Paradigm Targeting the Dorsolateral Prefrontal Cortex," *Frontiers in Behavioral Neuroscience* 17 (2023): 1014223, https://doi.org/10.3389/fnbeh.2023.1014223.

9. Lydia Hellrung et al., "Analysis of Individual Differences in Neurofeedback Training Illuminates Successful Self-Regulation of the Dopaminergic Midbrain," *Communications Biology* 5, no. 845 (2022), https://doi.org/10.1038/s42003-022-03756-4.

10. Dimitri van der Linden, Mattie Tops, and Arnold Bakker, "The Neuroscience of the Flow State: Involvement of the Locus Coeruleus Norepinephrine System," *Frontiers in Psychology* 12 (2021): 645498, https://doi.org/10.3389/fpsyg.2021.645498.

11. Ryan Holiday, *Discipline Is Destiny: The Power of Self-Control* (New York: Penguin Random House, 2022).

12. Shuki J. Cohen, "Cognitive Rigidity, Overgeneralization and Fanaticism," in *Encyclopedia of Personality and Individual Differences*, ed. V. Zeigler-Hill and T. Shackelford (Springer, 2017), 1–7, https://doi.org/10.1007/978-3-319-28099-8_834-1.

13. Christopher S. Kilham, *The Five Tibetans: Five Dynamic Exercises for Health, Energy, and Personal Power* (Rochester, VT: Healing Arts Press, 1994).

14. Fahimeh Haghighatdoost et al., "Drinking Plain Water Is Associated with Decreased Risk of Depression and Anxiety in Adults: Results from a Large Cross-Sectional Study," *World Journal of Psychiatry* 8, no. 3 (2018): 88–96, https://doi.org/10.5498/wjp.v8.i3.88.

15. Barry M. Popkin, Kristin E. D'Anci, and Irwin H. Rosenberg, "Water, Hydration, and Health," *Nutrition Reviews* 68, no. 8 (2010): 439–58, https://doi. org/10.1111/j.1753-4887.2010.00304.x.

16. Leandro Garcia et al., "Non-Occupational Physical Activity and Risk of Cardiovascular Disease, Cancer and Mortality Outcomes: A Dose–Response Meta-Analysis of Large Prospective Studies," *British Journal of Sports Medicine* 57, no. 15 (2023): 979–89, https://doi.org/10.1136/ bjsports-2022-105669; "5 Surprising Benefits of Walking," Harvard Health Publishing, December 7, 2023, https://www.health.harvard.edu/staying-healthy/5-surprising -benefits-of-walking.

17. Debra Umberson and Jennifer K. Montez, "Social Relationships and Health: A Flashpoint for Health Policy," *Journal of Health and Social Behavior* 51, no. 1 (suppl) (2010): S54–66, https:// doi.org/10.1177/0022146510383501.

18. John Stansfield and Louise Bunce, "The Relationship Between Empathy and Reading Fiction: Separate Roles for Cognitive and Affective Components," *Journal of European Psychology Students* 5, no. 3 (2014): 9–18, https://doi.org/10.5334/jeps.ca.

Chapter 10: Healing Your Brain Using Your Mind and Body

1. S. Vaynman et al., "Coupling Energy Metabolism with a Mechanism to Support Brain-Derived Neurotrophic Factor-Mediated Synaptic Plasticity," *Cellular Neuroscience* 139, no. 4 (2006): 1221–34, https://doi.org/10.1016/j.neuroscience.2006.01.062.

2. Laura Mandolesi et al., "Effects of Physical Exercise on Cognitive Functioning and Wellbeing:

Biological and Psychological Benefits," *Frontiers in Psychology* 9 (2018): 509, https://doi.org /10.3389/fpsyg.2018.00509.

3. Apoorva Shukla et al., "Role of Art Therapy in the Promotion of Mental Health: A Critical Review," *Cureus* 14, no. 8 (2022): e28026, https://doi.org/10.7759/cureus.28026.

4. Marnia Robinson, "Why Are Porn and Junk Food So Tempting?" HuffPost, updated November 17, 2011, https://www.huffpost.com/entry/300-vaginas-a-lot-of-dopa _b_730797.

5. Gregory Ciotti, "Supernormal Stimuli: This Is Your Brain on Porn, Junk Food, and the Internet," HuffPost, updated September 16, 2014, https://www.huffpost.com/entry /supernormal-stimuli-this_b_5584972.

6. Amy C. Reichelt and Michelle Rank, "The Impact of Junk Foods on the Adolescent Brain," *Birth Defects Research* 109, no. 20 (2017): 1649–58, https://doi.org/10.1002/bdr2.1173.

7. Fernando Gómez-Pinilla, "Brain Foods: The Effects of Nutrients on Brain Function," *Nature Reviews Neuroscience* 9 (2008): 568–78, https://doi.org/10.1038/nrn2421.

8. Vanessa Vigar et al., "A Systematic Review of Organic Versus Conventional Food Consumption: Is There a Measurable Benefit on Human Health?" *Nutrients* 12, no. 1 (2019): 7, https://doi.org/10.3390/nu12010007.

9. Raju Lal Bhardwaj et al., "An Alarming Decline in the Nutritional Quality of Foods: The Biggest Challenge for Future Generations' Health," *Foods* 13, no. 6 (2024): 877, https:// doi.org/10.3390/foods13060877.

10. Anne-Laure Tardy et al., "Vitamins and Minerals for Energy, Fatigue and Cognition: A Narrative Review of the Biochemical and Clinical Evidence," *Nutrients* 12, no. 1 (2020): 228, https://doi.org/10.3390/nu12010228.

11. A. Musetti et al., "The Interplay Between Problematic Online Pornography Use, Psychological Stress, Emotion Dysregulation and Insomnia Symptoms During the COVID-19 Pandemic: A Mediation Analysis," *Nature and Science of Sleep* 14 (2022): 83–92, https://doi.org/10.2147 /NSS.S348242.

12. Paula Alhola and P. Polo-Kantola, "Sleep Deprivation: Impact on Cognitive Performance," *Neuropsychiatric Disease and Treatment* 3, no. 5 (2007): 553–67; Albertas Skurvydas et al., "One Night of Sleep Deprivation Impairs Executive Function but Does Not Affect Psychomotor or Motor Performance," *Biology of Sport* 37, no. 1 (2020): 7–14, https://doi.org /10.5114/biolsport.2020.89936.

13. Alhola and Polo-Kantola, "Sleep Deprivation."

14. Farah Younes et al., "Internet Addiction and Relationships with Insomnia, Anxiety, Depression, Stress and Self-Esteem in University Students: A Cross-Sectional Designed Study," *PLoS One* 11 (2016): e0161126, https://doi.org/10.1371/journal.pone .0161126.

15. Pawel Dobrakowski, Michal Blaszkiewicz, and Sebastian Skalski, "Changes in the Electrical Activity of the Brain in the Alpha and Theta Bands during Prayer and Meditation," *International Journal of Environmental Research and Public Health* 17, no. 24 (2020): 9567, https://doi.org/10.3390/ijerph17249567.

16. Ampere A. Tseng, "Scientific Evidence of Health Benefits by Practicing Mantra Meditation: Narrative Review," *International Journal of Yoga* 15, no. 2 (2022): 89–95, https://doi.org /10.4103/ijoy.ijoy_53_22.

17. Neil D. Shortland et al., "The Effect of a 3-Minute Mindfulness Intervention, and the Mediating Role of Maximization, on Critical Incident Decision-Making," *Frontiers in Psychology* 12 (2021): 674694, https://doi.org/10.3389/fpsyg.2021.674694.

18. John W. Pelley and Bernell K. Dalley, *Success Types in Medical Education: A Program for Improving Academic Performance* (Lubbock, TX: John W. Pelley, 2008), https://www.ttuhsc .edu/medicine/medical-education/success-types/documents/stsinmeded.pdf.

19. Taylor M. Blose et al., "The Enneagram and Its Application in Medical Education," *Baylor University Medical Center Proceedings* 36, no. 1 (2022): 54–58, https://doi.org/10.1080 /08998280.2022.2132591.

Chapter 11: Creating Healthy Sexuality

1. Patrick Carnes, *Out of the Shadows: Understanding Sexual Addiction*, 2nd ed. (Center City, MN: Hazelden, 1994).
2. Patrick Carnes, "The Anatomy of Arousal: Three Internet Portals," *Sexual and Relationship Therapy* 18, no. 3 (2003): 309–28, https://doi.org/10.1080/14681990310153937.
3. Taha F. Rasul et al., "The Potential Cutaneous Effects of Pornography Addiction: A Narrative Review," *Cureus* 14, no. 12 (2022): e33066, https://doi.org/10.7759/cureus.33066.
4. Todd Love et al., "Neuroscience of Internet Pornography Addiction: A Review and Update," *Behavorial Sciences* 5, no. 3 (2015): 388–433, https://doi.org/10.3390/bs5030388.
5. Agnieszka Sorokowska et al., "Love and Affectionate Touch Toward Romantic Partners All Over the World," *Scientific Reports* 13, no. 5497 (2023), https://doi.org/10.1038/s41598-023-31502-1.
6. Helen E. Fisher et al., "Defining the Brain Systems of Lust, Romantic Attraction, and Attachment," *Archives of Sexual Behavior* 31, no. 5 (2002): 413–19, https://doi.org/10.1023/a:1019888024255.
7. Lara Maister et al., "The Erogenous Mirror: Intersubjective and Multisensory Maps of Sexual Arousal in Men and Women," *Archives of Sexual Behavior* 49, no. 8 (2020): 2919–33, https://doi.org/10.1007/s10508-020-01756-1.
8. Justin R. García et al., "Sexual Hookup Culture: A Review," Review of General Psychology 16, no. 2 (2012): 161–76, https://doi.org/10.1037/a0027911.
9. Billie E. McKeen, Ryan C. Anderson, and David A. Mitchell, "Was It Good for You? Gender Differences in Motives and Emotional Outcomes Following Casual Sex," Sexuality and Culture 26 (2022): 1339–59, https://doi.org/10.1007/s12119-022-09946-w; "Domestic Violence Statistics," National Domestic Violence Hotline, https://www.thehotline.org/stakeholders/domestic-violence-statistics/.
10. Adelaida Irene Ogallar-Blanco, Raquel Lara Moreno, and Débora Godoy-Izquierdo, "Going Beyond 'With a Partner' and 'Intercourse': Does Anything Else Influence Sexual Satisfaction among Women? The Sexual Satisfaction Comprehensive Index," *International Journal of Environmental Research and Public Health* 19, no. 16 (2022): 10232, https://doi.org/10.3390/ijerph191610232.
11. Stephen W. Leslie and Thushanth Sooriyamoorthy, "Erectile Dysfunction," StatPearls, updated January 9, 2024, https://www.ncbi.nlm.nih.gov/books/NBK562253/.
12. Tim Jacobs et al., "Associations Between Online Pornography Consumption and Sexual Dysfunction in Young Men: Multivariate Analysis Based on an International Web-Based Survey," *JMIR Public Health and Surveillance* 7, no. 10 (2021): e32542, https://doi.org/10.2196/32542.
13. Todd Love et al., "Neuroscience of Internet Pornography Addiction: A Review and Update," *Behavioral Sciences* 5, no. 3 (2015): 388–433, https://doi.org/10.3390/bs5030388.

Chapter 12: Building Intimacy in Your Life

1. Kathleen C. Light, Karen M. Grewen, Janet A. Amico, "More Frequent Partner Hugs and Higher Oxytocin Levels Are Linked to Lower Blood Pressure and Heart Rate in Premenopausal Women, *Biological Psychology* 69, no. 1 (2005): 5–21, https://doi.org/10.1016/j.biopsycho.2004.11.002.
2. Leili Panaghi et al., "Living with Addicted Men and Codependency: The Moderating Effect of Personality Traits," *Addiction and Health* 8, no. 2 (2016): 98–106, https://pmc.ncbi.nlm.nih.gov/articles/PMC5115643/.
3. Ingrid Bacon and Jeff Conway, "Co-Dependency and Enmeshment—A Fusion of Concepts," *International Journal of Mental Health and Addiction* 21 (2023): 3594–3603, https://doi.org/10.1007/s11469-022-00810-4.
4. Cynthia J. Price and Carole Hooven, "Interoceptive Awareness Skills for Emotion Regulation:

Theory and Approach of Mindful Awareness in Body-Oriented Therapy (MABT)," *Frontiers in Psychology* 9 (2018): 798, https://doi.org/10.3389/fpsyg.2018.00798.

5. Breanne E. Kearney et al., "How the Body Remembers: Examining the Default Mode and Sensorimotor Networks During Moral Injury Autobiographical Memory Retrieval in PTSD," NeuroImage Clinical 38 (2023): 103426, https://doi.org/10.1016/j.nicl.2023.103426.

6. Jennifer P. Schneider, Robert Weiss, and Charles Samenow, "Is It Really Cheating? Understanding the Emotional Reactions and Clinical Treatment of Spouses and Partners Affected by Cybersex Infidelity," *Sexual Addiction & Compulsivity* 19, no. 1–2 (2012): 123–39, https://doi.org/10.1080/10720162.2012.658344.

7. Carolin Kieckhaefer, Leonhard Schilbach, and Danilo Bzdok, "Social Belonging: Brain Structure and Function Is Linked to Membership in Sports Teams, Religious Groups, and Social Clubs," Cerebral Cortex 33, no. 8 (2023): 4405–20, https://doi.org/10.1093/cercor/bhac351.

8. Rocco S. Calabrò et al., "Neuroanatomy and Function of Human Sexual Behavior: A Neglected or Unknown Issue?" *Brain and Behavior* 9, no. 12 (2019): e01389, https://doi.org/10.1002/brb3.1389.

9. Marnia Robinson, *Cupid's Poisoned Arrow: From Habit to Harmony in Sexual Relationships* (Berkeley, CA: North Atlantic Books, 2009).

Chapter 13: Your Future: Hardwiring Your Brain for Lasting Success

1. Julie A. Kauer and Robert C. Malenka, "Synaptic Plasticity and Addiction," Nature Reviews Neuroscience 8 (2007): 844–58, https://doi.org/10.1038/nrn2234.

2. Eric J. Nestler, Michel Barrot, and David W. Self, "DeltaFosB: A Sustained Molecular Switch for Addiction," Proceedings of the National Academy of Sciences of the United States of America 98, no. 20 (2001): 11042–6, https://doi.org/10.1073/pnas.191352698.

3. K. M. Sheldon and T. Kasser, "Coherence and Congruence: Two Aspects of Personality Integration," *Journal of Personality and Social Psychology* 68, no. 3 (1995): 531–43, https://doi.org/10.1037//0022-3514.68.3.531.

4. E. T. Berkman, "The Neuroscience of Goals and Behavior Change," *Consulting Psychology Journal: Practice and Research* 70, no. 1 (2018): 28–44, https://doi.org/10.1037/cpb0000094.

Conclusion

1. Kenneth Blum et al., "Addressing Cortex Dysregulation in Youth Through Brain Health Check Coaching and Prophylactic Brain Development," *INNOSC Theranostics and Pharmacological Sciences* 7, no. 2 (2024): 1472, https://doi.org/10.36922/itps.1472; Hope E. M. Schwartz et al., "The Brain Health Champion Study: Health Coaching Changes Behaviors in Patients with Cognitive Impairment," *Alzheimer's & Dementia: Translational Research & Clinical Interventions* 5, no. 1 (2019): 771–79, https://doi.org/10.1016/j.trci.2019.09.008.

ABOUT THE AUTHOR

DR. TRISH LEIGH is a world-renowned educator, speaker, and practitioner who holds professional certification as a top-tier brain health, neurofeedback, and sex addiction recovery coach. In her easy-to-understand, inspiring, and empowering way, Dr. Leigh has taught millions of people worldwide how to rewire their brains and recondition their minds to leave behind self-sabotaging habits as they learn to fulfill their true, authentic purpose.

In addition to the plethora of free content she provides, Dr. Leigh offers paid online educational programs, personal neurofeedback coaching, and in-depth sex addiction intensive sessions to create a massive ripple effect of positive change.

STOP THE STRUGGLE.
START LIVING.

The constant battle with urges and unhealthy habits ends here.

Dr. Trish Leigh's program helps you transform your screen use and sexuality—no prescriptions, no sponsors, no suffering in silence.

☑ Reset pleasure pathways for healthy real-world pleasure.

☑ Restore intimacy and confidence with simple, science-backed strategies.

☑ Overcome neurological dysfunction caused by explicit matter.

☑ It's time to turn your struggle into success.

Dr. TRISH LEIGH

Enroll today and experience the difference.
Visit drtrishleigh.com.

FEEL AND PERFORM BETTER. FAST.

Overcoming hypersexuality and sexual arousal dysfunction can feel overwhelming. But it doesn't have to be.

This program is not like others you've tried. Dr. Trish Leigh uses advanced neuroscience technology to:

- ☑ Help you overcome cravings and compulsions.
- ☑ Rewire your brain for healthy pleasure, clarity, and happiness.
- ☑ Restore your confidence, intimacy, and sexual satisfaction.
- ☑ Healing is closer than you think. Take the first step today.

Transform your brain and your life—start now. Visit drtrishleigh.com.

Dr. TRISH LEIGH